Smokies & 'Pies

(with a hint of ~~Tartare~~ Tartan Sauce)

By Mike Gyles

British Library Cataloguing in Publication Data.

A catalogue record for this book is available from the British Library

ISBN 978 0 86071 835 2

A Commissioned Publication Printed by

MOORLEYS
Print, Design & Publishing
info@moorleys.co.uk · www.moorleys.co.uk

For Alex, Fin, Dan & Saul

Even though this book was specifically written with the four of you in mind, as I write (1st August 2020), it's far too early for you to appreciate. However, I'd like to think that in years to come you'll be able to relate to some of the experiences and adventures that Grumps has enjoyed.

Of more immediate importance, I'm hoping that this coming Monday morning there is a small paragraph somewhere at the back of the Premier League obsessed print media, confirming that Notts County FC are, once again, officially recognised as the oldest football League club in the world.

A review of

Smokies & 'Pies (with a hint of ~~Tartare~~ Tartan Sauce)

If you're someone for whom sport has been an important part of your personal journey through life, you'll be able to relate to Mike's story. In his entertaining memoir, you can follow the highs and lows of a lifetime in which sport has taken him to six of the seven continents of the world.

From his early days in Scotland using either thumb, bike and the occasional train or car journey, we discover how determined he has always been to get his regular football fix. Then, after his move south of the Border, we read of how his love affair with the FA Cup winners (of 1894) evolved.

Those looking for more tales of sex, drugs and rock'n'roll, as featured in his first memoir, will undoubtedly be disappointed. If that's what you're after, you've picked the wrong book. If you're into sport however, I can guarantee that the reader will ride the full gamut of emotions as they:-

- *hear of his 'severe' dressing down at school, simply because of his love of football*
- *admire the bravery of his wife as she confronts hooligans 'out for his blood'*
- *share his pain as he loses a £1 on the Dartford Crossing*
- *learn of his interesting 'chats' with Graham Taylor, Steve Cotterill & Big Sam*
- *feel unashamed anger at how he was duped by a pair of conniving Welshmen*
- *share his joy as he manages to smuggle a teasmade into Craven Cottage*
- *marvel at how he successfully scales the perimeter fence at The Valley*
- *be impressed when you read of how he escapes a mugging in Malaga*

- *reel with shock (& share his embarrassment) as he recalls his unwitting naked exhibitionism as a 17 year old, prior to a big game at Elland Road*

This is a book that could have been written by countless sports fans across the world. However, when his being raised in Arbroath, home of the record breaking Red Lichties, is combined with a move south of the Border and the conscious decision to follow Notts County, Mike's tale has a somewhat unique perspective.

He may have had to endure a lifetime of people looking at him sympathetically and asking "why?", but he has remained optimistically philosophic throughout. His Presbyterian acceptance that 'Wi wirnae put oan this planet to be happy and enjoy wirsels", has helped him to overcome just about every sporting disappointment he has had to endure.

Despite the seemingly endless doom and gloom, there are the occasional passages of unrestrained joy. You may have to look for them, but they're well worth finding, and on that basis, I strongly recommend this book. It's a bit of an emotional roller coaster, but when you've finished, you'll realise just how fortunate you've been in the life choices you've had to make for yourself!

Mr **Bill Ashrub** **(Psy.D)** - Professor of Psychology (& *anagrams*!), Bath University

PS – it's his wife I feel sorry for. That poor woman!

Acknowledgements

Whilst any personal opinions expressed in this book are open to challenge - and I'd be happy to enter into friendly debate at any time - I'm hoping that there are very few factual errors. The memory does play tricks on you as you get older, and although I've tried to ensure that any names, dates, results, locations etc., are accurate, if I have made mistakes, my only defence is that they are genuine. I've certainly not tried to deceive or in any way 'gild the lily'.

In addition to the specific sources referred to below, I've 'googled away' to my heart's content to supplement my memory, particularly from the early years. This makes me reasonably confident that there won't be many coming back to tell me that I've got things wrong. Inevitably there will be some, but I reckon I've drastically limited their number.

I'm indebted to Tony Brown for his *Official History of Notts County (1862 – 1995),* an invaluable reference book and mine of information that I've referred to on numerous occasions to either confirm or re-evaluate memories of my first twenty five years of following Notts County.

I've also gleaned useful information from the game by game account of a number of seasons found on *Notts County FC Match Line-Ups and Details* listed on the carousel.royalwebhosting.net website. Whichever fellow 'Pie has done this work deserves all the credit he/she deserves.

Nick Richardson at NCFC and Richard Bell, a fellow Red Lichtie, kindly provided the digital photos of Meadow Lane and Gayfield respectively.

Alistair McGrady who, for a number of years, has occupied a seat next to me at Meadow Lane, and as a result, has had to put up with my occasionally sardonic take on all sorts of topics, deserves a big thank you for reminding me of some of the details relating to club ownership.

Not forgetting of course that, despite the offer of a free copy of this book - should it ever be published! - a few volunteers still came forward to proof read individual chapters. I, more than most, recognise the sacrifice they have made and think it's only right that the wider public do too. Let's hear a loud cheer then for the aforementioned Alistair McGrady plus Phil Mansfield, Alan Baldwin, John Olney, Dan Brunning, Paul Kirkland (& his Dad), John Mostyn, Brian Chesworth, brother Alan, sister Dawn Hammond and not forgetting our first born, Ailsa, who took on the onerous task of checking the longest chapter.

It would be remiss of me not to acknowledge the help, advice and encouragement that I've received from Patrick Mancini and his team at Moorleys, the print, design and publishing specialists in Ilkeston. Tom Leleux, a fellow *92 Club* member, put me in touch with them. I owe him a big favour – how about treating you to a midweek game at Meadow Lane some time Tom? – as they've been brilliant.

Finally, although she doesn't make an appearance until Chapter 5, the young lady who rescued me nearly 50 years ago deserves a special mention. I hate to think where I would have ended up had it not been for Helen. She has deserved more than spending frequently uncomfortable afternoons in the likes of Berwick, Barnsley and Burslem over the years. I can only hope that the visits to Brazil, Barcelona and ....Brechin, in some small way, have made up for it.

Mike Gyles

August 2020

Contents

Picture Credits

Gayfield (Outer Cover and page 303)

A seagull's view of Arbroath v Dundee from 23rd July 2011. Watched by 1761, the visitors won this Ramsdens Challenge Cup Tie 2-1 in extra time. On page 303, you will note that the seagull has a full panoramic view of a large area of Arbroath and is probably thinking about dropping down for a teatime treat of discarded chips.

Meadow Lane (Inner Cover and page 302)

An aerial view from around 2013. If you look closely (& know where to look!) you can spot Helen and myself alongside Dave Allsop, Neil Wass, Richard & Jess Kerry and Alistair McGrady.

Four Boys (page i)

Taken on 4th July 2020. Finlay & Alex aged 8 at the back with Saul and Daniel aged 5 in front.

Mr & Mrs Gyles - San Francisco 1994 & 2015 (page ii)

It's easy to detect the impact on facial features of following Notts County for 21 years.

The Prologue

In 2017 I self-published a memoir, entitled *Processed Peas, Macaroon Bars, Warm Pork Pies and Well Made Bras*. I've heard it described as a riveting read, particularly for those who are into Sex, Drugs and Rock'n'Roll. If that's you, and you're desperate to read it, copies can probably still be found in good charity shops.

The aim of that first book was to ensure that I'd left something that might be of interest to future generations of my family and provide them with some understanding of their ancestry and of how they came to be. For the immediate family it was intended to provide memories (mostly happy I hoped) and insight into what influences shaped me as a husband/father/uncle/Grumps.

One of the frustrating elements in committing my life story to print however, was avoiding talking about sporting experiences. It was impossible of course to omit all references, as those of you who have already read it will be aware. With a Dad so keen himself on the likes of football, cricket, horse racing, boxing etc., I guess it was inevitable that in such an environment, the Gyles' kids (brother Alan, sister Dawn and myself) would follow suit. Nonetheless, I made a conscious decision in writing the first book to restrict sporting references to the very minimum as I thought there would be sufficient material - and you'll be the judge of whether or not I was right - for a second book. Whatever, *Smokies & 'Pies (with a hint of ~~Tartare~~ Tartan Sauce)* is the outcome.

Like most of us who, as youngsters, might have hoped to pursue the 'career of their dreams', I was never good enough at any of the sports that I played to have serious aspirations of becoming a success. I had my moments, and if I'm honest, was disappointed that the SFA never came 'calling' to enable me to fulfil my destiny and become the first man wearing dark blue to lift the World Cup.

When I started running to keep fit in my mid-forties, I gradually improved and set myself a target of competing in the 2012 Olympic (my 'home') Games in London. I reckoned that I would just about be reaching my peak in August of that year and dreamt of glory. To the best of my knowledge, no Team GB selector even came to see me. *Perhaps they did but got fed up waiting for me!*

There have been too many instances of my limited sporting prowess being ignored for me to record, but as I don't want you to get the impression that I'm bitter about this, I'll just give one more example. In the summer of 1988, as England battled with a West Indies side at their peak, and lost 4-0 in a series of five Tests, they used four separate captains. Peter May, then Chairman of Selectors, knew that I was not only in good form, but available. Did he give me a call? No he didn't, and like you, I can only assume that attendance at Arbroath High School was not deemed appropriate enough for a captain of the England cricket team.

There you have it then, with a lifetime of personal sporting ambitions seemingly constantly thwarted, almost all of the sporting highs and lows to be found in this book, were gained as a spectator. I don't suppose I'm alone and would guess that the majority of people reading this will be in the same boat, i.e. frustrated sports men and women who have lived out their dreams through watching their heroes, whilst standing on a terrace, sitting in a grandstand or in front of a television screen. If you're one of them, I'm confident that you'll find something in the following pages that you can relate to.

Chapter 1

Discovering my limitations

I can't remember exactly when I realised that I was never going to be a sportsman, although I reckon the seeds of doubt would have been planted by the age of five. Whatever, by the time I left Arbroath's Hayshead Primary School in June 1962, there were realistically only three career options left open to me. I could either become a successful criminal, a much sought after gigolo or simply knuckle down and enjoy a lifetime of conventional work.

It's possible that my fairly strict God fearing Presbyterian upbringing may have played a part in determining which of the options I would follow. However, whilst I'm convinced that I could have been a success in whichever of those career paths I chose to follow - and even now, it may not be too late to give the first two a go - I'd like to think that I preferred the personal challenge of making a more conventional contribution to Society. Was it worth it? Readers of the first book can judge.

Up to the age of around 6/7, the lads (& some of the lassies) living at the top end of Benedict Road in Arbroath, would play all sorts of games, some of which involved a ball. There was nothing sophisticated or remotely organised and we'd just kick or throw a ball around as we began to develop the basic skills of cricket, rounders and football etc. Other than the ball and a rudimentary bat, the only other equipment we used were lampposts. They would serve as stumps for the first, bases in the second and as one of the goalposts when we attempted the latter.

In that small corner of town, and without blatant blowing of my own trumpet, I would confidently assess my level of ability amongst my peers as being…………………………average. There were some things I was particularly good at like 'swinging and missing' with either bat in hand or foot anywhere near ball, but just occasionally, I'd make a great

1

save or hold a catch that in today's parlance would be described as a 'worldy'. The early signs were that if I was ever to make a name for myself, it would be either as a goalkeeper, catcher, wicketkeeper or circus performer.

I can remember the day, and this will have been before starting school, when I managed to perfect the art of consistently kicking a ball back over my head. Had there been any scouts in Arbroath at that time who had been briefed, "Find us a young kid who can lob the ball back to the goalie without having to turn round and look at him", who knows how my career path would have panned out? We can only guess.

On the back green and along the side passage between shed and front door of 56 Benedict Road, Alan and I would practise our skills. I can recall the 1958 World Cup held in June in Sweden when Pele first emerged as an eighteen year old superstar. There was no television coverage back in those days - certainly not in our house - so we were reliant on radio (wireless as was) and newspaper reports to provide a mental picture of what our heroes were doing in that seemingly far off country.

We were certainly no 'glory hunters' as we tried to imagine ourselves as some of the greats of that tournament. Yes, we were interested in how the likes of Pele, Just Fontaine and Raymond Kopa were doing, but our heroes were the likes of Bill Brown, the Arbroath born goalkeeper who was playing for Dundee, Harry Haddock, the Clyde left back and Graham Leggat, the speedy Aberdeen winger.

Sadly, manager Dawson Walker only played Leggat in the first two games, Brown in the last and poor Haddock never got a game. No wonder Scotland floundered (that's deliberate folks!) and as has been the case ever since, Scotland were denied their rightful place in the knockout stages when, despite an encouraging opening draw against Yugoslavia, defeats to Paraguay and France sent the plucky Scots home.

Undaunted, Alan and I immediately switched our allegiance to Northern Ireland, the land of our birth, and amongst others, our heroes became Harry Gregg, Alf McMichael, Peter McParland and the like, as the Irish reached the quarter finals after a dramatic play-off victory over Czechoslovakia, only to lose 4-0 to France.

On the green at the back of the house, we would develop our cricketing skills, but as is the way with all young lads, we were not interested in perfecting our solid forward defensive technique. If the ball was there to be hit, who could blame us if that was exactly what we did. I have one distinct memory of pulling a full toss from Alan over the midwicket boundary.

Now then, I may not have mentioned the dimensions of our cricketing arena, but I guess the boundary, the edge of the house, must have been a good eight yards away from the crease. Unfortunately, it also contained the window of the master bedroom in Mr & Mrs Cant's (and their daughters Sheena and Constance) downstairs flat. Just as the ball smashed through the window, Mr Cant happened to walk in. What a timely entry! There was no escape or excuse. We couldn't say that it was a) an act of God or b) some bad boys from Abbotsford Road who had done it. I've no idea how this was resolved but I suspect that Dad had to do a bit of overtime down at Northern Tool & Gear to settle the debt with our downstairs neighbour.

It wasn't until we got to our third year at school that the first signs of structure, self-discipline and of playing within the rules surfaced. In part, this will have been a result of us boys becoming a Life Boy, like me, or in other cases, a Cub, and being asked to make up the numbers as we joined the older members of those organisations in 'proper' games. We may still have been at the stage where we ran around and collectively chased the ball, but the bigger boys were showing - and probably before Alan Hansen was out of nappies back home in Sauchie - that there was more to be gained for the team from 'passing & moving'.

By the age of ten, we were organising our own games of football, and to a lesser extent cricket, after school. Some of us even had ....football boots or ....cricket bats.

Between years 5 & 7 at primary school, it was clear that some of us boys had more natural ability than others. Those who won selection to one of the school teams thought that they had become part of a select sporting elite. In reality, Mr Robertson, who had perhaps upwards of 120 boys to choose from had a far better chance of achieving success than Jim Mann, the Life Boy leader, who always appeared grateful just to have 11 boys turn up and be prepared to suffer regular heavy and humiliating defeats.

In truth, almost all of the boys picked for one of Hayshead's three teams, were picked from either Year 6 or 7. I can recall only the one exception and that was Tommy Walker who, although two years younger than most of us, was already a class act and went on to become a part-timer with Arbroath FC before being transferred to Airdrieonians and a full time professional playing career in the Scottish First Division.

By Primary 6, I was a regular member of the 'B' team, playing mostly in goal. I did have a couple of games on the right wing, but after two spectacular shows of mediocrity, I was given the woollen roll top goalkeeper's jersey on a permanent basis.

I can't remember how we did competitively in 1960/61 but the following year, Hayshead won the League and Cup double with me making a contribution as the last line of defence. My memory may be letting let me down, but I think we won every league game we played. Whatever, I must have impressed someone because I was selected to represent the Arbroath & District Primary School Football Association in a match against their counterparts from Dundee. The match was played at Ogilvie Park in Arbroath, and whilst the final score escapes me, I know that I did suffer from that complaint that all goalies have to put up with from time to time viz. a bad back. If I didn't before, I now knew that I was just not good enough.

Incidentally, in a conversation with Don Masson recently, he told me that he had a similar reality check type experience when playing (as an outfield player) for Kincardineshire Primary schoolboys. As the best player I've ever seen wear the black and white stripes of Notts County,

4

he obviously got over it quicker than me or.....................perhaps he was just more talented!

The 'double' was sealed as Hayshead beat close rivals, Inverbrothock Primary, 4-1 in the Watters' Cup Final at Gayfield on a warm summer evening in June 1962. I was a hero to many on that night, making a number of useful contributions including saving a penalty when the game was 'in the balance'. However, I was wholly responsible for allowing what proved thankfully to be no more than a consolation goal, by allowing a weak shot to pass through my legs and into the net. That just about summed up my playing career - up one minute but down the next.

I was still at Hayshead when an exciting new feature was added to Springfield Park (Springy), viz. the pitch and putt course. I spent hours on there trying to develop skills that might allow me to a) see the world and b) earn lots of money. Sadly, I was never going to make a good golfer but it was fun, and in adult life, although I've never got any better, I've infrequently enjoyed hacking my way round 18 holes.

Moving on to secondary school (Arbroath High), I was a member of most sports teams, most notably football and cricket, and after becoming Southesk House Captain, felt obliged to represent my house by competing at the annual Sports' Day, swimming gala and rugby union six-a-side tournament. Looking back, I suppose the phrase, 'it's not the winning, it's the taking part', was probably coined as some sort of consolation for the likes of me.

I guess there was some minor glory in twice coming third in the one mile race which was open to all boy pupils of the school, regardless of age. It not only gained some points for Southesk, but in both years, I was then asked to represent the school as a 'miler' at the Angus Schools event. I took some pride in that although I was later to discover that those who were ahead of me by some distance at the AHS Sports' Day, had been offered the chance, but had found some reason - make that excuse - not to be available on the nights in question. They knew what they were doing, as on both occasions up in Forfar, I was a distant last and out of my depth.

Looking back now, I suppose my 20/day smoking habit - you may wonder how I could afford that as a teenager and you'll just have to read the first book for an explanation - didn't help, but there was much more to it than that. I had the stamina but just didn't have the speed.

As if to reinforce that last observation, I once left school at around the normal finishing time of 3.45pm, and having quickly changed at home on Keptie Street, ran all the way to Monifieth in time to catch the 6.05pm train back to Arbroath. Some of my Monifieth based AHS school friends had bet me that I couldn't do it, and I think I gained a packet of 10 Park Drive Tipped as a result of proving that I could.

In addition to playing for school teams, I also competed in various sports, although primarily football, as a member of the 5th (Abbey Church) Boys' Brigade. As a group we had our successes and failures and I suppose that 'win some/lose some' habit has helped develop the philosophic outlook that has comforted me as I experienced the occasional highs but much more frequent lows in later sport watching life.

As an adult, and particularly in the ten/fifteen years or so after leaving Scotland, I turned out on the odd occasion for college or work teams in various sports. For a brief time I was even manager of a team competing in the Mansfield & District Sunday League. My tenure only lasted a few games. Indeed, only until such time as I conveniently found that I had other things to do on Sundays, and resigned before the chairman had the chance to give me a very public 'vote of confidence'.

Chapter 2

Earliest memories of watching fitba'

Whilst the details are somewhat sketchy, all the evidence appears to suggest that the first game of professional football I ever watched was at Gayfield Park in the 1953/54 season as Arbroath took on Dumbarton in what was then known as the Scottish 'B' Division. I'm basing this, admittedly very loosely, on my recollections as a three year old, details of which can be found in Chapter 4 of the first book.

Thereafter, if I'm honest, I've no recollection of any specific games until the 1958/59 season. I have however a distinct memory of looking out of the Arbroath Infirmary window one morning in September 1958 and seeing smoke rise from the remnants of Gayfield's fire ruined main stand.

NB – in truth, other than some covered terracing, this was the only stand.

This followed a Scottish League Cup Tie against Partick Thistle. Arbroath had reached the Quarter Finals and having lost 2-1 at Firhill in the first leg could only manage a 1-1 draw in the second. On that sunny 18th September 1958 morning, the Club had not only missed out on a possible semi-final tie - Partick Thistle progressed to the Final only to lose to Hearts - but their stand had disappeared.

NB – if you want to find out why I was in hospital and not at the previous night's game, you'll just have to get yourself a copy of Processed Peas.....etc. OK – I promise not to mention it again!

The fact that Arbroath had shown some early form was promising and this developed into the first season that I can recall with any clarity as, with Dad and brother Alan, notwithstanding just the one instance of hospitalisation of course, we watched almost every home game and celebrated with Red Lichties all over the world as the Maroons regained their rightful place in the Scottish 1st Division.

They had been in the top division at the outbreak of WW2, but following cessation of hostilities, had been demoted. There is no evidence to support my theory but I detect the heavy influence of both Rangers and Celtic in this arbitrary decision. Historically, they have paid lip service to the lesser clubs in Scotland, and in my opinion, have been ruining the game north of the Border for years. Besides, and I can perhaps relate to this a little, they just never fancied an away trip to Gayfield in February when, with a cold wind blowing in off the North Sea, there were occasions when, with a particularly heavy tide, spray could drench both players and spectators alike if they happened to be in the north east corner of the ground.

As the season drew to a conclusion, Arbroath were fighting for the runners-up spot - Ayr United were runaway leaders - and although they looked fairly secure in second place, there was still a chance that Stenhousemuir or Dumbarton could catch them.

Following postponements as a result of a hard winter, the end of the season was proving to be a demanding challenge for many Scottish clubs, and Arbroath's last four games were played in a period of nine days. The first of these, an away trip to Stenhousemuir on Monday 20th April 1959, saw them lose 7-0 to their promotion rivals. This set the nerves jangling in one eight year old boy in particular.

When, forty eight hours later, Arbroath returned from Douglas Park (Hamilton Accies) having been beaten 4-0, it proved almost too much for this young fan. Were we to be denied the glory we had fought for all year, and should we prepare ourselves for anti-climax and another season up against the likes of the bridie munchers from Forfar? I expect, dear reader that the tension is even getting to you right now!

Well, you can relax, because in front of a crowd of 3,894, on Saturday 25th April 1959, Arbroath FC gained sweet revenge for the defeat seventy two hours or so earlier, and defeated the Accies 6-0 in the return game at Gayfield. For the first time in my life, I experienced the joy that only true followers of any sport will recognise. The terraces may not have bounced to the tune of "We ..are ..going ..up.. say..we.. are.. going.. up!" that afternoon - too early for such musical (?)

celebrations - but I reckon there will have been many a dram, no doubt washed down by copious pints of heavy and/or light, in the town that night.

The celebrations continued until the following Wednesday night, when Arbroath completed a momentous season with a 3-1 win over Tayside rivals, St Johnstone. For the first time in nearly twenty years, or in some cases (like me) within living memory, Arbroath would be competing at the same level as the giants of Scottish football.

One other aspect of that memorable year was the exploits of Dave Easson. Throughout 1958/59 there was a contest between the Arbroath centre forward and his main challenger, Peter Price of Ayr United, to see who would become that season's leading scorer in British football. Well, the Honest Men from Ayr may have gone up as champions, but the bustling Dave Easson, with 52 goals, took the scoring honours. There was no 'golden boot' in those days, but I'm sure Dave will have received the equivalent accolade (a mock chop supper perhaps?) in recognition of his achievement.

By the start of the new season, and despite now being a mature nine year old, I was not allowed to attend the first game away at Partick Thistle. It ended as a 2-0 defeat. In fact, I didn't get to any of the away games - not even Dundee - that year. It would have been an adventure, although with a record of

P17 - W0 - D2 - L 15

it would have been a chastening experience for a naïve young supporter who, all summer, had been imagining Arbroath FC challenging for the title. It has to be remembered that, other than Arbroath, all other teams in the top division were full time professionals, and for the Maroons to be even competing at that level was a remarkable feat in itself.

Despite creditable draws at both Pittodrie (Aberdeen) and Ibrox (Rangers), the rest of the campaign away from Arbroath was a bit of a disaster and included defeats such as 8-1 at Love Street (St Mirren), 7-1 at Cathkin Park (Third Lanark), 6-0 at Fir Park (Motherwell) and a

9

succession of 5-0 losses at the likes of Dens Park (Dundee), Starks Park (Raith Rovers) and Easter Road (Hibernian).

Arbroath had a better - although in reality only marginally so - experience when playing at home as the following record illustrates:-

P 17 - W 4 - D 5 - L 8

OK, it was clear from around February that Arbroath were destined for relegation, but for me as an impressionable lad, there were a number of memorable highlights.

It was the first full season that I can recall being allowed to stand wherever I liked on the terraces. Prior to that, and my memory may be letting me down here, both Alan and myself would sit with Dad in the stand. After the fire the previous September, whilst standing, we had still been under Dad's watchful eye.

The crowds averaged around 4,700, and despite results, never dropped below 3,000. This of course was in a burgh with a population of around 20,000, so you can imagine the buzz in the town on the day of a home game. The highest crowds, understandably I guess, were when Celtic (10,135) and Rangers (6,025) arrived with their entourage of 'cerry oot' carrying fans. It was, for me, my first real experience of the differing sectarian views sung in drunken harmony by both sets of supporters. A real eye opener to a wider malaise that continues to counter Scotland's reputation as an open minded and welcoming country.

As for the games at Gayfield, the first on 5th September, saw Arbroath recover from the opening day defeat at Firhill, to beat Stirling Albion 4-3, followed a couple of weeks later by a 1-1 draw with Airdrie. A succession of defeats (more like hammerings!) followed until 28th November when a 2-1 victory over Third Lanark raised hopes of a recovery.

This was followed by a narrow and controversial defeat to Hibernian - to this day I remain convinced that their winner in a five goal thriller should have been disallowed for a foul on Bobby Williamson! - and a run of six unbeaten (2 x wins and 4 x draws) home games. Motherwell were beaten 3-1, and St Mirren 6-2 (some revenge for that 8-1 thrashing in September?) and there were honourable draws with Partick Thistle, Ayr United, Dunfermline Athletic and Dundee.

This was all to no avail however, as the away form was such that the inevitable return to the lower division was confirmed before the end of March. With a record of 38 goals scored and 106 conceded, it is clear that the part time defence, despite the aforementioned Williamson, was not quite up to 1st Division standard.

By the end, at a time when 2 points were awarded for a win, Arbroath finished on 15, with Stirling Albion on 22 and three teams (Airdrie, Aberdeen and St Mirren) a distant 13 points further away. For the record, Hearts won the 59/60 Scottish Championship with Kilmarnock as runners up. Those were the days when, despite the Old Firm dominance in terms of support, there remained a competitive edge to Scottish football.

Whilst all this was a fantastic experience for a football mad wee boy, there was one other football related development occurring in 1958/59 viz. I bought my first ever programme. In fact, I have one for every home league game for that season. This was a new venture by the Club and I'm not aware of them ever having been any available prior to that, at least not during the 1950's, and for over sixty years now, where programmes have been produced, I have tried to get one from every game that I've attended. There are currently, almost 3,000 dating back to 5th September 1959, in my cellar.

Chapter 3

Earliest memories of watching other sports

I can't remember the first time I was taken to Lochlands to watch Arbroath United play competitive cricket in the Strathmore Union. Until 1959, I have only vague memories of playing impromptu cricket with Alan and other young lads - I suspect Ian Robb will have been there as his dad was one of the mainstays of the club - around the side of the pavilion. This, plus having catching practice using an old discarded slip cradle. Watching the cricket would have been of secondary importance to our main source of pleasure which was creating our own games.

Amongst the names that I can remember, and who in my mind will always be associated with that period in the club's history, were the Sievwrights, Vannets, Somervilles and the aforementioned Robbs. This was a very successful time for the Club, with the 1st eleven winning the Strathmore Union in 1959 - *what a sporting year that was in Arbroath!* - made up almost entirely of local players. The one exception was a former Northamptonshire player named Doug Greasley who, after 55 first class games, retired in 1956 and took on the role of professional and coach with Arbroath United.

I suspect that, like the arrangement south of the Border in the Lancashire and Yorkshire leagues, Mr Greasley's appointment will have come with the offer of full time employment. Whatever, he held the role between 1957 and 1966.

The outstanding memory of the championship winning season was attending the professional's benefit game when an Arbroath United X1 played a game against some of the better players competing in the Scottish Counties Championship. These included the then professional at Aberdeenshire, Rohan Kanhai, who was already an established Test player. I've no recollection of how he performed on the day, but have vivid memories of a large crowd and of how we queued up to get this future West Indian captain's autograph. Whatever happened to that?

Other than trips to Lochlands, I used to listen to cricket commentary of England's Test Matches and can recall the long record breaking partnership between Peter May and Colin Cowdrey which helped save England in the 1957 Edgbaston Test v West Indies. This was not only Rohan Kanhai's first Test, it was the very first of what has since become a cricketing institution, viz. Test Match Special. Yes, in between going to school, I heard some of that first ever broadcast, and I've been tuning in ever since.

56 Benedict Road joined the rest of the human race at some time in 1959 and had a television set installed. It must have been early in that year as I can recall occasionally watching televised horse racing – my Dad was a big fan – on Saturday afternoons when Arbroath were playing away from home.

Two key early memories give rise to contrasting emotion. The first was of seeing Dad's reaction during, and immediately after, the televising of the 1959 Grand National. I think he must have been working that Saturday morning and had a drink on the way home after placing his bet on the day's big race. We lads picked out our own fancy, only for fun of course, but were mesmerised by how Dad willed Oxo on to win. I've no idea how much he had wagered on the horse, but we were allowed to go round to the shops on Mayfield Terrace and buy all sorts of treats.

The second memory was much less enjoyable. We were watching the racing one Saturday afternoon - I've just checked and it was the day Arbroath lost by the only goal away at Ayr United - when one of the horses threw his jockey. From memory, the horses were on their way to the start when this incident occurred, and the television camera remained focussed on the prone jockey lying close to the rails, whilst commentators speculated on what had happened and on the health of the jockey.

I can't recall the exact sequence of events, but I seem to think that after a few minutes during which attention was on the horses lining up for the start, the television picture returned to the scene of the incident and showed a sheet being placed over the jockey and him being

13

stretchered away. The commentator(s) then said that they had heard that the jockey had been kicked in the head by his mount and it had been reported that he had died instantly. This sadly proved to be correct and the unfortunate jockey was Manny Mercer, brother of the subsequently better known Joe Mercer.

Chapter 4

Football in the 1960's – there's life beyond Angus

Apart from a lengthy spell in hospital during the 1962/63 season, and a couple of years when my Saturday responsibilities as a message boy for the William Low & Co grocery branch on Keptie Street severely limited my football watching opportunities, I was a regular attender at Gayfield, and increasingly, other grounds. Unfortunately, as not all Scottish clubs produced programmes in the 1960's - to the best of my knowledge, Arbroath just issued the one in 1960/61 - I only have my memory to rely on.

I can say with some certainty that my first visit to Dens Park, Dundee was in April 1961 when a busload of young boys (& possibly a few girls) travelled from Hayshead Primary School to see a Schoolboy International between Scotland and Northern Ireland. I have the programme, and although some of the youngsters on the park that night went on to play professionally, none of them became big names or gained senior international recognition. The Scots won 4-1 although this was theoretically a disappointing result for me as Mum had sent me off wearing green in an attempt to show support for the land of my birth.

My antics that night must have been somewhat embarrassing - in fact Mr McGregor, the Head, quietly informed me as such - but I took some consolation on the bus journey back up to Arbroath, as Mr Robertson told me that two of Scotland's goals should have been disallowed. In effect, it should have been a defeat by just the one goal.

Meanwhile, despite my stay in Bridge of Earn Hospital, up until the 1964/65 season, I was at Gayfield every other Saturday and making trips on my bike to Montrose, Brechin and Forfar for Angus derby games. I've no record of these but I can recall in January 1964 hitch hiking (yes I was 13) to Brechin to see the locals take on Dundee, then

Scottish champions and en route to a European Cup semi-final, in the 2nd Round of the Scottish Cup.

It was a very cold day, and in my mind's eye I can still see the snow-capped Angus hills to the north and west as whoever picked me up headed into Brechin. As for the game, unsurprisingly the senior team won, but with Alan Gilzean scoring four goals in a 9-2 victory, it was a hammering.

My next programme confirms that I then went to Dundee under my own steam - can't remember if it was bike, train or a lift - to see Dundee in a home Scottish Cup Q/F tie with Motherwell. This game was a draw but Dundee won both the replay and semi-final before losing 3-1 to Rangers at Hampden Park in front of over 120,000. I was a bit envious of my pal, Peem Low, who was a genuine Dundee fan and who went to the Final with his dad. My trips to Hampden were to come later.

Thinking of the Scottish Cup, there was great excitement the previous season (62/63) when, following a hard winter and a number of postponements, Arbroath eventually took on 1st Division Partick Thistle in the second round. Following a 1-1 draw away at Firhill, and a 2-2 draw in the replay, because of the unavailability of a neutral venue as a result of the backlog of games, Gayfield was chosen for the third game.

I can remember this for two reasons. Firstly, I'd not long been released after five months in hospital and this was my first game since September. Secondly, as Gayfield had no floodlights, the kick off was set for, from memory, 3.30pm. Now, this caused a problem at Arbroath High School as we'd normally not have been released by that time. Despite overtures from senior pupils - remember I was just a 1st year pleb then and had only returned to school a few days earlier - there was to be no mass early exodus of excited youngsters.

Whatever, as soon as we were 'set free', I ran down Keptie Street as fast as my recovering legs would carry me, and there was Mum at the front door with my scarf. I can't remember how much of the game I missed, although I reckon I was probably the first AHS schoolboy to make it, but sadly not the only one to traipse home disconsolately afterwards following a 3-2 defeat.

There was a similar experience in 1965/66 when, in a Preliminary Round tie, Arbroath were paired with Cowdenbeath. After a 2-2 draw at Gayfield, the Maroons travelled to Central Park and played out a 1-1 draw. This time, a geographically suitable neutral venue was available, and on a midweek night, I biked down to Dundee to see the third game under the Tannadice Park (Dundee United) floodlights. Again, in dramatic fashion, Arbroath were to be on the wrong end of a five goal thriller.

With a good tail wind, as I pedalled back up the A92, I surmised that it was highly unlikely that I'd ever see my home town team win the Scottish Cup. Still, I made good time and was back home at the Station Hotel approximately one hour later. In fact, I was able to not only tell the regular drinkers the outcome of the game, but I'd beaten those of their pals who'd travelled down to Dundee on the train.

One of the punters in the famous 'wee room' was Bob McLean, a free-lance journalist. He was so impressed with my achievement, and having heard of how I'd followed Arbroath all over the county on my bike, thought that this was newsworthy. So it was then, that following a press photograph of myself and bike, there was a short article in praise of my efforts in both the Arbroath Herald and Dundee Courier. The short lived publicity and praise was all well and good, but if I'm honest, I'd much rather that Arbroath had made it through to the next round and a home game v St Mirren!!

Whilst on the subject of Scottish Cup Ties, my very first trip to Hampden Park was for the Rangers v Celtic Final in April 1966. A chap called Walter Edmonds (always known as Wattie), who was a former barman at the Station Hotel, had a spare ticket and asked if I'd like to go. Well, he knew he was onto a winner there and we travelled through on the train. It was a jam packed journey with a) supporters of both persuasions crammed into the various carriages and b) carrier bags of sufficient alcohol to have kept a small nation in booze for a year.

There was no bother on the way through, but after the game which ended as 0-0 draw, there were a few from the 126,552 in attendance who were clearly 'the worse for wear', and unlikely to be going home that night. Not that I witnessed any violence or crimes being committed, but there was such an alcohol infused atmosphere that I'd not have been surprised to have read of trouble as I delivered my papers the next day.

The replay was played the following Wednesday night with Rangers lifting the trophy after a 1-0 win. The only goal of the game came from the Dane, Kai Johansen. I only saw this on television of course, but can confirm that it was a 25 yard screamer.

Despite going on to reach the final of the European Cup Winner's Cup the following season, that was the last Scottish Cup Tie that Rangers were to win for almost twenty months. I just happened to have been at Parkhead on 28th January 1967, watching Arbroath lose 4-0 to Celtic in the first round of the 1966/67 Scottish Cup.

Memorable though that was, by the midway point of the second half, the match taking place before us was no longer the focus of interest for the majority of fans present that day, as word came through of how another game taking place that afternoon was unfolding. Yes, this was the day when the 'mighty' Rangers travelled across the Border to face 'wee' Berwick Rangers, and suffered a 1-0 defeat. Probably, the greatest ever shock in Scottish FA Cup history prompting never to be forgotten celebrations amongst the Celtic supporters.

One final personal memory of the Scottish Cup in the 1960's is of Arbroath's visit to then non-league Elgin City in February 1968. Arbroath had caused a surprise by beating Ayr United away from home in the 1st Round and were expected to easily secure their passage into the 3rd Round after then being drawn away to Elgin.

There had been a lot of snow in the week leading up to the game and there was a threat of more as I walked up the Montrose Road on the morning of the game, looking for a lift north. Within minutes a car pulled up and I was on my way.................at least to Montrose. I had quite a long wait standing by the A92 before the next driver took pity on me. Hallelujah, I had hit the jackpot. En route to Elgin himself, the driver had spotted my scarf and not only picked me up but promised to meet me after the game to get me back to Arbroath.

Unfortunately, that is as good as it got. In what was then, and remains to this day, a record crowd of 12,650 at Borough Briggs, Elgin produced the shock of the round - although no way near as cataclysmic as in the previous year at Berwick! - and won 2-0.

NB – in 2016 I took Helen for her first ever (& my second) visit to that ground. Before joining 859 other spectators at the game, we spent some time in the supporters' bar. I got talking and mentioned that I had a programme from that record breaking game of almost 50 years before. "How much do you think" I asked, "would this highly collectable programme, in mint condition, fetch today?" I was somewhat chastened by the reply, "Ach, thirs hunerrds o' them aboot in the toon. Ye've proabably goat a chance o' getting 50p!"

Whilst most of those with a keen interest in football living in Arbroath wished the local team well, it is a fact that many of them had a regular top division team that they also followed. I personally had no problem with that when it was the likes of Dundee, Aberdeen, or even as the 1960's developed and Dundee United progressed, the team from Tannadice Park. I did have a problem though with the hordes who professed to a lifelong support of either of the Old Firm teams.

Seeing at least one bus, crammed with supporters of either Rangers or Celtic, leave the town every week to travel to wherever either of the two teams were playing, just didn't seem right to me. In my youth I was probably a bit naïve and didn't fully appreciate the historical sectarian reasons for the level of mass support (and indeed deep rooted antipathy of the other team) for the two Glasgow based giants.

It dismayed me then, and even more so now, to hear commentators suggest that the two teams were 'good for Scottish football'. Taking a detached view, this has never been the case, although I do accept that without their high profile, the rest of the world would probably be blissfully unaware of the game in Scotland.

I'm giving these personal thoughts because, in part, they explain how I came to be a Kilmarnock supporter. During my formative years, under Willie Waddell as manager, the Ayrshire club were beginning to emerge as one of the leading sides in Scotland. However, just like Leeds United south of the Border a few years later, whilst they threatened to win trophies, they never quite succeeded and were perennial runners-up.

As someone who has always favoured the underdog – no glory hunter me! – and perhaps the fact that supporting them made me different and stand out in a crowd, I became a keen follower of Kilmarnock FC. *NB – although this coincided with Arbroath having a few 'fallow' years floundering around near the bottom of the 2nd Division, they remained my 'proper' team.*

I started to go to a few away games to watch Killie, primarily when they were in Dundee, although I did see them at least once at Aberdeen, St Johnstone and at Montrose in a Scottish Cup Tie. Not only that, I bought a tie, badge and a scarf, each of which became key elements of my outward appearance during the mid-sixties, and all of them remain in my possession to this day. The scarf was one of those faux silk designs featuring the club badge. I wore this in classic student fashion with one end flamboyantly thrown over my shoulder. All I needed was a duffle coat and I'd have been regarded as a fashion icon.

Sorry – I digress.

The 1964/65 Scottish Football League season is remarkable for a number of reasons. Firstly, it is the only occasion in the entire history of the competition when neither one of Rangers or Celtic have finished in the top three. Secondly, as it came to a conclusion, it featured three teams, two of whom had never previously been champions, all in with a chance of winning the title.

As the season reached its finale, Dunfermline Athletic drew their penultimate game with St Johnstone and this meant that the best they could do was finish as runners-up. Their final league game, at home to

Celtic, should have been played on Saturday 24th April 1965. However, they were to play this same team on that day in their first ever Scottish Cup Final. *NB – they lost that 3-2 but gained some revenge the following Wednesday by beating the Bhoys 5-1 in the re-arranged game at East End Park.*

All of this meant that the League could now only be won by either Hearts or Kilmarnock. As it was, the Edinburgh team were two points ahead on the morning of the last game when they were to face ....Killie at Tynecastle. In the days of two points for a win, all the Jambos needed was a draw or to make sure that if they were to lose, it was by no worse than 2-0, to win their fifth Championship on goal average. NB – under the vagaries of that old system, any other defeat by two goals, e.g. 3-1, 4-2 etc., would have been good enough for Hearts.

Were it not for the fact that my responsibilities as Willie Low's message boy operating out of the Keptie Street branch took precedence - I did, without success, look around for someone to cover me on that afternoon - there would have been one additional, nearly fifteen year old schoolboy, squeezed into the 37,000 in attendance that day.

Although the radio coverage concentrated on the Cup Final - it did feature Celtic after all - I managed to get regular updates on how the 'Championship decider' was going. This meant me going out on the bike with a little transistor radio in the basket. I can remember I'd just dropped off some 'messages' at a house on Nolt Loan Road, when news came through that the game at Tynecastle was over, and for the only time in their history, Kilmarnock FC were Scottish Champions. They had defeated Hearts by exactly two goals to nil and had a goal average of 1.879 compared to that of Heart of Midlothian's 1.837.

I'm sure I'm not the only one in Arbroath who can vividly recall a somewhat tousled message boy racing down Keptie Road/Street that late afternoon. With his blue college scarf flapping away vigorously behind him as the bike reached unheard of before speeds, he could be clearly heard loudly singing/screaming celebratory songs.

Kilmarnock, like many Scottish League sides back then, achieved some success in European football. In that 1964/65 Championship winning season they appeared in the Inter-Cities Fairs Cup, the predecessor of the UEFA Cup/Europa League. It looked as if it would be a short lived campaign as they lost 3-0 in the first leg of their opening tie away to Eintracht Frankfurt, European Cup finalists a mere four years previously.

It wasn't until I called into Yules for my paper round - yes I had two jobs back then - in the morning following the second leg, that I became aware of Killie having achieved a footballing miracle. Despite conceding an early goal at Rugby Park, they went on to gain a 5-1 (5-4 on aggregate) win over the German giants. This got me thinking, 'next time - I want to be there'.

Well, I didn't make it to the 2nd Round tie v Everton, which they lost 6-1 on aggregate, nor did I get to the famous 2-2 draw in the home leg of the game against Real Madrid (lost 7-3 on aggregate) in the following year's European Cup. I had to make do with the 1966/67 campaign, once again in the Inter-Cities Fairs Cup, before I made my own European debut.

I can't remember the circumstances, although I think Dad arranged for me to get a lift through to and from Glasgow, with an overnight stay thrown in, with one of the whisky travellers. Whatever, and unfortunately I have no programme from that game, I saw Kilmarnock defeat La Gantoise of Belgium, 1-0 in the 3rd round home leg before going through 3-1 on aggregate. They then met and defeated Lokomotive Leipzig in the quarter final to set up a tie with Leeds United, who stood in the way of the wee Ayrshire club making it to a European final.

NB – in that same competition in that year I went down to Dundee to see United defeat Barcelona and then Juventus at Tannadice in the home 2nd & 3rd round games. Although the Italians won the 3rd round tie on aggregate, I make the point to illustrate that a) Scottish club football was a force to be reckoned with and b) as a 16 year old schoolboy, I was happy to travel anywhere to see a game of football.

Kilmarnock's ties with Leeds were fixed for Friday 19th May (away) and Wednesday 24th May (home). I resolved to get to both of them.

I'd completed my Highers, and like many in 5th Year, was very much killing time at school until the summer holidays. On that basis, I decided to set off hitch hiking on the Thursday morning before the first leg. Dad had arranged for me to get a good start as one of the regulars at the Station was a lorry driver who had a delivery to make in Airdrie that morning. I met him at about 6.30am and he left me at a big transport café a couple of hours later. Following the A74/A66/A1 route I crossed into England for the first time in my life and reached Leeds around 6.00pm.

I found myself a shared room in a very cheap B&B and set off for a pub. Yes, I'd only just turned 17 but you'd be naïve if you thought that I'd had a sheltered upbringing!

I can't recall what part of Leeds I was staying in, but the most striking visual recollection is of the number of black people in the neighbourhood. That is not intended as a social comment but an observation from a teuchter who had probably only ever seen a couple of black men/women in his own non-diverse part of the country.

Whatever, I found a pub and asked for a Black & Tan. Now this was a popular drink at the time for us underage drinkers up in Arbroath and comprised sweet stout (usually William Youngers Sweetheart) and cider. That was what I expected but it is not what I got. Now whether or not it was the three pints of **Guinness** and cider, or the fact that I'd hardly eaten all day that made me 'come over all queer', we'll just have to surmise. Anyway, having drained the last of those three pints, I staggered to the door - it was one of those saloon swing type efforts - and threw up all over the pavement. As the door swung back and forth, I could hear a voice from the bar saying something like "Eeh, them bluddy Scotchmen, they canna hold their drink!" *NB – apologies for the poor attempt at a West Yorkshire accent.*

Although it was dark by this time, and despite my inebriated state, I managed to find the B&B. I had no key, and had to ring to get the landlady to let me in. My companion for the night was already in his bed as I stumbled about in the dark, took off my clothes and climbed into mine.

Well, I'm sure that many readers will be able to relate to what happened next. After probably only a couple of minutes, with my head spinning and a growing desire to retch, I had to sit up to try to overcome the feeling that I was going to be sick. That was having no effect and conscious that being sick all over the floor (or indeed my apparently sleeping but no doubt alarmed roommate) might result in me being thrown out onto the streets, I had to think of something.

Now, you might have thought, find the bathroom. Well, I had an even better idea. Just open the window, and if I was going to throw up, at least I wouldn't be troubling my landlady. The idea seemed sound at the time although there was an immediate problem. The window was one of those old fashioned double paned sash types and I couldn't lift the bottom pane. After a struggle, I managed to lower the top pane by a few inches and was able to stick my head through the gap I'd created.

To do this, I had to stand on the window sill. There I was then, stark naked, standing upright with my head hanging out of the window as I looked out upon that dark Leeds street. Now, I'll never know, but I reckon there may well have been a few locals who just happened to be passing by at that time. Had they looked up and got a good view, I reckon they've probably since required psychiatric help. If not them, just think about the poor guy I was sharing the room with. There is no way he could have slept through the commotion I was making, and you can just imagine what was going through his mind as he got a rear view.

Well, the good news is that after what was probably ten minutes or so, the powerful urge to be sick was overcome and I dropped down off the window sill, and back into bed.

In the morning, and you'll not be surprised to hear this, it's fair to say that 'Ah wiznae feelin' too guid'. After a bit of breakfast, I headed off into the unknown. My first priority was to find the ground. After asking for directions on a few occasions I eventually found Elland Road. My memory may be playing tricks on me but it seemed like I'd walked for miles which, now that I know Leeds fairly well, would suggest that I'd spent the night in the north or east of the city.

Having established the location of the ground, I walked back towards the city centre and found a cinema which was showing films that afternoon. I spent a couple of hours in a café - sipping very slowly on a large mug of tea - before going to the cinema. Some of you will remember that you could spend nearly all day in a picture house in 1967. The adverts, supporting film and main feature were on a continuous loop. Despite falling asleep for a short period, I reckon I probably sat through two whole circuits of the loop before leaving around 5.30pm.

Given the fact that the game would finish around 9.15pm and that it would be getting dark at that time, I had been thinking about how I was to get 'back on the road'. I reckoned that there would be a long walk and struggle to get to a place where I could thumb a lift and feel confident that I'd was heading back to Scotland. I had however come up with a simple plan. I would find a group of Kilmarnock supporters at the ground and see if I could talk myself into getting a lift back over the Border. It was ingenious and......................it worked.

Before the game I asked a few supporters wearing blue and white scarves - no replica shirts in those days - and was eventually directed towards Wullie and Dougie *(NB – that may not be their proper names. I can't remember. I'm just painting a picture!)* who had travelled down from Mauchline that afternoon. When I told them my tale they were more than happy to give me a lift back to Scotland and suggested that I join in with their larger group of pals during the game and we return together to the large car park outside the ground afterwards.

As for the game, Leeds, under Don Revie, were challenging for the English League title at that time and were a team to be feared. Within 30 minutes they were 3-0 up with all three goals coming from Rod Belfitt. Killie kept at it though and didn't let their heads drop, eventually losing 4-2.

The advantage was most definitely with the English side, but with the return leg a mere five days away, the tie was far from over. Wullie, Dougie etc., were confident that Kilmarnock would reach the Final as we were funnelled out of the ground. Unfortunately, I lost them in the throng and had no idea what kind of car they were driving or where it was parked. Now, it may have been that, suspicious of my story viz. a schoolboy from Arbroath of all places, hitch-hiking down the day before to see a team from Ayrshire play football, they considered me a risk. I'll never know and I suppose it may just be possible that the two of them waited all night by their car expecting me to turn up. Whatever, I had an immediate problem.

Thinking quickly, I came up with plan B. In those days, it was quite easy to tell where a car had been registered. This could be done either via the VRN with many Scottish registrations having an 'S', e.g. Angus was SR, or via the tax disc which had the stamp of the issuing office. My plan then was to scour the large car park outside Elland Road to see if I could find a Scottish, and hopefully Ayrshire, registered vehicle in the hope that a) they were heading north and b) had room for a fellow supporter who was desperate to get back over the Border.

My luck was in, as I found a couple of cars side by side with both having been registered in Cumnock. Surely, these belonged to Killie supporters. After a few minutes, six blokes turned up and yes, they were going straight back to Ayrshire. After hearing my story, and having had a wee discussion amongst themselves – I'll admit now, after all these years, it must have seemed a bit strange - I was told to jump in the back and Jimmy & Shuggie *(once more possibly not their real names but you get the picture)* would drop me off on the A74.

With me in the back, we chatted away like old pals as the car headed on through the night, out of Yorkshire/England, and into Scotland. It was still dark when they dropped me off just over the Border as their route took them north westwards via Dumfries and the A76 to Cumnock.

If you've never tried it, you won't need me to tell you that hitch-hiking in the dark can be a bit 'iffy'. Not only are there fewer vehicles on the road in the wee small hours, but drivers are less likely to interrupt their own journey to pick up some ragamuffin standing by the roadside.

My hitch-hiking technique was to wait on the downside of a roundabout to catch traffic as they pulled away, or on the slip road exit from a transport café/service station. If neither option was possible the best course of action I felt was to head off walking in the right direction. I decided upon the latter and must have walked for about three miles when, just as the first glimpses of a new day were beginning to show in the east, I heard the welcome sound of a 'pip' from a horn and the even more welcoming realisation that a vehicle was slowing down behind me.

Looking round, I saw a bus, with the driver pointing to a spot further up the road. He passed me but pulled up in a lay by about 100 yards away. As I approached I could see from the back that it was a Wallace Arnold bus from............................Leeds, and there appeared to be no-one on it. The passenger door was open and the driver, having asked me where I was heading, invited me on board, indicating that I sit in the front seat above the steps.

After telling me that this was a replacement bus heading for somewhere near Loch Lomond, and that he'd drop me off at a transport café near Glasgow, he wanted to know what I was doing hitch-hiking up the A74 at that time of night/day. When I told him the whole tale, he said that he thought I'd been at the game the night before - as had he! - and that having seen my blue college style scarf in the early morning light, he had put two and two together. Well he'd actually made five because he'd assumed that I was heading for Ayrshire and not the north east coast.

By the time I got off his bus, the Saturday morning sun was shining brightly even though it was probably no more than 5.00am. I treated myself to something to eat/drink and asked around the few guys reading a paper/having a bit of breakfast if there was anyone heading towards Dundee. One chap volunteered to take me part of the way and about half an hour later I was standing by a roundabout outside Cumbernauld.

I wasn't waiting long when a car pulled up and a man got out and asked me where I was going. On hearing 'Arbroath' he said he'd take me as far as Perth. That was fine by me, as from there I'd probably need no more than two lifts to get back home. His wife was with him, so I sat in the back and told them where I'd been and what I'd been up to. They seemed elderly, although as I write this now having recently passed 70, I realise they were probably only middle aged.

Whatever, they seemed to take a keen interest in my story. So much so that the driver said they'd change their route and instead of heading off from Perth to Blairgowrie and beyond to reach Aberdeen, they'd take the coast road via Dundee and Arbroath. First though, they were going to stop at the big transport café in Perth - for those of you who can remember, it was on Edinburgh Road near the prison - for a spot of breakfast. When they pulled up, I said that I'd already had something to eat and asked if it was alright if I stayed and had a bit of a sleep in the back of the car. The answer was a short, but polite 'no' and I joined them inside.

NB – this made me think later that they may have thought my tale just a bit too far-fetched to be plausible and they were not prepared to take a risk on me actually being some innocent looking (& sounding), but inventive young criminal.

After their short break, we carried on, and true to their word, they dropped me off in Arbroath around 8.30am. Less than 12 hours previously, I'd been at Elland Road!

As for the return leg, Dad had arranged for me to stay overnight with a family from Rutherglen who were regular visitors to the town (& the Station Hotel) during long weekends, Glasgow Fair etc. Again, I hitch-hiked through to Glasgow, caught the bus that I'd been advised in advance to take, and arrived at their house in the early afternoon. They made quite a fuss of me, told me where I could catch a bus to take me to Kilmarnock and insisted on me meeting the wider family and having a meal.

Well, they overdid it to the point that the game was already underway when I reached Rugby Park, and not only did I not get a programme, but when I eventually got in, I could barely see anything. As it happens, it was a scoreless draw so it could be argued that I didn't miss much as Leeds went through to the Final where they lost over two legs to Dynamo Zagreb.

After the game I had to rush back into town to get the last bus back to Glasgow. I managed this and was dropped off at what I thought was the correct bus stop. However, whether or not I'd made a mistake, I'll never know, but it quickly became apparent that I had no idea where I was. Not only was it dark, but with it being past 11.00pm, there was hardly anyone around. I can't remember now the name of the street that this family lived on, but after asking some of the few people who were about, I was eventually re-directed away from Rutherglen towards Croftfoot, a mile or so further away. I appears that not only had I been dropped off at the wrong stop, it was the wrong suburb in the Glasgow conurbation.

I got to my overnight lodgings around 1.00am to find the 'man of the house' waiting anxiously for my return. Looking back now as an adult and dad myself, I guess he'll have been mightily relieved that, having offered to 'put me up', he was not having to report a 'missing schoolboy'. I was given a lift to the outskirts of the city in the morning and got back to the Station Hotel in the early afternoon.

Now then, it just so happens that as I got home, who should be enjoying a lunchtime drink in the 'wee room' but Bob McLean. You'll remember him - providing you've been paying attention of course! - from a couple of years earlier when he had submitted an article praising my bicycling efforts to watch Arbroath. Well, as Dad told him what I'd done over the past week, his freelance journalistic ears pricked up and the upshot was the wide readership of both Arbroath Herald and Dundee Courier being informed of my exploits. The text came with an accompanying photograph of myself proudly wearing my precious blue and white college type scarf.

Now then, what astute readers will have been thinking to themselves is, 'shouldn't he have been at school?' and....................they'd be right. Although, we were now at that time in the summer term when there was a relaxed atmosphere and a lot of comings and goings, there was still a need to properly record all non-attendances. Aware of this, I'd arranged for a self-penned note (from Mum!) to be sent to Mr Gracie, Head of Fifth Year, asking that Michael be excused on Thursday and Friday of the first week, because he was attending a family wedding in Inverness.

The following Wednesday, Mr Gracie received another note in Mum's 'handwriting', saying that Michael had caught a cold up in Inverness and had been advised to take a couple of days off school. All being well, he should be back on Friday.

Well, as all children are told, lies will invariably come back to haunt you and so it was that I was summoned to Tom Gracie's room in the week following publication of the article. Mr Gracie would have been in his fifties - he had a son at School in the year above me - and was a fine Mathematics teacher with a reputation for discipline. I won't say that he was feared, but he was certainly respected, and on that basis, no-one liked to disappoint him.

Having knocked, probably timidly, at the door, through the glass panel I could see him beckoning me in. I stood in front of his desk where lay three pieces of paper. Two of them I instantly recognised - I'd written them myself! - plus a page from a newspaper containing a picture of someone I also instantly recognised.

He told me of how the article in the Herald had been brought to the attention of Rector Hay and that he had been told to 'deal with me'. I had what could best be described as a severe telling off as I was reminded of the reputation of the School and of how my absences may be interpreted as an indicator of a lack of discipline. I was further reminded that although we were approaching the end of the academic year, he was aware that I was likely to be a member of the 1967/68 sixth form and that were there to be any further examples of unacceptable or disreputable behaviour, I ran the risk of expulsion.

NB – as any readers of my first book, Processed Peas etc., can attest, there could have been any number of reasons for expulsion in the coming twelve months.

Our meeting probably only lasted around five minutes before, with me looking suitably reprimanded, Mr Gracie ended it with a "...............now be off with you!". However, as I put my hand on the door handle, ready to escape the verbal mauling, he shouted "Michael!" I turned round to see him, with a half smile on his face, as he asked, "Michael, why Kilmarnock?" I muttered some incoherent reply but could detect just a slight twinkle in his eye, which led me to believe that Mr Tom Gracie, a well-known and life-long Hibernian supporter was, in his own way, either winding me up, or secretly admiring what I'd done/become.

As a footnote to this tale, I arrived back in Arbroath after Kilmarnock's second leg of their European tie with Leeds on Thursday 25th May 1967, and that night watched on television as Celtic became the first British team to win the European Cup. As, in the previous month, Scotland had travelled to Wembley to inflict England's first defeat since 30th July 1966, thereby themselves, according to the Scottish press, becoming unofficial World Champions, these were indeed heady days.

Now, no longer a message boy, I was able to attend games on any day of the week and whilst it was generally Arbroath home and occasionally away, I was also regularly travelling down to Dundee to see 1st Division football. However, under Albert Henderson who served continuously as Manager/Secretary of the Red Lichties between 1962 and 1980, there were the first signs of a revival in fortunes beginning in 1966/67.

With local lads Tom Cargill, Ian Stirling and Jimmy Cant, supplemented by the likes of Eric Sellars, Dennis Bruce and especially Jimmy Jack, Arbroath finished only a point behind second placed Raith Rovers to be denied promotion back to the 1st Division.

The following season, Arbroath made good on the promise they had shown the year before and with Bruce and Jack a free scoring front pairing, they finished four points clear of third placed East Fife, and would once again be playing the likes of Aberdeen, Hearts, Hibs,

Kilmarnock, and the two Dundee teams. Not forgetting of course, the other two from Glasgow,

An abiding memory of 20th April 1968, when a 2-0 victory over Ayr United at Gayfield confirmed promotion with one league game to go, was of hearing Cliff Richard singing *Congratulations* over the tannoy at the end of the game.

The following season was only marginally better than Arbroath's last in the top flight, inasmuch as they gained 16 points, and were much closer to the second bottom side than back in 1959/60. My programme collection suggests that I went to most home matches - it's possible that I didn't manage to get one at every game - and a number of away games, principally on the east coast. In truth, there were few highlights, although I can say that I was there when Colin Stein, having been sold by Hibs during the week, made his debut for Rangers. He scored a hat-trick in a 5-1 victory!!

As the 1960's drew to a close, in many ways I was a bit of a free spirit, and with the purchase of my first car (VRN 142 EGG), my footballing horizons became much wider. In 1969, in my ultimately unreliable Ford Anglia, I made trips to Aberdeen, Dundee, Perth and even as far as Glasgow where I saw Scotland thrash Cyprus 8-0 in a World Cup Qualifying match.

This was my second time at Hampden Park for a Scotland game. In February 1968, having received a ticket from Mr Dave McKechnie, our PE Teacher and director of Arbroath FC, I had gone by train to witness a 1-1 draw with England. In front of a capacity 134,000, this was a big disappointment as the failure to defeat the 'auld enemy' on this occasion meant that it was England who qualified for that year's European Championships and not Scotland.

Chapter 5

1960's – other sports

In truth, I can't remember watching any live sport, other than football (& two others that I'll cover shortly), during my teens. However, with a television set in the Gyles' household from the previous year, when other commitments allowed, I'd watch whatever sport was being transmitted during this decade.

My first memory is of John Surtees winning the *Sports Personality of the Year* award in 1959. As almost any sport worth watching was shown on the BBC at that time, the annual awards evening was a 'must view' occasion for sports fans of all shapes, sizes and sporting preference. The highlights of the year had invariably been captured by the BBC cameras and this was a TV watching highlight for at least one young lad in Arbroath. *NB – this remains the case to this day, despite much of the coverage now available on other, mainly satellite stations.*

The winners throughout the 1960's were largely predictable and included gold medal winning Olympians, Wimbledon winners, and World Cup winning captains. OK – just the one of those!

Alongside the likes of Anita Lonsbrough, Mary Rand, David Hemery, Ann Jones and Bobby Moore were Henry Cooper and Tommy Simpson. The boxer, later Sir 'Enery, who won the award again in 1970, was not too much of a surprise, but the cyclist certainly was.

Whether or not it was a sign of emerging and thrusting manhood, I have particularly vivid memories of Maria Bueno's tennis successes at Wimbledon. Although she won the Championship just twice (beaten finalist on two other occasions) she not only appeared a very attractive young lady, she was a mighty fine player.

BBC TV coverage of Test Cricket, with Peter West as the main presenter and Jim Laker and Richie Benaud as commentators, was another 'must watch' whenever I was able to get in front of a set. Failing that, the ball by ball coverage from TMS (Test Match Special) would replace those infuriating times when the words "Sorry, but we're going to have to interrupt coverage of the Test to go over to Newmarket for the 2.30 feature", or whatever, were uttered.

One early memory, is of the 1963 Test Series v West Indies. Having lost the first Test, England were in a position to win the second and tie the Series as play drew to a close on a rain affected fifth day at Lord's. Back from school, and with message boy duties not due to start until later that year, the television was switched on as soon as I got in. England were batting, needing 234 to win and looked as if they would do it. However, they were one batsman short as Colin Cowdrey had suffered a broken arm earlier in the innings. A ball from Wes Hall had done the damage.

As England inched towards victory they were losing wickets at regular intervals. With rain clouds gathering, the last over saw England require eight runs with two wickets (one of whom was Cowdrey!) remaining, for victory. West Indies, given Cowdrey's injury, would have felt that only one further wicket was required.

Well, in such drama that the BBC News was delayed - a previously unheard of occurrence - and with all four results still possible, England gathered a further two runs but lost a wicket via a run out on the fourth ball of the over. The Nation waited to see if Colin Cowdrey would emerge from the England dressing room. To rapturous cheers, and with his arm in plaster, he did. Fortunately, as a result of the run out he was at the non-striking end and was able to watch as David Allen successfully defended the final two balls of the match. It was a draw and Kenneth Kendall, Richard Baker, or whoever, was finally able to present the BBC News.

Olympic coverage of the Rome games in 1960 suited television viewers in the UK. The key events were being held at a time when we were 'up & about' and able to watch live.

I can recall seeing Anita Lonsbrough win her swimming gold medal and Don Thompson wearing some form of towel under his cap to protect himself from the sun/heat as he won the 50km walk.

Brian Phelps, the diver, who I think won a bronze medal, was another British personality from those Games, although of much more local interest, was Dick McTaggart. He was a lightweight boxer who had won gold at Melbourne four years earlier. I'd no personal recollection of this but was aware of him via the almost saturation coverage in the Courier. In Rome, he won bronze, which whilst a disappointment for him and the good citizens of Dundee and the wider locality, did not deny him almost hero status. Younger Dundonians, who will have no recollection of his boxing career, can at least now develop their gymnastic skills at the Dick McTaggart Centre in the city.

Sports fans were given advance notice of the pending Tokyo Olympic Games in 1964 listening to an instrumental hit from Helmut Zacharias called *Tokyo Melody*.

British gold medal winners in these Games included the long jumpers Mary Rand and the Welshman Lynn Davis, plus 800 metre runner Ann Packer and Ken Matthews in the 20km walk. From memory, the only medallist from north of the Border was Bobby McGregor who gained a swimming silver in the 100 metre freestyle.

As for Mexico City in 1968, a combination of the time difference and the fact that I had started work, limited the live viewing of these Games. I did stay up to watch David Hemery win the 400 metres hurdles and Chris Finnegan his gold as a middleweight boxer.

As referred to earlier, having secured my first car, I was able to travel further afield for my fix of football. In addition, my Ford Anglia, on most Sundays, could be seen travelling over the Tay Road Bridge heading towards Cowdenbeath and the regular Stock Car Racing at Central Park. With then girlfriend Jackie, and occasionally sister Dawn, I really enjoyed these outings.

Unlike F1, where, unless you are watching on TV you cannot get the whole picture and see the drama unfold, with stock cars all of the action was there before you. I particularly liked the 'reverse grid' element in which the faster, or higher graded vehicles, started at the back and had to use skill to manoeuvre their way up to the front of the field. That to me, was the thrill of these events. I was not however, particularly keen on the 'banger' races when drivers seemed simply to take delight in barging out of the way any car that inconveniently happened to be in front of them. Not sport to me!

It was a good summer and in addition to George Findlay (car number 128) who was from Arbroath, I can vividly remember the leading drivers of that era viz. Tennant Douglas (31), Gordon McDougall (41) and Alan Neilson (119). Sadly, the Ford Anglia's days were numbered and that summer of 1969 was a 'one off'.

The other sport that I briefly glimpsed was hurling. As a family, we were in Ireland in September 1961 for my Uncle Bobby's wedding. On a day out with my Dad driving - that was a sporting experience of sorts in itself! - we stopped off in Navan for some reason and passed by a sports field where two teams were playing a weird game. Dad explained what it was and we watched, somewhat bemused, for about half an hour. I was none the wiser!

Chapter 6

The 1970's – falling in love (twice!)

As I've been working away here, I've slowly come to the conclusion that I'm going to have to cut back a little or else this sporting memoir will end up so long that it will cease to be of any interest to anyone other than myself. *NB – I know what you're thinking. You're probably right, but I'll carry on anyway.*

Having made the decision, my plan is, with the exception of 1970 (below), from here on in, I'm just going to recall a few memorable games from each year, adding casual observations/experiences on whatever relevant topics come to mind. This should come easy enough to me, particularly as that's how I normally hold a conversation.

1970

Up until September, I continued to live and work in Arbroath. I no longer had a vehicle of my own, and was restricted to hitch hiking to any games outside the town. With the Red Lichties back in the 2nd Division and only producing the occasional programme during the 1969/70 season (none apparently available at any of the away games I went to), I have next to no record of games I attended in the very early part of the new decade.

Generally, when Arbroath were too far away for me to guarantee getting there and back in a day, I'd simply hitch - usually one lift only required either way - down to Dundee to see whichever team was at home that weekend. I'm not aware of any memorable games, although the latter stages of the Scottish Cup were the highlight of the closing months of that season.

I'd seen Arbroath knocked out in the 1st Round, losing 2-1 at home to Clydebank and then Dundee defeat Airdrie (3-0) in the 2nd Round. The quarter final ties saw Kilmarnock - they remained my 'second' team - drawn away to Motherwell.

OK, it was pushing it a bit, particularly in February, but as I'd never before been to Fir Park, I set off early to make my way to the west of Scotland. I must have made good time because I can remember, after probably more pints than was advisable for a nineteen year old, that I got into deep conversation with a number of Killie fans in a pub before the game. I can just imagine some of them later that night, telling their wives that they'd met up with a young guy from Arbroath who'd tried to convince them that he'd hitch-hiked to Leeds three years before! Well, I knew it was true.

Kilmarnock won the tie 1-0. I can't remember the scorer, which might have had something to do with my pre-match intake of anaesthetic, but arrived safely back in Arbroath that night looking forward to finding out who Kilmarnock would draw in the semi-final. Whatever, I was going.

There was some good and bad news. They were to play Aberdeen - they had missed all-conquering Celtic - so, like the Motherwell tie, this was winnable. The choice of neutral venue, Muirton Park in Perth, was also good news as it was easy for me to get to. The downside to that though was that it was also very easy for Dons' fans to make the trip. So it proved to be. On 14th March 1970, there were probably four times as many Aberdonians in the crowd of 25,812 as had travelled up from Ayrshire.

I got a lift both to and from Perth with a couple of Aberdeen fans who frequented the Station Hotel. We stood together on the terraces as their team deservedly won, albeit narrowly, courtesy of the one first half goal from Derek McKay. I came home disappointed but resolved that I'd go to the Final - inevitably against Celtic - and take 'ma wee sister' Dawn, who, at thirteen, was at an impressionable age and had convinced herself that she was a fan of the Glasgow side.

The night before the Final was spent at the head of Glen Clova. Jake Nangle - you'll have to read my first book to find out more about him - was the following week heading off for a new life in England, and a gang of us had decided to give him a different sort of leaving 'do'.

We arrived there early that night and set up a tent for the four of us in a field across from the Glen Clova Hotel. We then went on to please the bar manager by more than doubling his takings for a normal Friday night. *NB – if you're not familiar with the Glen, it is a dead end with, other than the odd farming family, no-one living within about five miles. Anyone using the bar will have had to make a conscious decision to be there.* Well, we certainly had!

I've no idea how much we drank, but I felt worse than terrible in the morning. Still, I'd promised my sister that she was going to Hampden to see Celtic win the Scottish FA Cup and I just had to get back to Arbroath. I wasn't going to spoil her day!

As it happens, in front of 108,434 at Hampden on Saturday 11th April 1970, Aberdeen shocked Celtic by winning 3-1 with two of the goals coming from McKay and one from Joe Harper. Bobby Lennox pulled back a late goal to make the score 2-1, but McKay got his second even later to send Rangers supporters across the world wild with delight.

In addition to Dawn, I took my then girlfriend - they were both making their first trip to Hampden - and we travelled in style. Well, although we joined a trainload of heavy drinking football fans in Arbroath, at least both mothers would have been pleased that we weren't hitch-hiking.

Now, I can't remember the full circumstances, but there came a time late in the game when Dawn became alarmed - no, it was more like panic stricken - at the movement of the crowd and I had to force a gap to squeeze the two girls out to the back where they could breathe more easily. We could hardly see a blade of grass down below of course, but sometimes sacrifices have to be made!

Looking back, I reckon this came about as a result of the sheer size of the crowd. Everyone's first experience in a seething mass of humanity, the likes of which is no longer allowed at sports stadia, can be daunting, to say the least. That is not up for debate. However, I reckon part of Dawn's discomfort could have been the result of seeing her beloved

Celtic, behind from the 27th minute, well beaten by the underdogs. She'll never admit it and......we'll never know.

That was the last game of the 69/70 season for which I have a programme although, as it was 11th April, I reckon I probably saw at least a couple more. Whatever, from this point onwards, things were about to change. I saw a few Scottish games at the beginning of the 1970/71 season, but on Sunday 13th September, I boarded the overnight sleeper service to England, and less than twenty four hours later, saw only my second ever game south of the Border.

I had been working for Metal Box in Arbroath for a couple of years. Career opportunities were limited at this small site, and as a result, I was transferred to the significantly larger plant, based in Sutton-in Ashfield, Nottinghamshire. I got off the train at Grantham - it must have been about 4.00am - and waited for an hour or so for the first to run to Nottingham. A driver from the factory met me and took me to the White Swan in Mansfield where I'd been booked in for the first two weeks. I checked in, dropped off my bag, and from there he took me the three miles over to Sutton for my first day as a Shift Quality Controller. *Don't ask, it wasn't particularly exciting!*

An induction programme had been arranged which, for this very first day, took account of the fact that I'd already had a long day (& night), and by 4.00pm, I was heading back to Mansfield on one of the many Midland General bus services that then ran between the two towns.

As you'd expect, having done my research, I knew that Nottingham Forest were at home that night. *NB – I'm not sure why the game was scheduled for a Monday night. They were at home again the following Monday and yes, before you ask, I was at that one too.*

Whatever, on Monday 14th September 1970, Forest played a 1st Round 1st Leg Texaco Cup tie against Airdrie. It was a 2-2 draw, but other than the score, I can't recall too much of the game. I got back to Mansfield fairly late and surprised my new colleagues the following day when I told them of how I'd spent my first night. They were soon to learn, as before the end of the year, I'd become a regular visitor at all three senior Nottinghamshire grounds.

The first of, as I write, a subsequent 1,200 and rising visits to Meadow Lane, was on Wednesday 23rd September. I'd seen Wrexham at Mansfield on the Saturday and Huddersfield at Forest on the Monday before seeing the 'Pies defeat Newport County 2-0 (Richie Barker & Jon Nixon) in front of 8,445. Notts County had made an encouraging start in this, their first full season with Jimmy Sirrel as manager. I make the point because, as I now know, this was a much higher mid-week attendance than they would have expected during the previous decade. In fact, another home mid-week fixture against the same opponents the season before, had drawn a crowd of only 4,394. As I was about to discover however, although expectation in how Notts are doing has historically seen a rise in interest when they are doing well, it is often temporary in nature and very rarely sustained.

I alternated my Saturday and mid-week football trips (NB – after the first fortnight, I was working on afternoon shift every other week and this was somewhat limiting) between, Field Mill, City Ground and Meadow Lane. However, I increasingly found my journeys to see Notts, the more enjoyable. Yes, they were playing well, and eventually won that season's 4th Division title by some distance (I guess that leaves me open to the allegation that I was simply a glory hunter!) but there was more to it than that.

Standing around the halfway line on the covered County Road terrace, with the Ivor Thirst half-time scoreboard on top of the huge open ended Kop to my right, regardless of result, evolved into my idea of a couple of hours well spent.

Like most love affairs, which in practice are rarely 'love at first sight', as Mama Cass sang, this one 'just started quietly and grew'. I suppose the first real indication was when I took up the offer of Martin Turner, who not only worked at Metal Box, but was a fellow resident at my 160 Diamond Avenue, Kirkby-in-Ashfield bed-sit, to travel up to Bury (his home town) to see Notts in a 2nd Round FA Cup Tie on 12th December.

For me, this was the first of, at the time of writing, nearly 800 away games.

The game ended in a 1-1 draw and I knew I was hooked when, back up in Scotland early for the forthcoming holiday, I nervously listened to the radio four days before Christmas, to find out what had happened in the replay. Notts won 3-0 and were drawn away to Leicester City in the 3rd Round. I was still in Arbroath when that took place and probably just as well. Had I gone, I'd have seen them lose for the first time as they went down 2-0. I've made up for it ever since of course, having probably seen more defeats than victories over the last 50 years.

NB – this FA Cup tie took place on Saturday 2nd January 1971, the day of the Ibrox disaster. I'm glad I wasn't there either!

1971

Having settled into life in the East Midlands, I began to spread my wings a bit, and for the first time, saw games at the likes of Derby County, Leicester City, Chesterfield and Sheffield Utd. I also made my first trip to Old Trafford (on a Rams supporters' bus) and the Dell (to meet up with Jake in Southampton)

Looking back, despite visits to new grounds being memorable if for no other reason than they were the first, the key game from this year took place on 1st May, when Notts drew 1-1 against Exeter City. The result may have been a surprise and, given the euphoric atmosphere around Meadow Lane, disappointing for most of the 18,002 present, but it ensured that a) the Club had remained unbeaten at home all season and b) finished a full nine points (remember - only two for a win) ahead of second placed Bournemouth.

This was the second highest Meadow Lane crowd of the 70/71 season and it was perhaps fitting that Tony Hateley scored that final goal. It was his return to the Club in November that saw 21,012 turn up for his first game back since leaving for 1st Division football (Aston Villa, Chelsea, Liverpool, Coventry City and Birmingham City) in 1963. Despite playing in only 29 games, he still finished as top scorer with 22, one of five Notts players to score ten or more goals that season.

1972

This was an unusual year. The previous September I had left Metal Box - didn't I say that the job was not particularly exciting - and after an abortive attempt to transfer to a position within the organisation that better suited my skills and temperament, I resigned and enrolled as a student at the Eaton Hall (near Retford) Teacher Training College. By now 21 years of age, I had become a 'mature' student, a term that some of my mainly younger colleagues, felt was a bit of a misnomer. My earlier memoir, provides a number of clues as to why they'd have thought that.

In January 1972, I had just begun my first teaching practice at a secondary school in Mansfield. I'd only been there a week when I got a call from my brother, recently married and still living in Arbroath, to say that both parents had been hospitalised and not only was Dawn (now 15 but still our wee sister) on her own, but the family business was only ticking over through the efforts of part time staff. Having got the OK from both College Principal and Head of my school, I travelled up to Scotland to, within a few weeks, become licensee of the Station Hotel. It's a long story, but I remained up there for eight months before starting afresh as a Year 1 student in September.

As a result, most of my football in this year was north of the Border. Arbroath won promotion back to the 1st Division in 1971/72 and I saw a number of their games during the second half of the campaign, notably a crucial 2-0 away win at relatively close rivals Cowdenbeath. In the early weeks of the 72/73 season I followed Arbroath to, amongst other clubs, my first ever visits to both Dumbarton and Falkirk.

However, the memorable match that year was at Hampden. Having, three weeks earlier, taken Dawn through to Glasgow to see her second Scottish Cup Final, this time witnessing a 6-1 victory for Celtic over Hibs, we returned on Saturday 27th May for her first full International.

It was disappointment for us both this time as, in front of 119,325, she saw (well actually she didn't but more on this later!) England secure a narrow 1-0 victory over the ever plucky Scots. The teams that day included some of the greats of both nations with Gordon Banks, Bobby Moore, Colin Bell playing for England and Billy McNeill, Billy Bremner and Denis Law featuring for Scotland.

People who know me well will know that I'm an objective watcher of football. I tend to look at both teams, and if my side play badly and lose, or are simply beaten by a better team on the day, I'm generally philosophic about it and very rarely look for excuses. On the other hand, if they've played well and lost, whilst I can't change what happened, I do feel a bit aggrieved. That, as all true fans can relate to, is just part and parcel of the game.

I'm making the point because on this particular day, Scotland got nothing from a game that they, by and large, controlled. Gordon Banks, although not having to make any Pele 'out of this world' type saves, denied Scotland time and again. He was inspired. To rub salt into an open wound, Alan Ball, having clearly fouled Bobby Clark in the home goal, scored in the 28th minute. Sergio Gonnella, the Italian referee, failed to see what approximately 119,319 others in attendance could, and allowed the goal to stand. That solitary goal was enough.

Now then, back to the teenage Miss Gyles and her first ever International game. After about twenty minutes she told me that she felt a bit sick and faint. I could see from her pallor that she was not joking. We were about half way down the open terrace behind the goal where, in addition to the aforementioned Bobby Clark, there were a number of St Johns Ambulance men/women. With some difficulty I managed to squeeze Dawn down and through to the front of the crowd and caught the attention of one of the St Johns helpers.

They came across and helped me to lift the now distinctly wobbly Dawn out and on to the grassy area behind the goal. There they laid her down, loosened some of her clothing and gave her smelling salts and the like to help revive her. She was clearly not feeling very well and her mood was not helped by me soon telling her that Alan Ball, only a few yards away from where she lay, had just given England the lead.

Now, standing behind the goal, I had a good close up and was probably in the best position in the whole ground to see what the carrot topped England midfielder had done to the unfortunate Bobby Clark. Mr Gonnella, I'm an objective fan and it was as clear as day. How could you not see it? Well, injustice though it may have been, there's not much that I can do about it now.

As a postscript, the prognosis of the St Johns Ambulance team was that Dawn had probably become weak and faint as a result of a lack of nourishment and that was put down to me. Well, how was I to know that, unlike her protective big brother, she needed regular intakes of food and was unable to survive a full day on little less than a peanut?

1973

There were so many memorable games that I could write a book on this one year alone. In any other year, seeing Notts clinch promotion to the 2nd Division with a last day 4-1 victory over Tranmere Rovers in front of 23,513 would have been the obvious choice.

That's not taking account of my first ever visit to that most scenic of towns, Burslem, in the Potteries, to see Notts gain a valuable point as they put together their promotion clinching run.

Nor indeed, of seeing crowds at Meadow Lane exceed those of the club across the River Trent. I saw Forest defeat Millwall 3-0 in front of 11,317 on 6th October, whilst Notts drew 12,243 for their home game with the Londoners on 3rd November. *NB – full disclosure. I didn't actually see that game at Meadow Lane as I was playing for a college team that afternoon. I make the point because, under normal circumstances, the crowd would have increased by at least one more!!*

I ought to also make the point that, by now, I was a Notts County season ticket holder. The run in to promotion at the end of 72/73 had convinced me that this was now my club and, as I write, coronavirus permitting, I'm about to renew for 2020/21. That will be 48 consecutive seasons.

My first season ticket cost £12 - a lot for a poor student, but I did have my priorities! - and came with a seat in the old wooden Main Stand on the Ironmonger Road side of the ground. I used it for the first home game of the new (2nd Division) season sitting in my allocated seat to see Sunderland win 4-1. That was a 'one off', as for the rest of the season I simply used the ticket to gain access to the ground, electing to stand back in my favoured spot on the County Road.

Yet, despite it being a fantastically successful year for Notts County (& for Arbroath who cemented their position amongst the Scottish elite) my match of the year was an international.

On Wednesday 26th September 1973, Hampden Park welcomed 95,786 - if you were to believe everyone who has since claimed to have been there that night, it would have been the highest attendance ever at any sporting event anywhere in the world! - for the World Cup Qualifier between Scotland and Czechoslovakia.

In an earlier chapter, I made reference to Scotland's appearance at the 1958 World Cup held in Sweden. They had since missed out in 1962, 1966 and 1970. They'd come close to qualifying in 1966, but an unexpected home defeat to Poland proved to be their downfall. Despite having a decent set of players for each of the three qualifying groups, they failed to fulfil their potential.

This particular campaign had started well with Tommy Docherty managing a side that in a three nation group, had defeated Denmark home and away. To Scotland's great joy, the Danes had secured a home draw with Czechoslovakia. This meant that, come autumn 1973, the Scots had two opportunities to defeat the Czechs to seal their passage to Germany the following summer. The first of these two games was to take place in Glasgow, with the second scheduled for three weeks later in Bratislava.

I travelled up to an expectant Scotland the day before the game. I had a young sister (well she was 16 by this time) who was beside herself with joy and excitement that her big brother had got a spare ticket. She was still attending Arbroath High School, and as part of the package, I had agreed to provide her with a letter explaining her absence. I may have been found out a few years earlier with my own written lies, but this time there was nothing particularly newsworthy in Dawn attending a game that the entire nation was eagerly anticipating.

By this time, Tommy Docherty was no longer the Scotland team manager. He had been lured south of the Border attracted by a) the money he had been offered by Manchester United and b) the attractive Mrs Brown although, to be fair, we didn't know that at the time. The new manager was Willie Ormond, a famous player with Hibernian in the 1940's/1950's, a Scottish International (six caps including two in the 1954 (Switzerland) World Cup finals) and latterly a successful manager with St Johnstone.

He was much more of a thinking manager, unlike his ebullient and self-promoting predecessor, and to the best of my knowledge, never took a fancy to Mrs Brown. In fact, I'm not sure what he took a fancy to as he never married.

Whatever, he quietly went about his job, and with a starting eleven that featured only two (Billy Bremner and Denis Law) of those who had started in that game v England less than fifteen months before, he was prepared to let his team do the talking.

On the night, the Czechs took the lead, and probably deservedly so as Scotland, with the nervous hopes of the Nation perhaps getting to the players, looked very shaky in defence. Dawn and myself, were beginning to ask ourselves how we might get to Bratislava for the second chance to qualify when, four minutes before half-time, big Jim Holton forced home the equaliser. The sense of relief around Hampden was well.............. you can imagine.

In the second half, although it was end to end and exciting, neither side appeared to have a player with the composure to either create or finish a good chance. This was when Willie Ormond saw something that we nail biting supporters hadn't. He took off Kenny Dalglish, probably the one player who you would have thought was capable of 'seizing the moment', and replaced him with Joe Jordan.

Now Jordan was little known in Scotland, having played only eight times for Morton as a teenager before being sold to Leeds United in 1970. He was still only 21, and to many in the crowd, it looked like a big gamble by the manager. Regardless of whether or not it was, it was truly inspired as it was Jordan who scored what proved to be the winner in the 72nd minute.

Billy Bremner had just seen a shot hit the post and run along the line before being cleared as far as Willie Morgan. The Manchester United winger swiftly sent over a cross where, at the far post, Big Joe leapt like a salmon to head home.

Throughout the nation, those last eighteen minutes probably resulted in a record number of cardiac arrests over such a brief time period. For those who survived through to the final whistle, for they were in the majority, the next couple of days passed by in a largely alcoholic haze followed by plans for a co-ordinated invasion of West Germany.

Dawn and myself made our way back to the car, and amid a cauldron of noise, set off on the return journey arriving in Arbroath at about 1.00am.

As it happens, Dick Scott, old school pal and now fellow resident of 160 Diamond Avenue, Kirkby had also managed to get a ticket but had made his own way there. Nonetheless, we met up on the Thursday, adding to the alcoholic haze, and then travelled back down to Kirkby together on the Sunday. There, we joyously marched into our communal lodgings, draped in Saltire and Lion Rampant flags singing triumphalist songs forecasting how Scotland were 'gonnae win the Cup!'

This was the first night at these premises for a fellow student of mine from Eaton Hall who was joining me on teaching practice at Kirkby Woodhouse Primary School. Should Barrie Howard, from Benfleet in Essex, ever get to read this, please accept the belated apologies from Dick and myself. If we made any references to England not having qualified - at the time they still had a chance - we didn't really mean them!!

1974

I'd met my future wife the previous year whilst we were working together as part time staff at the Leg of Mutton. I reckon she must have been thrilled to bits when I took her, aged 21, to her first ever football match. Helen won't remember, but she saw Les Bradd score the winner as Notts beat Bristol City 2-1 on 27th April.

That was the last game of the season, one in which Notts finished in a comfortable mid-table position. Since then, like me, I'm sure that she's often lain awake in the middle of the night and asked herself "Notts County - WHY?" It may be no consolation, but at least I can argue that she knew at a very early stage what she was letting herself in for!

We split up for a period in the summer of 1974. It's a long story, and my fault entirely, but once we got back together again in September, she began to accompany me to wherever I was going. As a treat - yes I know it's debatable - for her 22nd birthday, I took her to her very first Notts away game. At Villa Park we stood on the Holte End and watched David Needham score the only goal of the game. Since that away victory, Helen has now seen the 'Pies win on over 70 different grounds.

There were a number of highlights that year, but the truly memorable games were undoubtedly four that I never got to.

With Scotland having qualified for the World Cup Finals in June, I had managed to get a pair of tickets for all three qualifying games in West Germany. Dick Scott and I had planned to join the *Tartan Army* and just 'rough it' for a fortnight. As the day drew near however, I had to face up to some realities. Not only was I falling behind with a number of college assignments - partly a result of too many 'extra-curricular' activities and undertaking various part-time jobs to remain solvent - but I owed my long suffering landlady a considerable sum of money.

The upshot was that I had to make some serious decisions. These entailed relinquishing all of my jobs, including the Leg of Mutton, having a difficult conversation with Helen, spending all waking hours trying to catch up with college work and lastly, deciding to give up my tickets for the games v Zaire (Dortmund) and Brazil and Yugoslavia (Frankfurt).

49

That resulted in another painful face to face conversation, this time with Dick. It didn't make any difference to him though. He was dead set on going.

I'd finally come to the decision (some would say my senses) early in May and with a spare ticket for each game wrote to Albert Henderson (Arbroath FC Manager) asking him if he knew of any Red Lichtie who could use them.

A few days later I was contacted by a guy from Dundee who said that he and his mate had been planning on going regardless of whether or not they could get tickets. I explained that I'd only got the one spare for each game, but in his view, that was better than nothing and he'd take them. The story gets a bit bizarre now because he rang the following day to say that as they intended being part of the 'advance guard' of the *Army*, they would be travelling down through England en route to the ferry that coming Saturday and could we meet up to exchange/pay up? This was Saturday 18th May and the first game v Zaire was scheduled for 14th June. Well, it was not up to me to question either their plans or how they intended to subsidise their trip.

I explained that I'd be at Hampden that day (for the record, Scotland beat England 2-0) but should be back in Kirkby around midnight. In light of that, it might be better for them to leave the pick up until the Sunday. He seemed happy enough with that suggestion and I thought no more about it.

The trip back from Glasgow was a bit quicker than I'd anticipated - I reckon you drive a bit faster after a good win! - and I pulled into Nest Avenue at around 11.15pm. There was a car parked just outside the house, and when I got out I was approached by a young lad I'd never seen before. "Are you Mike?" was the question, "Ehm Dougie fae Dundee. Hiv ye goat thae tickets?"

Yes, it was the two guys and after I'd gone into the house to get him the tickets, and the money had been handed over, Dougie said that they were a bit concerned that I might have got a better offer *(NB - I only ever intended charging face value)* and were not prepared to take that chance. I must admit, that were I in the same situation, I'd most probably have done the same.

Anyway, I was sad to see the tickets go but wished them (I never did find out the other guy's name) well as they set off. They'd managed to swap their ferry time for an early Sunday morning departure, and set off to drive through the night to Dover. I may have seen the two of them at future Scotland games, but after our brief meeting under a Nest Avenue lamppost, if I had done, I'm not sure I would have recognised them.

I hope they enjoyed the trip and Scotland's acclaimed performances in the three games. As was to be the case in a number of future World Cup tournaments, they were unfortunate not to reach the knock-out stages. 1974 was probably the closest. Brazil, Yugoslavia and Scotland easily disposed of Zaire and drew the games against each other. In the end, just one goal was the difference. Scotland played Zaire in their opening game and won 2-0 before the draws with first Brazil and then Yugoslavia. Brazil went on to beat Zaire 3-0 in their final game. That one goal swing was crucial.

Still, we could take some pride in the fact that Scotland had returned home unbeaten, the only one of the sixteen teams throughout the Tournament to do so.

The other memorable game **that I didn't go to** took place across the River Trent at the City Ground on Saturday 28th December 1974. I was up in Scotland for the Christmas/New Year holiday. I'd got myself seasonal work with the Post Office, and in between shifts, was doing a bit of decoration at 6 George Street where Mum was effectively living on her own as Dad was working away. As a consequence, I missed Notts County's away derby game with Nottingham Forest.

By this time, Notts were the top team and were flirting with promotion to the 1st Division. Forest on the other hand were struggling, although they had enjoyed a good FA Cup run the previous season. I'd seen them defeat Portsmouth and Manchester City in the 4th & 5th rounds with Duncan McKenzie emerging as a good prospect, before they took on

Newcastle United up at St James' Park in the quarter final. I travelled up to that game on a Forest supporters' bus.

There were 52,551 there, most of whom were distinctly unhappy as Forest took a 3-1 lead in the second half following a converted penalty. To make matters worse for the Geordie (as opposed to the original and best) Magpies, their skipper, Pat Howard was sent off for arguing with the referee.

A few minutes later, irate fans began spilling over from the Leazes End and onto the pitch, before running towards the Gallowgate Terrace. I had a good view from that end, and it's probably fair to say that the majority of them were not coming over to congratulate the Forest fans on their team's showing. Whatever, the referee took the players off for ten minutes whilst order was restored.

When the action resumed, despite being a man short, in an intensely hostile atmosphere, Newcastle staged an incredible come back, scoring three times to win the tie 4-3 and advance to the semi-finals. Or so we thought! In addition to having a window smashed on our bus as we headed out of the city, there were ructions over the coming days and calls for Newcastle to be thrown out of the Competition, or at least for the game to be replayed.

The FA carried out a quick investigation and decided, rather than award the tie to Forest, which to me as an objective observer would have seemed fair, to arrange a replay at a neutral venue. This took place at Goodison Park, where, after a draw, a second replay saw Newcastle progress.

Anyway, where was I?

Forest had failed to build on that FA Cup run, the 1974/75 season was not going well and the natives were getting a bit restless. Still, they had a home game against Notts to look forward to between Christmas and New Year. Surely that would provide the win to see them go on a good run and lift them up the table.

It wasn't to be, as goals from Les Bradd and Steve Carter saw Notts secure a deserved (not being at the game, I am of course basing this upon the objective opinions I heard expressed when next at Meadow Lane) 2-0 victory. Within a few days, 3rd January 1975 to be exact, the Nottingham Forest committee informed the manager, Allan Brown, that his services were no longer required. Three days later, the club announced the appointment of a certain Brian Clough.

It has become increasingly difficult as the Nottingham Forest fan base has got younger - well at least in comparison to me! - to convince their supporters that the two stars that they now proudly display over their badge are arguably there courtesy of the country cousins from across the river. Losing to Jimmy Sirrel's side was the ultimate insult for many a club at that time, but for Forest it was the straw that broke the camel's back and the sacking of the manager became inevitable.

It may seem a bit obtuse, but it would probably have been to Notts County's long term benefit not to have won that game. We'll never know of course, but that won't stop me from arguing the point that the success at the City Ground that followed in the late seventies and throughout the 1980's would probably never have happened had Notts lost that day.

One final memory from 1974 before I continue. On the day of that game at the City Ground, I travelled down to Dens Park to see Dundee take on Airdrie. Standing just down from the Red Lion Caravan Park thumbing a lift, I noticed a car pass by and then turn round and come back. The window was wound down and I was asked "Where you going Mike?" When I replied, "Dens Park", the answer was, "You're in luck, 'cos so am I."

I hadn't recognised the driver, but when he swung the car round I could see that it was Tommy Walker and realised that he was not only going to the game but that he'd be playing. The last time I'd seen him he was wearing the maroon of Arbroath FC as a teenager and was clearly a good prospect. Ian McMillan certainly thought so and was prepared to pay Arbroath a good sum (£16,000) to back his judgement. He went on to be a key midfield player for the Diamonds for ten years.

Well, not only did he give me a lift to the ground but he continued the favour after the game. Dundee had scored the only goal of the game so we shared a somewhat downbeat conversation on the way home, and after a couple of pints back in Arbroath, went our separate ways. I never saw Tommy Walker play again.

1975

This was the year when following Notts to away games became the norm. Memorable away victories were gained at high profile venues like, Hillsborough, Elland Road and the City Ground...... ......again. Yes, despite Mr Clough being manager now, it was becoming a habit.

We also travelled down to Fratton Park for a game against Portsmouth. It may have been a drab 1-1 draw, but it was the perfect opportunity for Helen to meet her future sister-in-law, as Dawn was down that way undergoing training as a future, albeit short lived, Wren.

Perhaps most importantly, it was the year when I bought Helen her first season ticket. She has told me since, that at the time she confided to friends that "I think he's getting serious!" Well I was, but it was November before I got round to suggesting we get married. After all, if a girl was prepared to travel with me to such exotic footballing locations as Orient (as they were then), Oxford and Blackpool, it was time to cement the deal.

Manchester United, already assured of promotion, were the last team to visit Meadow Lane that season. Wherever they had played throughout the previous nine months, they had been followed by thousands of fans determined to see their side regain their 'rightful place' in the 1st Division. This was at a time when football hooliganism was an ever present problem within the English game and the reputation of some Manchester United supporters went before them.

On this day, 19th April, they surpassed themselves. For reasons that defy belief, after a 2-2 draw, which admittedly was a disappointment after being 2-0 up at half time - and at that time guaranteeing that they would go up as champions - a number of their fans decided to have a riot.

A lot of damage was caused to the ground and there were running skirmishes with police in various parts of the city afterwards. There were injuries to police, innocent bystanders and the occasional fan, and although many were arrested, there will have been a great deal more who escaped to 'fight another day'.

I was shocked, so appalled in fact, that I wrote a letter to Tommy Docherty. He had annoyed me earlier in the season when he had made a glib remark concerning the trouble, grief and general mayhem that marauding fans of his club were causing, suggesting something along the lines of 'I'd rather have this lot in their thousands than none at all'. I took issue with this, and via my letter, told him so. I'm still waiting for a reply.

To be fair, in the aftermath of the Meadow Lane riot, when the full extent of the damage and injury caused became clear, he did issue a statement condemning the actions of a 'few' of his club's supporters, expressing concern about what might happen the following year, when they were back in the big time.

Notts, in their second year back in the 2nd Division, had a reasonable season, and had been in with a possible chance of promotion for much of the time. However, a run of only one win in their last nine games saw them slip away to finish in fourteenth place, thirteen points behind Norwich City who occupied third spot. As a result, it was the Canaries who were to play 1st Division football in 1975/76.

It was, nonetheless, a disappointing end to the season but we could take pride in the fact that, despite the 'green shoots of recovery' showing across the river, Notts were still the higher placed of the two Nottingham teams. That was 45 years ago and was to happen again the following season, but sad to say, I can predict with complete confidence, that I'll never see that again.

In addition to a satisfactory start to the 75/76 League season, Notts had a good run in the League Cup. After defeating Sunderland at home in a 2nd Round tie, the reward was a trip to Elland Road, to take on the mighty Leeds United, European Cup finalists a mere five months before.

We (i.e. Helen and myself) travelled up to Leeds on a supporters' bus for the Wednesday night game. It was a night that Notts' fans who made it will never forget as a solitary Ian Scanlon goal was enough for a shock result. Sadly, it was the last victory under Jimmy Sirrel in his first spell at the Club, as after a 1-0 home defeat to Oxford United three days later, he left for Bramall Lane. His assistant, Ron Fenton was installed as his replacement.

The League Cup run continued however. After a 2-2 draw at Goodison Park, Notts won the replay 2-0, and the following week went up to Newcastle for the Q/F tie. Standing once more at the Gallowgate End, I watched in horror as the otherwise excellent Eric McManus failed to catch a long throw in and effectively dropped the ball into his own net for the only goal. It was a shame that the run had come to such a sorry end. Newcastle went on to the Final where they lost to Manchester City.

1976

By now, Helen and I were a) saving up for a wedding and b) looking for somewhere to stay. These tasks were made much more difficult by me having difficulty in settling down to do a proper job. I'll spare you the embarrassing details, but having abandoned teaching, in sequence, I was a painter and decorator, trainee executive officer for the Department of Employment, a packer at a lemonade factory and finally, seven weeks prior to the wedding, a wages clerk for a Jacksdale based company. Throughout of course, I maintained the most significant of my part-time jobs as a Littlewoods Pools collector. Something, apart from a short break of a few months, I was to do for 42 years.

Don't get me wrong, I was never ever out of work, always leaving one job and going straight to the next, and was serious about securing enough cash to enable us to settle down to married life in some degree of comfort. So much so that at 11.50pm on Sunday 29th February, I had my last ever cigarette. The habit was costing me approximately 50p/day and I was disciplined enough to put that amount in a jar at the end of each day. Over the next few months I had accumulated enough to buy something for Helen. She wears it on the third finger of her left hand to this very day.

The other cost saving measure was to reduce the number of away games we went to. In fact, in the period up to the wedding on 30th August - Helen had suggested a Monday, in part to avoid missing a game - we managed just the three, Carlisle (to meet up with friends Rud and Jenny who had moved from Kirkby to take up teaching positions in the town), Blackburn Rovers and Oldham Athletic.

We saw the New Year in up in Arbroath and pulled in Helen's first visit to Gayfield where she saw Morton win 1-0. That date, 3rd January 1976, is however notable for another reason. South of the Border that day, Notts County's FA Cup campaign was ended before it had effectively begun as Leeds United gained revenge for the League Cup defeat from a few weeks earlier, winning 1-0. The reason that is significant is simply because it is the last time that Notts have been eliminated from 'the world's oldest cup competition' ™, without me being present. It's not a record I'm particularly happy with, but as I write, I've been present when Notts have been knocked out of the Cup on 44 (& rising) consecutive occasions.

We still saw at least one game a week, and generally when Notts were playing away, Mansfield Town were conveniently at home. The Stags were beginning to put together a side that would achieve promotion to the 2nd Division for the only time in their history and were a joy to watch.

Notts County had enjoyed a 'much better than average' season in 1975/76, and come May, finished a mere four points away from West Bromwich Albion who, in third place, secured the final promotion spot. It wasn't until late in that year that the 'Pies fell away giving rise to the inevitable grumbles on the terraces that 'they don't want to go up'.

Although Notts had been serious challengers for promotion to the 1st Division, for much of that year, from memory, 1976/77 was less successful. I note however from the records that we secured just one fewer point so it couldn't have been that bad. In fact, we again finished a mere four points behind the third placed side. Unfortunately, for the long term future of Notts County, that final promotion spot was secured by Nottingham Forest. There are plenty of books available recording exactly what happened next on the other side of the River Trent, and yes, lest ye forget, the 'Pies had played their part in bringing about that success.

The long hot summer of 1976 ended just a couple of days before our wedding, held at St Thomas Church, Kirkby on the late summer Bank Holiday Monday. Amongst the cards and telegrams read out at the reception by Best Man, John Peebles, was one from Notts County Manager, Ron Fenton. I can't remember his exact wording but it was something along the lines of '...........if you support each other through married life with as much enthusiasm as you support us, you'll be just fine.'

With money tight upon our return from honeymoon in Wales, we continued to restrict our attendance at away games. These were limited to Derby County (League Cup), Sheffield United and Charlton Athletic. Unfortunately, having hired a car for the weekend, we found that this last game had been postponed as we travelled down the M1. Well, as we were meeting up with friends Tony and Ann and staying overnight with them at their place in Enfield, we carried on, and rather than waste the afternoon, went to Upton Park to see West Ham beat Liverpool 2-0. The first of many games over the years where we've ended up somewhere other than we had intended.

The most memorable game of this year was however, a trip to London in November to see Notts at Craven Cottage. At this time, the Club arranged special trains for selected away games and we took advantage of that. The train times had been set to allow supporters the chance to do whatever they fancied in London before the game. From memory, we were scheduled to arrive in London around 11.00am, with the 'special' leaving from St Pancras at 7.00pm for the journey home.

This suited us, and as we'd not yet bought a Christmas present for Helen's Mum & Dad, we planned to do a bit of shopping. It didn't take us long to find what we thought would suit Ken & Betty....... a teasmade.

Remember them? Well, this particular product was stretching our available funds to the limit, but what the hell, they'd been really good to us in the period up to and immediately following the wedding, so it was a price worth paying.

Besides, I did some quick calculations and worked out that if we just got a one way tube ticket to Fulham, limited our food intake, and were prepared to walk the relatively short distance from the ground back to St Pancras, we should not only be back in time for the train, but crucially, we could afford it. We handed over the money, and for the one and only time in my life, I was later to carry a teasmade into a football ground.

Before I get to the game, there was one other episode that day that's worth recording. Neither Helen nor I knew London particularly well at the time, and we'd never been to Harrods, so went in search of the 'top people's' shop. Having found the store we walked around amazed at both what was on offer and the prices. Did you know, for instance, that you can buy bananas that have been grown in the store? No, nor did we.

As we walked around, Helen nudged me and whispered that she thought we were being followed. It appeared as if 'security' had been notified that there were a couple of dodgy looking football types walking around carrying a teasmade. Had they nicked it? We were never actually approached, but did the decent thing anyway and made a purchase. With extremely limited resources we could only manage a box of Oxo cubes. Even they were about twice the price we'd have expected to pay anywhere else, but they did come in a small - it was exactly the right size for the pack - green and gold Harrods' plastic bag. Something else I'd never before (or since) carried into a football ground.

Fulham that year had invested in a number of proven internationals in the belief that their experience and talent would see them return to the 1st Division for the first time since the days of Johnny Haynes, Tony Macedo, Bedford Jezzard and the like. Big crowds were turning up at Craven Cottage to see, amongst others, Bobby Moore, Rodney Marsh and George Best. Unfortunately for them, despite Best scoring, Notts recent signing Martyn Busby was the star of the show, getting one goal himself and setting up a couple for Mick Vinter. We, that's Helen, myself, teasmade and Oxo cubes, left the ground at around 4.50pm having seen Notts eventually win 5-1.

The route back to St Pancras seemed straightforward enough from the *A to Z*. Indeed it was, but it was a damn sight further than I'd imagined. That was not an issue for me, but by 6.00pm I realised that it was for Helen. To be fair, she was carrying the Oxo cubes!

In a phrase that she (and later Ailsa & Heather) were to become familiar with, I kept telling her that "It's not far now" whilst encouraging her to walk just a little bit faster. I'd clearly underestimated both the distance and what I was asking the recently married Mrs Gyles to do. By the time we got to Euston Road, it was 6.55pm and Helen was trailing about 100 yards behind me. I shouted that I'd now run and see if I could stop the train from setting off. I was concerned that our tickets would only be valid for the 'special' and that if we missed that, having no money, we'd be in trouble. I'd visions of me trying to hawk a teasmade to the highest bidder on the station concourse to secure sufficient funds to pay for a later service train.

When I got to St Pancras, the big clock was showing 7.04pm. We were too late and I was in big trouble.

I went back out onto Euston Road to wait for Helen, wondering how I was going to get out of this mess. As I waited, I saw a couple of Notts supporters that we'd got to know on our travels and shouted over to them that they were too late, the train had gone. For a moment, they looked as flustered as I felt. "What?" they exclaimed, "25 minutes early? It's not due to leave until 7.30pm." One of them went to check and came back with the news that it was on Platform whatever and would be leaving on time.

At this, Helen appeared, somewhat bedraggled. If she'd had feathers she'd have been spitting them. When I tried to get round this self-made debacle by saying that I'd led her to believe that the train was departing at 7.00pm, knowing full well that this would ensure that we'd at least make it well before the actual time of 7.30pm, she developed a look that most husbands will have experienced at least once in their married life. I knew however, that she wouldn't murder me there and then. Besides the fact that there were witnesses, I was carrying a very expensive teasmade.

It all ended well enough, although the train had reached Loughborough before Helen felt able to talk to me. Apparently, she claims that there have been numerous occasions since, when I've come close to being a divorcee. From my perspective, that was quite possibly the closest. And do you know what, I'm not sure that Betty and Ken ever made full use of that bloody teasmade!

1977

Although we were living in rented accommodation, our plan was to save enough for a deposit for a house of our own as quickly as possible. We lived fairly frugally in that period with Helen walking to work at her new job in Kirkby, and courtesy of father-in-law Ken, and the gift of a renovated second hand bike at Christmas, I pedalled over to Jacksdale on a daily basis. We had no television, limited our nights out to Saturdays only, and took it in turns to read the affordable *SUN* at night.

Meanwhile, my earnings from Littlewoods Pools collections were, to the exact halfpenny, deposited with the Derbyshire Building Society every Saturday morning without fail. I had developed and built up the round to a level where Helen was drafted in as a helper - I'd have been out knocking on doors at 11.00pm without her! - and our joint commission was averaging £15/week. By early 1978, we'd got over £1,000 in our 'house fund'.

Despite this background, football attendances didn't suffer. Throughout the year, I managed 55 games with Helen only missing a few. One Saturday we did miss out on was 12th February and that might have been a blessing as Notts suffered a 4-0 thrashing at Burnden Park, Bolton. We've got to be thankful for Dawn's wedding to Mark Hammond in a very cold and wet Arbroath that afternoon, for denying us that pleasure (?).

We stayed in Arbroath for the week, and although we'd seen no game on the Saturday, Dundee were at home to Queen of the South on the Tuesday. Too good an opportunity for Mrs Gyles to miss! Dundee were to lose 2-0 in a game which, for most of the 4,635 at Dens Park that night, will have been forgotten by the weekend.

Not for me however. Dundee had a little ginger haired midfielder who was far and away the best player on the park. I'd never seen or heard of him, but before the match was over said to Helen "We must let Ron Fenton know about this player. He's just what Notts need right now!" *NB - this is absolutely true. Helen will back me up!* Well, to my regret, I never got round to it and by October, not only was Ron Fenton no longer manager of Notts County but................. Gordon Strachan, for he it was, had been signed by Billy McNeill for Aberdeen.

Who knows how many European trophies Notts County would have won if I'd just had the courage of my convictions? As it happened, after a poor start to the 77/78 season, Jimmy Sirrel returned to Meadow Lane. His stay at Sheffield United had lasted less than two years and poor results resulted in the inevitable sacking. *NB – rumour has it that he might have been a success at Bramall Lane but the players 'cuidnae unerstan a bluidy wird he wiz sayn!'* We'll never know.

Ron Fenton had done reasonably well the previous season - indeed, as I've indicated, better than my memory had led me to believe - and on Easter Monday, Helen and I travelled to Molineux to see Notts play Wolves. Although it was a satisfactory outcome for Notts, the 2-2 draw was a disappointment for the home side. In the end however, it didn't matter, as Wolves were to be promoted as champions.

This game is memorable for another reason however. It was the first time that I had personally been subjected to the blight of the English game at that time viz. football hooliganism. Dawn had knitted me a long - it must have been 10 foot in length! - black and white scarf which I wore to games home and away. It had never been a problem until then, and because we never associated with the rowdy element of Notts fans, always making our way to and from grounds on our own, we were clearly not one of those fans who'd be 'looking for a fight'.

On this day, as we walked back to the car that Ken had let us borrow, Helen became aware of some young Wolves fans following us. I wasn't bothered, but could hear them muttering as they quickly caught up with us, and before I knew it, were trying to trip me up. They wanted the scarf as a 'trophy'.

This could have become serious but Helen turned round and bawled them out. I can't remember exactly what she said but it seemed to do the trick. They continued making the kind of puerile comments that cowards such as these used to say to give the impression that they were hard, but at least they backed away. They'd met their match in Mrs Gyles! We managed to get to the car and escaped without further incident.

I managed to get to two Scotland games in 1977. The first, at Wembley, took place in June in front of 98,103 spectators, of whom it appeared, at least 70,000 were hoping for an away win. They were not disappointed as the Scots secured a 2-1 victory, much more comfortable than the narrow score line suggests.

The game is however, best remembered for the post-match celebrations. Many jubilant - I reckon a couple of thousand - tartan clad fans ran on to the pitch at the end of the game and proceeded to help themselves to mementoes. There must be little patches of green throughout Scotland that the owner claims is genuine Wembley turf, brought back from England that day.

Perhaps more famously, although undoubtedly apocryphal, is the tale of the wee guy who that summer was to be seen on Glasgow's Sauchiehall Street selling boxes of matches. Nothing unusual in that you'd think, but he was claiming that they had been made from the Wembley goalposts that had been triumphantly carried back over the Border.

I'm not condoning what I witnessed at Wembley, but it was a) very funny and b) there was no violence. I've been with the *Tartan Army* many times and whilst I'm not happy to be associated with some of the anti-social behaviour I've seen, I've never witnessed fighting or felt that we were not welcome. OK – I'll qualify that and exclude London from this unashamed generalisation.

The other Scotland game that I attended was a World Cup Qualifier that took place on 12th October. This was an away game against Wales, but as the Welsh FA wanted to maximise revenue, was staged at Anfield in the hope that they'd have perhaps twice the attendance they could have expected had the game been played in Cardiff, Swansea or Wrexham. It was a decision that was to rebound on them as, just like Wembley a few months before, Liverpool was invaded and there were probably 40,000 Scottish supporters in the 50,850 crowd.

I feared I was going to miss out on this crucial game which, if Scotland were to win, would see them qualify for their second consecutive World Cup Finals tournament. I tried a number of avenues and contacts but couldn't get a ticket and was resigned to listening to the game - remember, we'd got no television - which, as any true fan will tell you, is purgatory.

Well, a week before the game, I was sitting in our rented home (1 Kingsley Street, Kirkby) playing cards with Helen and my Mum who'd come down for a week, when there was a knock at the front door. It was Dick Scott who, with a big beaming smile came in and engaged in small talk to begin with before asking what I was doing next Wednesday. If I wasn't doing anything special, would I fancy going to Anfield as he'd got a spare? Oh Dick Scott, you beauty, you knew the answer!

He may have told me how he'd come across these tickets but I wasn't really listening. I can remember him saying though that there was just one problem and my heart missed a beat. He was going to say that they cost £50 or the like. No, it wasn't that bad, but the spare ticket was for the home end. Apparently, the Scottish FA had only been allocated tickets for the Anfield Road end and he'd got tickets for the Kop. We'd be enjoying the game surrounded by our Celtic cousins from the other side of the Severn Bridge/Offa's Dyke etc. As I've already hinted at, that turned out to be far from reality.

As for the game itself, Scotland won 2-0 courtesy of Joe Jordan's fist and a Kenny Dalglish converted penalty. Both goals were up at the other end and we were unaware at the time of the controversy over the first goal. The first I knew was when Derek Radford, Accounts Office Manager, accosted me when he arrived at work - I was always first in - the following morning and asked if I was proud to have seen my country cheat in order to get to Argentina the following summer.

I had no idea what he was talking about - I reckon he thought I was just being obstreperous - but probably made the situation worse by naively asking how England had got on. NB - as it happens, England had also secured a 2-0 victory away to Luxembourg in their World Cup Qualifier the previous night. It wasn't enough, as they were ultimately left with having to beat Italy by six clear goals in the last qualifier to make it through. They did win that final game, but only by 2-0.

I genuinely hadn't meant to cause offence Derek, and in the unlikely event that you ever get to read this - I reckon you'll be about 105 now - I apologise most sincerely if I did. I've now seen the Joe Jordan goal on TV many times and accept that had VAR been in operation in 1977, that first 'goal' would have been disallowed. Good job we scored a second then! Clearly that doesn't make life any easier for Welshmen, and as you'll eventually find out, in 1985, a couple of them took pleasure in extracting some form of revenge...............on me!

1978

Nottingham Forest clinched their first, and given the way football has changed in the intervening years, only ever English Championship, following a scoreless draw away to Coventry City on 22nd April. On that day, Mr & Mrs Gyles were amongst 7,710 others at Meadow Lane to see the home team defeat Crystal Palace 2-0.

It's fair to say that whilst the home fans were happy with a victory in what had been a relatively poor season, there were no wild celebrations at the ground when news of Forest's success was confirmed. Now I'm not one of those who gets all hung up about my team's closest rivals. There are plenty around Meadow Lane on a

Saturday afternoon who take some form of perverse delight when, regardless of how Notts have done on the day, they hear that Forest have lost. I'm not one of those (*NB - I happily went to all the home European Cup games over the next two seasons*), although I do feel just a little bitter that there appears to be no acknowledgement amongst devout followers of the *Tricky Trees* of the part Notts County played in their success. OK, I won't mention it again!!

On the domestic front, we'd bought our first house and moved into 10 Bunyan Green Road, Selston on Saturday 29th April. For no other reason than you may be asking the question, we missed a 1-1 draw at Stoke City's Victoria Ground on the day. From memory, it seems as if the flit was carried out whilst listening all day to *Rivers of Babylon* by Boney M. *Isn't strange how you come to associate certain songs with specific events in your life?*

We had a week's holiday in Scotland planned for the second week in May and managed to see all three of that year's Home Internationals played at Hampden Park. NB - the situation in Northern Ireland at the time was such that Scotland's away game at Windsor Park was re-scheduled. This was the first game and ended in a 1-1 draw. The midweek fixture v Wales was heading for a narrow but deserved single goal victory for the Scots, until Willie Donachie scored a bizarre 90th minute own goal. 1-1 again.

On the Saturday, England headed north, and courtesy of a late Steve Coppell goal, most decidedly against the run of play - look I was there, you weren't! - gained a shock 1-0 victory. England beating, what we were led to believe were the clear favourites for the World Cup to be held in just a few weeks' time, was nonetheless a shock. Still, undaunted, following a subsequent pre-tournament 'victory parade' in front of thousands at Hampden, those members of the *Tartan Army* making their way to South America - there were rumours that some of them had hi-jacked a submarine from the Holy Loch - set off in high spirits.

Back to reality. As you've read, we had saved hard to get this first house. That had been our aim since the wedding and we'd achieved it.

Sadly, there was not enough money left over to pay for a two week holiday in Argentina. In order to see *Ally McLeod's Tartan Army* lift the World Cup for Scotland, we had to do the next best thing and get our very first television set. Rented from and installed by the Co-op, it meant that Helen and I had something else to keep us occupied of an evening. I know what you're thinking, just don't ask.

With Dick Scott now living on Mansfield Road in Selston, we decided to alternate between our respective houses to watch each game in what we just knew (because Ally had said so) would be a glorious campaign. Well, I'll spare you the drama - it's been well recorded - but after a disastrous defeat (Peru) and hard fought draw (Iran) Scotland had to defeat Holland in the final group game by three clear goals to qualify for the knock-out stage. At one stage they were winning 3-1 and the impossible looked distinctly probable but.................it wasn't. The game ended 3-2 and Scotland were once again eliminated on goal difference.

My birthday that year fell on the Saturday of the FA Cup Final. Helen had contacted Notts County a few weeks before and asked if it might be possible for a ticket from the Club's allocation to be made available for me as this would be the perfect present. She was successful. What a woman!

Because of the logistics, I was made aware of this in advance, and with Ken letting us borrow his car - what a father-in-law! – and Helen and her mate's mother accompanying me, we set off. I was going to see Arsenal v Ipswich Town and they were just as excited. They were going shopping!

I parked up near Dollis Hill, saw them safely onto the Tube and then walked over to Wembley. I'm assuming that most of you reading this will be interested in sport generally and football in particular. On that basis, I'm sure you'll be aware that it was an historic day with the underdogs, viz. Ipswich, dominating the game but requiring a sole 77th minute goal from Roger Osborne to win their first ever major trophy. It was a memorable day.

Years later, whilst at a social function attended by many of the key figures at Celestion Industries Ltd, owners of the Nottinghamshire based clothing company I was then working for, I found myself at the dining table sitting next to the then Chief Executive, a Mr Charles Ryder. He was a rare visitor to our business and this was the first opportunity that I'd had to have a proper conversation with him.

As the way of these situations go, he asked about my family and interests away from work. NB - that was a good one because, although he may not have known it, I was then spending about 60/70 hours a week doing my bit for what, like many British clothing manufacturers at the time, was effectively a failing business. His failing business indeed which not long afterwards was sold!

Whatever, when he found out - and it generally doesn't take very long for strangers to establish this fact when they first meet me - that I was interested in all sports and a long time Notts County season ticket holder, the conversation flowed. He revealed that he was a lifelong Ipswich Town supporter explaining that the factory producing Celestion Speakers, the initial core product of the organisation, was based in the town.

I waited my moment until the conversation died a little before suggesting that, with complete confidence, I could tell what he was likely to have been doing on 6th May 1978. This threw him a bit - well it was a bit random! - but his eyes lit up as he remembered. "I was at Wembley that day. How could you possibly have known that?"

When I told him that it was the first ever FA Cup Final that I'd attended and that it just also happened to have been on my birthday, he now realised that I was not some autistic Raymond Babbitt type character (played by Dustin Hoffman in *Rain Man*), but had a very good reason to remember. We got on even more like a house on fire after that!

To come back to how Notts County were doing, in the early part of 1978, they enjoyed a good cup run themselves. We travelled to The Valley on 7th January to see a Mick Vinter double secure a 2-0 victory. As a result, like many other Notts fans, we set off on yet another 'football special' on Saturday 28th January for the 4th Round tie at Brighton. Unfortunately, as we travelled through the south London suburbs, someone with a transistor radio (remember them? The guy with a trannie was always a popular figure at games in those days!) heard that the game had been postponed. The Goldstone Ground was waterlogged.

Well, being on train, we couldn't just turn round. To make matters worse, because of scheduling, we'd have to not only carry on into Brighton, but couldn't resume the return journey until 5.30pm. This meant spending something like four hours at a windswept and wet south coast holiday resort. We made the best of that miserable January afternoon enjoying an ice cream as we strolled along the beach.

The game was re-scheduled for the following Tuesday night. There was no way we could make that. Besides the distance and work considerations, we had already agreed to go over to Selston to view what in April was to become our new home. After meeting Mr & Mrs Peat, the vendors, Helen & myself called into the Bull & Butcher, the local pub, for a drink and a chat about the house and whether or not we should put in an offer.

As you now know, we clearly did. However, the key memory I have of sitting in the lounge, was hearing Radio Nottingham in the background and Colin Slater commentating from Brighton. I couldn't really make out what was happening, but when we got home, I was pleased to hear that with Mick Vinter again scoring two goals, Notts had progressed to the 5th Round following a 2-1 victory.

Next up was yet another trip by train to south London, this time to the Den to face Millwall. Although the journey was uneventful, the game was a bit of a let-down and despite a late consolation from Sammy Chapman, who had been released by Nottingham Forest, Notts lost 2-1. At that stage, it looked as if any slim hope I had of seeing the Wembley final that year had evaporated. Little did I know.

1979

The year started with a spell of bad weather. We'd hired a Mini and driven over to Stoke to see Notts lose 2-0 at the Victoria Ground on Saturday 30th December, before heading up to Helensburgh to spend a night with Dawn and Mark. The plan was that we'd drive to Arbroath the following day to see in the New Year over there. Dick Scott was also up there with wife Jackie and their first child, the infant Kirsty. I'm not sure how the Scott clan got up there but we'd agreed in advance to take them back to Selston.

We woke up on Hogmanay morning to see that there had been a significant fall of snow overnight. No-one said anything, but I reckon that there was a general feeling amongst my passengers that 'we'll never make it'. I thought otherwise though, and despite twice having to reverse out of packed snow as we made our way towards Glasgow, we eventually got onto clearer roads and reached Arbroath after about three hours. It wasn't pleasant, and despite the concerns raised, my view was that we'd only worry about the return journey when we had to.

Disappointingly (for me at any rate) the weather had not only put paid to any football, but the usual New Year celebrations were a bit muted. In fact, it was a bit of a damp squib all together. Still, we had the cosy return journey to look forward to!

On 2nd January, six adults, plus Kirsty, plus luggage, plus embryo (we found out a few weeks later that Dawn was already pregnant with first child Carey) squeezed into the car. It's not really relevant but you might like to know that it was a bright yellow Mini. We again drove across country to Helensburgh to drop off the Hammonds, and then headed south for a considerably more comfortable journey with significantly less ballast. With apologies to Mark and Dawn of course, as that is not intended to be a dig at them! Well, we made it back to Selston all right and I returned the car - I'm sure it was relieved - to Kennings in Alfreton the following day.

The big freeze covered all of the UK and the 3rd Round of the FA Cup taking place on the Saturday was badly affected. Notts home tie v Reading was postponed, but the weather having relented, was played the following Tuesday night. By that time, we knew that the reward for our 4-2 victory was a trip to either Arsenal or Sheffield Wednesday.

The two sides had managed to play in Sheffield on the Saturday but had drawn 1-1. There then followed a drama the likes of which we'll never see again. The first replay was another 1-1 draw. The second replay was a 2-2 draw. The third replay was a 3-3 draw. Five days before the day of the 4th Round, a fourth replay took place on a Monday night. It was only then, after a 2-0 victory for Arsenal, that we 'Pies found out we'd be heading to Highbury on the Saturday.

Don't get too excited, there was no FA Cup glory for us as we lost 2-0. Arsenal went on to make up for the shock defeat to Ipswich the previous year to beat Manchester United in what, for the Gunners, was the second of three consecutive Finals.

Once again, Notts had a disappointing finish to the season. They'd never really looked like serious promotion candidates, but with only one win from their final eleven games, any remote chance was extinguished. They still managed to finish sixth in the 2nd Division which, for a club with such limited resources, was a good effort.

Iain McCulloch had been signed from Kilmarnock towards the end of the 77/78 season and it was hoped that his all action aggressive style would improve the side. Well, he scored two goals in his first league start, the opening game of the 78/79 season (sadly a 5-2 defeat at Upton Park) and looked a very good prospect. Mick Vinter and Paul Hooks were also scoring goals regularly in the early part of that season, but come the turn of the year, it all just fizzled out.

With hindsight, Jimmy Sirrel accepted that he'd released Les Bradd too early and his replacement, Ricky Green, just failed to fulfil his promise. The fact that Eric McManus was named player of the year came as no surprise to those who saw Notts home and away. There was some good business carried out during the close season though with Vinter going to Wrexham and Trevor Christie joining from Leicester City, with Notts making a decent profit on the combined transaction. We weren't to know it at the time, but the nucleus of a challenging team was being put together.

Amongst the highlights was a 1-0 away victory at the Den. Jimmy Sirrel had spotted Ray O'Brien's ability from dead ball situations and it was from one of his free kicks that Notts secured the points. That was memorable enough in itself, but the fact that Helen and myself were standing along the touchline surrounded by Millwall fans left an indelible impression. When that goal went in, we didn't give away our allegiance - in 1979 that would have been even more stupid than it would today! - but I resolutely refused to engage in the abuse that was being directed to the small pocket of celebrating Notts fans behind the goal. In case you're wondering, so did Helen. Too refined a gal for that.

During the summer of this year we had a visit from my cousin, John Ross Emerson. He was a keen football supporter and decent player himself. We'd been over to Ireland for a holiday the previous year and when he'd mentioned that he was keen to see if he was good enough to play professionally, I suggested - without really thinking through the consequences - that he come over and spend some time with us. I'd see if I could get him a trial with Notts County.

Well, twelve months later, he took up the offer and stayed with us for about three months. He was an excellent lodger, not only getting himself a temporary job to pay his way, but accompanied us to a number of games. He even experienced cricket for the first time. Sadly, I was unable to fix him up with anything at Meadow Lane - no surprise there then Michael! - but he did get a couple of pre-season trial games with Chesterfield.

We went to watch him in one, a game against the now defunct Sutton Town at Lowmoor Road in Kirkby. He was clearly a good, fast and tricky winger but, as I'm sure the Chesterfield management team will have surmised, a bit too lightweight. Whatever, his playing dreams never materialised and he returned home to pursue a more conventional career path. At least, he'll have taken pleasure in seeing Manchester

United (eventually) become the top team in England under Alex Ferguson.

At the start of the 79/80 season, we'd settled into a routine, and besides the home games, went to as many away from Meadow Lane as we could manage. Towards the end of 1979 we were helped by a sales promotion from a leading soap powder manufacturer. It may have been Persil, but that doesn't really matter. The point is, in conjunction with British Rail, they were offering heavily discounted train tickets. I can't remember how much, but they were really cheap.

Well, we must have bought a year's supply of the product, whatever it was, exchanged the vouchers for inexpensive rail tickets and enjoyed trips to Fulham (another victory), Sunderland and Watford. We began and ended those trips from Alfreton (in those days it was known as Mansfield & Alfreton) railway station.

With the trip to Vicarage Road requiring us to go into London and then back out to Watford, to give us enough time, we had walked up to Leabrooks to get an early bus into town from outside the Tiger. By the time the return train arrived in Alfreton, all public transport had ended and we walked back to Selston, getting home around half past midnight. With Pedro Richards sent off, the ten men of Notts lost 2-1. Happy days!

I've saved the most memorable game of 1979 until the end. On Monday 3rd September, the entire workforce of James Oakes (Riddings) Ltd were called together and informed that the parent company, Hepworth Refractories, had decided to cease production of ceramic pipes at the Jacksdale site. With one or two exceptions, who might possibly transfer to the Ellistown Pipes division in Leicestershire, we were to be made redundant. This was a big concern for the two of us as our mortgage repayments seemed to be increasing every other month. Still, life had to go on.

We had already booked a day off (in my case a day and a half!) for the Wednesday, as we were travelling on the supporters' bus to Torquay for a League Cup 2nd Round 2nd Leg tie at Plainmoor. The first leg had been a dull scoreless draw. You'll just have to imagine our excitement levels!

Arriving at Victoria Centre Bus Station, we met up with the rest of the travelling 'Pies and set off for the English Riviera. There was a stop planned for an M5 service station (it may have been Gordano). Safely parked up we all trooped in having had the customary reminder from the driver, "You've got thirty minutes and no more."

After a few minutes, Helen and I could hear a bit of a kerfuffle and saw that a couple of our fellow passengers were being 'roughed up' just a little. It was all over in a flash, but when we went outside we could see a further confrontation taking place with a lot of aggressive shouting, swearing and arm waving. We went over to see what was happening.

It transpired that another bus, this one carrying Doncaster Rovers fans to their League Cup tie in Exeter, had pulled in. Some of them had apparently taken exception to the fact that we were supporters of another team, and decided to a) show how tough they were and b) secure a trophy or two.

I went over to try to sort the situation out. Now whether or not, the main troublemaker, a big bruising sort of a fella, saw me as a threat or not - I think know the answer to that! - he grabbed me by the shirt and pulled me towards him. "He's not getting his XXXXXXX shirt back and you can all XXXX off back to your bus", was his welcome greeting. Well, despite the fact that he'd ripped my own shirt, this seemed like sensible enough advice to me. I was all for leaving it at that. Not so Mrs Gyles.

Helen had established that one of our guys had lost his replica Notts shirt and this was now being provocatively displayed to us from the back seat of the Donny bus. At this, she climbed into the bus, determined to retrieve it. Well, I was not prepared to let my gentle wife go into the 'lion's den' without some manly assistance. In fact, I stood right behind her in the aisle of the bus!!

Having first shouted, "Call the Police if I'm not out this bus in a minute", and assured the young tyros that she was not leaving until the shirt had been returned, we had the usual foul mouthed response that you expect from cretins like these. Still, they eventually got the message, 'this lady was not for turning', and handed back their highly prized but criminally acquired memento. I quickly let Helen through and pass me by (I'm a gentleman after all!) before following her off the bus.

The shirt was returned to the young victim, we got back on the bus and carried on our journey. From memory, not much was said, but I reckon that most of the mainly male supporters were thinking what I'd come to recognise a few years beforehand, viz. whatever you do, don't mess with that woman.

As for the game, a Paul Hooks goal, was enough to see Notts progress and we arrived back at Victoria Bus Station at about 4.00am. We hung about for around 90 minutes for the first bus heading out to Selston. When we got home, Helen had a shower and went to work. As for me, I went to bed for a bit of kip, before walking down to Jacksdale for a shortened day.

Other footballing observations from the 1970's

I can't really move on without admitting that there were a number of games attended in the decade when, quite frankly, I was drunk. From a very early age, like many fans of the game, I've enjoyed a pre-match bevy. I still do, but in a much more controlled fashion than was the case during my late teens and twenties.

Whilst at the time I wasn't probably aware of it, I know that there have been occasions when I've been a bit of an embarrassment. Amongst the worst of these were:-

1 – a Scottish Cup quarter final tie between Raith Rovers and Kilmarnock in March 1972. Back then, it was still OK to take alcohol into football grounds. After I don't know how many drinks in the pub beforehand, I got myself a 'kerry oot' to keep me going during the game.

2 – a fifth Round FA Cup tie in February 1975 at Field Mill. Some of the 19,293 there that day, who saw Carlisle win through to the quarter final,

will remember the guy who was so drunk he could hardly stand on the terrace. Helen certainly does.

3 – England hammering Scotland 5-1 at Wembley in May of 1975 is but a blur, although I was sufficiently alert at the end of the game to secure a small piece of Wembley turf as a memento. Given the result, you may well question why.

There were others, although probably not to the same level, and I'm not proud of this and just happy that I have come through it. Others, many no longer with us, haven't.

One final point. May I remind you that 30th August 1976 was the day we were married. Despite spending our first anniversary at St Andrews, Birmingham (a 2nd Round League Cup victory by 2-0) and our second anniversary at Gresty Road, Crewe (a 2nd Round League Cup defeat by 3-0) we remain, surprisingly some might say, together. Just like on that bus at the service station, I'm still right behind Helen!!

Chapter 7

1970's – regularly crossing the River Trent!

Other than football, live sporting experiences in this decade were very limited. In truth, after leaving Arbroath in September 1970 and up until May 1978, even my television viewing of anything, never mind sport, was severely restricted. My landlady at 160 Diamond Avenue, Kirkby-in-Ashfield had a black/white television during my time there and she had no objections to me joining the 'family' to watch events like Cup Finals, the Grand National, Test Matches, Wimbledon etc.

Later, Helen's Mum and Dad welcomed me into their front room to see some events. Other than tennis, they'd got next to no interest in sport, but were prepared to indulge me. I caused a bit of a rumpus once whilst watching the Scotland v England Home International in May 1976. England took an early lead (Mick Channon) but were quickly pegged back by a goal from Don Masson (I'll just remind you that he is the best player I've ever seen play for Notts County, although at that time he was with Queens Park Rangers) and it was level at half time.

However, when Kenny Dalglish slipped the ball through Ray Clemence's legs early in the second half, I couldn't contain myself. I reckon I shocked not only everyone in 6 Victoria Road that afternoon, but probably most of East Kirkby, when letting out a loud shriek followed by my full repertoire of 'it's a goal' celebratory noises. There was no more scoring and Mr & Mrs Knight, who probably couldn't have given a toss, at least had a better idea of what their daughter was letting herself in for!

I was temporarily back in Arbroath during the 1972 Olympics, but as I was in the process of helping Dad dispose of the business was unable to pay too much attention to what was happening in Munich. Similarly, in 1976, the Montreal Olympics just passed me by as I was not only looking for somewhere to stay in advance of my wedding at the end of August, I was getting to grips with a new job. *NB – as a further money saving effort, and before I got my bike, I was walking to and from Jacksdale on a daily basis. It was time consuming, but I just had to cut down on bus fares.*

I did go through to Cowdenbeath for the stock car racing on odd occasions when in Scotland, but there was a 'first' for me in September 1972 when I went horse racing. The Station Hotel was being sold and two bookmakers from Arbroath were heavily involved in the transaction. They'd become regulars in the bar, and after I'd played a couple of rounds of golf with them in the summer of 1972, they asked if I'd like to join them on a trip to Perth for the racing.

Well, I'd always had a passing interest and at that time, like my Dad, could probably name all the winners of the big races since the War. Although I was no expert, I placed the occasional bet just for fun - it was difficult not to when surrounded by committed punters in the Station Hotel on a daily basis - and surprised everyone that year, by selecting the winner of the English Oaks. You're probably not interested, but just for the record, Ginevra came in at 8/1.

Anyway, back to Perth. My two new friends were working, so after being told what to do, how to place a bet with the on-course bookmakers etc., I was left to my own devices. I enjoyed the experience. The noise, colour and general atmosphere was so much better than going into a soulless bookies to place a bet. It may have taken a further 28 years before I set foot on another racecourse - that's another story and you'll just have to wait - so I can't claim to have become immediately 'hooked', but I did enjoy myself.

As it happens, from a punting point of view, I ended up breaking even on the day, although I can take no personal credit for that. In five of the six races I picked losers (not that I knew that in advance of course) but Dad had given me his 'tip of the day', and trusting his judgement, I was overjoyed to see this horse win at 5/1. I've tried googling, without success, for a record of racing results from 1972 to get the full picture for that day. There must be some way but life's too short to be wasting time on it. That being the case, I'll just have to satisfy myself with the knowledge that the successful horse had the word ice in its name. It may have been Ice Pick, but after all these years, who cares?

I was living and working in Birmingham for three months beginning April 1976. In addition to visiting St Andrews, The Hawthorns and Fellows Park (Walsall) for midweek games towards the end of that season, I also tried to get to Molineux for the Wolves home game v Liverpool on Wednesday 4th May. Liverpool only needed a draw to deny QPR the Championship to win it for themselves and the home side needed a win to have any chance of avoiding relegation. It was a big game. So big in fact, that for safety reasons, the gates were locked just as I got there and I missed the chance of seeing Liverpool win 3-1.

With the football season completed, I had to find something else to amuse myself on mid-week evenings whilst living away. From my lodgings in Kingstanding, the bus taking me into town passed the Perry Barr Stadium. I found out at work that the Birmingham Brummies speedway team raced there during the week. Just what I wanted to know.

I went to a few meetings during that hot summer. It didn't take long to get the hang of the sport and I looked forward to my visits. As it happens, the Brummies, other than the Graham (Alan and Andy) brothers, had a poor roster, and with one exception, were beaten every time I went. Still I enjoyed the experience and can claim to have seen both Peter Collins and Ivan Mauger racing when they were close to their peak.

Coming to Nottinghamshire in 1970 opened up opportunities that I was unlikely to ever see in Arbroath viz. first class cricket. I arrived at the back end of that season but resolved to get down to Trent Bridge whenever I could the following year.

Work commitments were clearly limiting but I managed to get to a few games in the John Player League in 1971. To say that Nottinghamshire were in the cricketing doldrums around that period would be an understatement. Despite having Garry Sobers, the rest of the squad captained by Mike Smedley was such that they rarely threatened to win any of the four competitions running at that time. Nonetheless, I did enjoy those Sunday afternoons watching the likes of Mike (Pasty) Harris, Basher Hassan, Carlton Forbes, Mike Tayler, Bob White, Barry Stead etc., competing alongside some of the home grown and overseas stars of the day.

BBC2 broadcast one game a week each Sunday with John Arlott and Jim Laker providing the commentary. I'd watched a few of these on television and knew that the routine was, regardless of location, to zoom in to the scoreboard at the end of every other over. Aware that the cameras were going to be at Trent Bridge one particular Sunday, I rang Dawn, and whilst acknowledging that she had next to no interest in the game itself, asked her to sacrifice fifteen minutes and tune in to BBC2 at 2.00pm. She did as she was told and rang back that night to confirm that, yes indeed, she'd seen me giving her a wave as I stood at the foot of the scoreboard.

With being in Arbroath next summer, I saw no cricket. However, in 1973, I picked up again, and in addition to Sunday League games, managed my first ever day of Test Cricket. England were hosting New Zealand that summer and I got down to Trent Bridge on Saturday 9th June for the third day of the 1st Test. Bowlers had been on top in the first two days and despite only scoring 250 in the first innings, John Snow, Geoff Arnold and Tony Greig had knocked over the Kiwis for 97, a lead of 153.

However, England were reduced to 24/4 on the Friday afternoon before Greig joined Dennis Amiss and began a recovery.

At the start of play on Saturday morning, as England continued from their overnight score of 72/4, I positively purred with delight as, sitting at the boundary edge, I watched the two overnight batsmen complete the recovery process with a stand of 210. When Greig was eventually out for 139, the remaining batsmen helped Amiss (he finished unbeaten on 138) extend the overall lead to 478 before Ray Illingworth's declaration.

As I went home that night, New Zealand were already 56/2 and it looked as if they had no realistic chance of victory. Well, with Bev Congdon scoring 176 and Viv Pollard 116, they came mighty close, taking the game into a fifth day by which time the improbable had become distinctly possible. They eventually fell away however to lose by a narrow 38 runs.

From a personal point of view, if I hadn't appreciated just how much I loved this game beforehand, especially the longer format, I certainly did now. I may not have told you when you were around Dad, but it's something for which I'm truly thankful.

My cricket watching continued to be limited to Sundays in the coming years, and by 1975 Helen was joining me. We used to travel down on the bus, taking a couple of deck chairs and settle down on the deep fine leg/long off boundary. Although Garry Sobers had left the Club and Mike Smedley remained as captain, the playing strength had been improved with a number of promising youngsters coming through. These included John Birch, Paul Todd, Paul Johnson and that bundle of nervous energy, Derek Randall. In addition, and as time was to prove, the most significant development was the recruitment of Clive Rice, the South African all-rounder.

1975 was the first of two consecutive long hot summers. I have a very painful and embarrassing reason for remembering this as, despite Helen advising me otherwise, on one Sunday afternoon I took off shirt, socks and shoes to reveal both pale torso and feet. A couple of hours later, all skin on display had turned a deep shade of crimson and I was suffering. On the way back up to the Victoria Bus Station I was in agony and began to feel physically sick as we headed out of town on the bus. We'd just passed the City Hospital when I told Helen that if I didn't get off there was a fair chance that I'd empty the contents of my stomach right there on the bus.

We both moved to the front and I asked the driver if he'd pull up at the next stop. He argued that he wasn't allowed to as he was not yet beyond the city limits. He relented when I told him that, unless he let me off, he was likely to soon have a noxious mess on the bus floor.

81

Whilst we waited for the next bus, I felt less nauseous, but my inflamed skin kept reminding me what an idiot I'd been.

One other memory of that season was the occasion when Derek Randall had a brief conversation with my future wife. It must have been late in the opposition's innings as he'd been sent out to patrol the long off boundary. As he came over, looking for something to remind him of where 'base' was, he looked Helen in the eye and said, "Please don't move from there!" Sure enough, two overs later, he gave her the 'thumbs up' as he made a bee-line for her.

Helen came through to join me in Birmingham one weekend the following summer. That Sunday there was a John Player League game at Edgbaston when, and I swear this is pure coincidence, Nottinghamshire were the opponents. Of course we went!

It was a high scoring game with Notts batting first, making 261 in their 40 overs (yes I know that doesn't look particularly high scoring now, but believe me, it was back then) with Basher Hassan making 93. In their innings, Warwickshire, with Rohan Kanhai - yes, he who I'd first seen in Arbroath 17 years earlier - scoring 93, secured the win with five balls to go. Although I was sorry to see Notts lose, I was most upset that I was still to see a batsman score a century. Yes, I'd seen Amiss and Greig in that Test Match a few years earlier, but both had already started their innings before I got there. In fact, it was 1985 before I finally witnessed a first class century from start to finish.

The Queen's Silver Jubilee year of 1977 saw the Australians visit the country for what proved to be a memorable Ashes series. The Third Test was scheduled for Trent Bridge and I'd managed to get tickets for all five days for Dad, with Helen and myself joining him on the Saturday. It was Ian Botham's debut, and although we didn't know it at the time, England's former captain, Tony Greig's Test career was soon to come to an end.

With the 1st Test drawn and England comfortably winning the 2nd, there was real hope (if not expectation) that the Australians might be handing back the Ashes. Those hopes were further raised after the Trent Bridge Test.

Australia were bowled out relatively cheaply (243) in the first innings with Botham taking 5/74. England began their reply that night and had reached 242/5 by close of play on the Friday, with Geoff Boycott on 88* and Alan Knott on 87*. This was a recovery following a batting collapse that had included Boycott being responsible for Derek Randall's run out. The stubborn and opinionated Yorkshireman had much to do to win over the Trent Bridge crowd.

On the Saturday, with Helen enjoying her first ever day of Test cricket, the recovery was completed with both overnight batsmen going on to make hundreds. England had a lead of 121 when Australia batted again. They made a better fist of it and set England a possibly tricky target of 189 to win the Test. They did with relative ease, with Randall and his apologetic partner Boycott at the crease, when the winning runs were scored.

Dad loved the whole experience - it was soon to become an annual visit - and had just the one regret. On each day of the Test, Geoff Boycott had been batting at some point. Unfortunately, on the first day, the light was not particularly good upon completion of the Australian innings, and on the assumption that there would be no more play, Dad had set off for home, missing the start of the England reply.

Incidentally, this was Geoff Boycott's 98th First Class Century. He famously secured his 100th in the next Test at Headingley, when another England victory secured the Ashes in a series which was ultimately won 3-0. As for Tony Greig, throughout the series he had been tapping up England players with a view to joining Kerry Packer's World Series Cricket. By the end of the summer he'd become 'persona non grata' to the cricketing establishment.

Just one final recollection of that summer. During the rest day of that Trent Bridge Test we were at a bit of a loss as to how to amuse Dad until I realised that Derbyshire had a home John Player League game that Sunday. You'll have to take my word for it but he didn't need any persuading. With deck chairs and sandwiches packed, all three of us set off in whatever car my father-in-law was driving at that time.

The County Ground at Derby was in no way comparable to Trent Bridge, but Dad was happy enough watching a game in which Middlesex were quite comfortable winners. If he was to never go to another cricket match in his life - as it happens there were plenty more - he could say that he'd seen such luminaries as Mike Gatting, Mike Selvey, John Embury, Phillipe Edmonds and........'Fartin' Freddie Swarbrook in action.

Chapter 8

1980's – all aboard the roller coaster!

Towards the end of 1979 we were once more looking for a house. Other than a straightforward redundancy, I was offered alternative employment at Ellistown Pipes HQ in Leicestershire. On the understanding that a suitable position be found for Helen, I was happy enough to accept the offer. She was given an interview and subsequently offered a job thereby leading to us house hunting in the likes of Ashby-de-la-Zouch, Woodville, Moira etc. during October/November.

However, while we were doing this, once Helen's employer heard that she was likely to be leaving soon, they tried to persuade her to change her mind. She explained that I'd been made a good offer and it was a career move that I was loathe to turn down. The upshot, and this probably says more about my wife's attributes than it does about me, was that I was offered a position there. They not only matched the new salary I had been promised, but if I took on the role, it would mean that we didn't have the hassle of moving.

We had settled in Selston with me now having a new local Littlewoods Pools round, and both Helen and myself had becoming increasingly involved with Selston FC. Besides, with Helen now an integral member of the management team at the largest employer in the village, we felt as if we belonged. Oh, and let's not forget, if we stayed, I would benefit from a redundancy package. Not a fortune, but you have to remember that although we could now afford a rented television, we had high mortgage commitments and were still restricted to public transport. We were not paupers by any means, but it seemed that if we were to stay, our circumstances would definitely be on the rise. Not forgetting of course, that for the time being at least, there were just the two mouths to feed, although we were hoping to make that three as soon as possible.

It was against this background then, that we began the new decade

1980

The 1979/80 season was the first when I felt that, as a small club competing for support with a much bigger rival that had just won the European Cup (as they would do again very soon), Notts County had probably peaked. In short, I'd probably have to get used to being a loyal supporter of a club that was the butt of jokes from most football followers in the area.

Results that year seemed to bear that out, and in truth, were it not for our top scoring left back, Ray O'Brien's ten goals, and new signing Raddy Avramovic's heroics in goal, we may well have dropped back to the Third Division. We survived, but there appeared to be few reasons to be optimistic as we renewed season tickets for the 80/81 season.

OK, with hindsight, there were a few. Gordon Mair, Brian Kilcline and Tristan Benjamin joined Pedro Richards as youth team players making regular appearances for the first team, and although they were prone to the occasional bad error, each looked as if they could make a career in the game.

On balance however, it seemed as if we were going to have to settle for memories of the good away wins at QPR and Swansea in January and February respectively, to sustain us through the close season.

That 1-0 win at Swansea was a day full of drama. The bus got us to The Vetch in plenty of time, and following Paul Hooks' late goal in a game that the home side had dominated, was filled by a band of happy 'Pies for the return journey. I knew we might be in trouble when the bus driver came off the M4 and travelled through Newport before returning to the Motorway and heading over the Severn Bridge rather than up towards the M50. I hope you're following this!

I can't remember if at that time there was a toll to leave Wales via the Bridge. There certainly was when travelling west and entering the Principality. Whatever, the coach driver was wasting good time, and after the obligatory service station stop, I was becoming increasingly

86

concerned that Helen and myself wouldn't get back to Nottingham in time to catch the last bus to Selston.

My worst fears were confirmed when, at about 9.30pm, the bus pulled over on to the hard shoulder of the M1 near Coalville. Our convoluted route home had resulted in the bus running out of fuel and the driver informing us that he'd have to summon a replacement to enable us to get home. About an hour later this arrived.

The end result however, was that by the time we got back to Meadow Lane, were it not for a very obliging fellow supporter, we'd have been either walking home - I don't do taxis! - or kipping down once more at the Victoria Bus Station. This chap - I never have got to know his name - went out of his way to drop Malcolm Shearstone off in Nuttall and then the two of us in Selston. What a guy.

There is a very sad postscript to this story. We heard on the Monday that a young guy who'd been on the bus, had committed suicide over the weekend. I can't remember the details other than that he was a student and that his parents, a Mr & Mrs Cameron, had donated some sort of trophy to be presented each year at the annual end of season awards night. Wonder what happened to that? Let's move on.

Whilst we fans had been preparing for what looked like an inevitable return to the lower divisions, there had been some quiet activity going on behind the scenes at Meadow Lane. Jimmy Sirrel had arranged for a new first team coach to assist him in managing the team, and it was clear from August 1980, that things might be about to change.

Other than Eddie Kelly, a former Arsenal player that Notts had signed from Leicester City, there were no changes in personnel. The key change however was the way the side was set up. After becoming an established full back over the past five seasons, Pedro Richards had been switched to sweeper. It proved to be an inspired move and the credit was all down to the new coach.

Howard Wilkinson was at the early stages of what was eventually to become a very successful career as football coach and subsequently manager. He'd managed in non-league football, most notably at

Boston United, but Notts provided the opportunity to prove himself at a much higher level.

Notts lost only one of their first eighteen league games - a four goal thrashing by West Ham on our fourth wedding anniversary! - but the pundits refused to take us seriously. When the last ten league games of the year resulted in seven draws, three defeats and no victories, it looked as if their scepticism was justified as Notts slipped out of the automatic promotion places.

However, there was clearly something stirring as they advanced to the 4th Round of the League Cup before suffering a 5-1 thrashing at Maine Road (Manchester City) and reached the final of the Anglo Scottish Cup. OK, promotion might have been asking too much, but under Jimmy Sirrel and Howard Wilkinson, the Club was definitely making progress.

Helen and myself were continuing to use a combination of public transport and supporters' buses to get to games home and away. There had been a significant development however earlier in the year. Let's hazard a guess and say that it must have been around the beginning of April, as Helen was now pregnant with our first child due on 31st December.

That didn't stop her however, and she continued to follow the team to the likes of Grimsby, Newport, West Ham, Swansea, Bristol City, Luton, Orient, Oldham, Manchester City, and Wrexham before her final game at Shrewsbury on 22nd November. Notts supporters of a certain vintage will remember Claude Bishop who used to organise the transport. He'd been doing it for many years, and keeping a keen eye on Helen's gradual 'expansion' as the weeks passed, I can remember him commenting that he'd never before been responsible for delivering a new Notts fan on his many journeys up and down the country. Well, fortunately it didn't come to that, as common sense prevailed and Helen missed trips (as indeed did I by the way) to Bolton, Watford, Bristol Rovers and Preston in the closing weeks of the year.

1981

I can't continue without first bringing you up to date on domestic developments. Ailsa Catriona Gyles was a little late in arriving, but finally made it at around 3.30am on Tuesday 6th January. I'm not going to take time recounting how tough it was during those early weeks/months because a) with a few exceptions, we've all been there and b) there is much more detail in my first book.

The winless run continued into the new year with a couple of home draws against Shrewsbury and West Ham. That changed on 31st January, in the thirteenth game of this depressing run, when I stood on the open Hillsborough Kop and saw Iain McCulloch hit the winner as Sheffield Wednesday were defeated 2-1. Notts were up and running again.

For obvious reasons that shouldn't need expanding upon, I was unable to get to as many away games as in the recent past. In addition to the Sheffield Wednesday game, during a visit to Letchworth to show Ailsa off to old friends the George's and their two girls, Tim and myself got to QPR (1-1) and I also managed the Baseball Ground to see a 2-2 draw. In the meantime, although West Ham were runaway leaders, Notts were 'hanging in there' still with a good chance of finishing in the top three and being promoted to the 1st Division for the first time in 55 years.

Away from the promotion race, and having been knocked out of the FA Cup at the 4th Round stage in a shock home defeat to Peterborough, Notts were short odds favourites to win the Anglo Scottish Cup, their first major trophy since 1894.

Notts had disposed of Kilmarnock and would meet Chesterfield, who had beaten the mighty Rangers in the other two legged semi-final. Chesterfield took a deserved, albeit narrow, one goal advantage from the first leg at Saltergate. Nonetheless, Notts were expected to overcome that the following week at Meadow Lane, and indeed they should have done.

Notts had been on top for much of the game, but it took a second half goal from Don Masson to level up the scores and take the final into extra time. Chances continued to come (and be missed) during the additional thirty minutes when, and this is something we 'Pies are used to, Alan Crawford scored in the 120th minute.

Now, people may question just how significant this competition was. Well, for those who do, may I refer you to the words of Brian Clough who, lest you have forgotten, became manager of Nottingham Forest courtesy of Notts County. He is on record as having said that of all the trophies he won whilst at that club, the most important one came after the defeat of Orient in the 1976/77 Anglo Scottish Cup Final. He justified this seemingly outrageous claim by pointing out "........because It was the first!"

Back to the 2nd Division and Notts travelled to Cambridge United on Easter Monday. I wasn't there, but following a Trevor Christie double in a 2-1 victory, and a check on other results that day, along with other disbelieving supporters of the 'oldest Football League Club in the World' TM, I realised that Notts had only to win one of their remaining three games to guarantee promotion.

The first of those was at home to Watford, a mid-table side with nothing to play for but who were destined for bigger things in the near future. Well, just like the Chesterfield game a few weeks earlier, I was one of many to return home that night questioning my sanity/loyalty. Despite a Mark Goodwin goal, Watford were worthy winners. To make matters worse, the Notts County end of season awards night was scheduled for that Saturday evening.

We'd planned for this and having brought Helen's Mum over from Kirkby in Ken's car, we had a) a vehicle to get back to Nottingham for what should have been a celebratory night and b) perhaps more importantly, our baby sitter for the night. We took Dick and Jackie with us and made the best of what was effectively a damp squib of an event. On the way back, it was starting to sleet and when we got up the following morning, there had been some serious snowfall. *NB – check it out, this was 26th April!*

Well, having mastered even worse conditions in Scotland just sixteen months earlier, I eventually managed to overcome the drifting snow and get Betty (& car) back home. I then trudged back to Selston on foot.

The problem now was that, having hoped to be present when Notts actually secured promotion, there were two games left and the first of those was away to Chelsea the following Saturday. I had a dilemma. I had a four month old baby at home and a young mother who was feeling the pressure that invariably all first-time mums feel when they're stuck in the house all day on their own. Should I go to Chelsea or not, and if I did, how was I going to get there?

Now, if you're a true football fan you might think that the answer is obvious. After all, this could be a once in a lifetime opportunity. I recognised this but, and you might question what I'm saying here, there is more to life than football. All week I wrestled with my conscience, and it was genuinely only on the Saturday morning that I made up my mind. I had to go!

I made a few telephone enquiries and found that I could get a train from Alfreton that would get me into London and leave enough time to get to Stamford Bridge. It was tight, but eminently doable. It's fair to say that having done this research and told Helen of my plans, her parting words were as far removed from "Bon Voyage" as you can imagine, and I set off in some trepidation. Yes, I was very nervous about the upcoming game, but whatever the outcome, I was more worried about whether or not the locks would be changed whilst I was away.

Well, with being nervous and all that, I just had to have a drink. I wasn't going to have time in London so I bought four cans for the train journey. This is something incidentally that I'd probably frown upon if I saw others doing it on a train journey now. Reckon I've become a bit of a snob!

Whatever, I'd downed three on the way to London and decided to keep one, which I was hoping would serve as a celebratory drink, for the return journey. It may seem unthinkable now but I carried that can into the ground in an inside pocket. I can't remember if I had to buy a ticket

91

beforehand or, as remained the case at many grounds in those days, pay at the gate. Whatever, I ended up in a seat in the upper Tier of the East Stand. It was about half way and gave me an excellent view.

Trevor Christie opened the scoring after fifteen minutes and whilst there was a lot of foul mouthed comment to be heard around me - Chelsea were having a really bad run, and regardless of that day's result, their fans were disgruntled - I just concentrated on the game. Half time arrived and although I was pleased with the score, I couldn't settle. To calm my nerves, I was tempted to find somewhere to swig down my liquid contraband. I resisted, but as you're about to find out, I now wish I had.

In the 57th minute Rachid Harkouk scored a second goal and I was surrounded by even more animosity. Not directed at me or my team but at the Chelsea FC owners. The fans had had enough of the Mears family and wanted them out. *NB – the following year, Ken Bates bought the club for £1*

The guy next to me asked why I was so quiet. I smiled and told him it was because I was nervous as my team were on the verge of promotion. That set him back a little but we got into a friendly conversation and he seemed a decent sort. So much so that with about fifteen minutes to go I produced my can and asked if he'd like to share a celebratory drink with me. He did, but after taking a swig, threw the can out of the stand and then got up and left. Now this was an almost full can, and from that height, could have caused some serious damage down below. I was shocked but can only assume that it landed safely.

The drama wasn't over. There were around ten minutes to go when, from the smaller West Stand opposite me, a few fans began to encroach onto the pitch. They grew in number as what looked like a very visible protest against Brian Mears (& co) took place. The game was briefly stopped, and with me thinking terrible thoughts that this could lead to an abandonment, our now almost certain promotion was temporarily put on hold. Thankfully, things calmed down, the idiots left the pitch allowing the restart, and the game was played to a somewhat surreal finish. Time to get home and face the music.

I phoned Helen from St Pancras. Let's just say that it was a one way joyous conversation but, and I may have been clutching at straws here, we were talking. No that's not quite right – she was listening.

The final game was the following Tuesday, and with the pressure off, it was a happy occasion made all the happier by a 2-0 victory over Cambridge United. I'd only been following the Club for ten years, and I was buzzing. However, I could see what it meant to those who could recall the Tommy Lawton glory years of thirty years before. They had never thought they'd see the like again and grown men and women were in tears.

Four days later I was at Wembley for my second FA Cup Final. This time I'd used my own initiative and contacted Notts well in advance of knowing who the finalists might be. I came up trumps and my ticket for the Manchester City v Tottenham Hotspur Final arrived in plenty of time. I can't remember how I got down there – Ken must have, once again, lent me his car – but, should I ever come across Tommy Hutchison, I'll be able to tell him that 'I was there' on 9th May 1981, the day he scored for both teams in a 1-1 draw.

Hutchison was one of the best attacking winger/midfield players I saw play for Scotland and yes, I'll accept that it's a matter of debate, but I'd claim that had he played from the start – he made only two substitute appearances – in West Germany in 1974, Scotland would not only have qualified, they'd have gone on to be World Champions. We'll never know now, but you'll have a difficult job in persuading me otherwise!

Back to 1981. In the replay the following Thursday night, which I didn't attend, Tottenham won 3-2 with Ricky Villa scoring **THAT** goal. I'm sure you know what I'm referring to, but if not, just check out YouTube footage of the 1981 FA Cup Final replay.

That's just reminded me of a sporting question that used to do the rounds a few years ago. The question was:-

If it was Sunderland in 1979, and Villa in 1981, who was it in 1980?

The answer of course being Brooking. Scorers of the winning goals in three successive FA Cup Finals were Alan Sunderland (1979), Trevor Brooking (1980) and Ricky Villa (1981)

That summer saw a number of riots across England. Starting in Brixton, but carrying on in other cities, primarily Liverpool (Toxteth), Birmingham (Handsworth), Leeds (Chapeltown) and Manchester (Moss Side) they also, to a lesser extent, affected Nottingham. After years of subjugation and police harassment, second generation immigrants were fighting back. It's not for me to argue the rights and wrongs, but it did put a bit of a damper on things for all, not just us 'Pies.

Still, once the 1981/82 fixtures were released, we could look forward to our first game back in the top flight. We'd visit the home of the current League Champions (and soon to be European Cup winners), Aston Villa.

Saturday 29th August 1981 was a memorable day. Betty and Ken had agreed to not only look after Ailsa for the afternoon, but we'd been allowed to borrow the car. This arrangement also suited a third party.

For a few weeks that summer, we had a lodger staying with us. With Helen no longer working, the extra income came in handy, and this young fella was one of many to stay with us over the years. She had noted an advert from a local company seeking accommodation for foreign exchange students for a few weeks. Well, we could take one, and subsequently Raymond, who was Hong Kong Chinese and studying at Aston University, became a temporary member of the family. Coincidentally, and fortunately for Raymond, he had to return to Birmingham on the weekend of the opening game.

With Ailsa safely deposited with her grandparents, and Raymond dropped off at his halls of residence, we made our way to Villa Park. ATV, the Birmingham based franchise, covered the game for its recorded highlights programme the following afternoon. No surprise really as this was the Midlands top team (Forest fans might have disputed that at the time) and current Champions first game of the season. The fact that they were playing a minor team from the same region was probably irrelevant. Villa at home just had to be covered.

Notts had made only the three signings, a pacy winger and two defenders, during the close season. John Chiedozie, a Nigerian international had been signed from Leyton Orient (no longer just plain old Orient!), Aki Lahtinen from Finnish club OPS and Nigel Worthington from Ballymena United. Of the three, Chiedozie was the only one to make his debut on this historic day.

In truth, it was one of those games which could have gone either way. However, midway through the first half, from a corner in front of the Holte End, Iain McCulloch headed the only goal of the game. This was not supposed to happen. Notts were everyone's favourites to be relegated and here they were, only denied being top team in the English 1st Division on goal difference. The realists among us knew that we had a further 41 games to go and that this was probably the high point.

The next two games were at home and after drawing with Manchester City and beating Coventry City in this, the first season in which three points were awarded for a win, we were still sitting third in the table with seven points. It wasn't to last of course and there were only two more wins, both at home, against Sunderland and Arsenal before the turn of the year.

As well as the additional point awarded for a win, another change introduced was the decision to allow clubs to retain all gate receipts from their home games. This was cynically a move to appease the so-called bigger clubs who thought it was unfair that the proceeds from an attendance of say, 40,000 at their ground, should be shared with the likes of Notts County. We weren't to know it at the time, but this was the first step leading to the inevitable creation of the English Premier League.

Scotland were still playing with my emotions. I'd been to Wembley in May to see a John Robertson penalty secure another win over the auld enemy and managed to get a ticket for the vital World Cup Qualifier v Sweden at Hampden in September. It just so happened that on the Sunday before that game, my two nieces, Carey and Zoe (Dawn's first two) were to be baptised at Faslane. With my brother then living at

Milton of Campsie, and with Ailsa in tow, we enjoyed a few days 'family time' in that part of Scotland splitting our time between the two.

As for the game, we knew beforehand that a Scotland win, whilst not making it a mathematical certainty, would very likely see them qualify for their third consecutive World Cup Finals tournament. On the night, goals from Joe Jordan and another from a John Robertson penalty, delivered a 2-0 win. We would almost certainly be going to Spain next summer. Helen was up for it, so why not? Watch this space.

1982

With apologies for the choice of language, the New Year appears to have gone off with a bit of a bang. You can take that however you like, but it is a fact that Heather Fiona Gyles was born on Thursday 30th September. She made her first appearance around 5.45pm, just as – and I promise this is most definitely the last time I'll mention it Heather! – I should have been busily collecting Littlewoods Pools coupons. At around 5.55pm that night, Helen told me "That's it, no more. You're off for the snip!"

As 1981 turned into 1982, Notts County were in lower mid-table with the main objective viz. survival, still uncertain. We were enjoying our season, getting the occasional mention on the back pages, although this was generally reserved for match reports involving one of the bigger clubs amongst the English elite.

If I wasn't aware of it beforehand, I now realised that the game was riddled with a form of latent arrogance. Many were openly questioning why it was that this little club with their rundown ground, manager who was unable to speak English properly and poor attendances which were only kept at a reasonable level as a result of the support of a couple of thousand veterans of WW2 who, even now, thought that life was a lot better when Tommy Lawton and Jackie Sewell were playing, should be allowed to compete with the likes of Arsenal, Liverpool, Manchester United etc. Over the years, this has just got worse, and according to many today, the game of football didn't really start until 1992 and the formation of the English Premier League. Don't get me started!

Well, one of the footballing elite visited Meadow Lane twice in the early weeks of 1982. Aston Villa, founder members of the Football League but, unlike Notts, winners of many trophies, were the visitors for a 3rd Round FA Cup tie. The original tie had been postponed for weather related reasons, and a crowd of 12,312 huddled together for warmth the following Tuesday night as Villa, with David Geddes scoring a hat-trick, won 6-0.

Fortunately, there was an almost immediate opportunity for revenge – for both sides as it happens – eleven days later, as Villa visited for the return league fixture. We may have shocked them on the opening day of the season, but the current Champions had recovered since then, and although they had no chance of retaining their title, they were through to the quarter finals of the European Cup. After the cup victory the previous week, surely this had to be an away win?

In front of nearly 3,000 less spectators than had attended the cup-tie, Trevor Christie scored the only goal of the game and Notts had secured their first league double. A few weeks later, courtesy of a 5-1 thrashing of Coventry City at Highfield Road, came the second.

After only one away win in the first half of the season, four followed the turn of the year. Under normal circumstances, were it not for the fact that it was becoming such a regular occurrence, the 2-0 (Hooks & Christie) victory at the City Ground would have been the pick.

Enjoyable though that was, in a shock that probably made people sit up and take more notice than at any time since the opening day, Notts went to Portman Road and returned with three points. I wasn't there, but the cameras were and it was gratifying, following the Sunday highlights show, to hear Bobby Robson, whose Ipswich Town were to finish as runners-up only four points behind Liverpool, claim that Notts were a much better team than pundits appeared to credit them. The third goal in particular in that 3-1 victory, when a slick passing move from defence involving a number of players, ended with Gordon Mair nonchalantly stroking the ball past Paul Cooper, was a joy to watch. I just wish I'd been there.

There were a few more ups and downs before the end of the season, but Notts were never in any serious danger of relegation, and the likes of Leeds Utd, Wolves, Sunderland and West Brom ended with less than the 'Pies creditable total of 47 points as they finished in 15th position.

For me, it was a short close season. I was lucky enough to get a ticket for my third FA Cup Final. Well, I thought I was, but the Tottenham v QPR final, for the neutral, did not live long in the memory. There were no goals in ninety minutes and for the second consecutive year extra time was again required.

Glen Hoddle scored to give Tottenham the lead with only ten of the extra thirty minutes left. That should have been it, but Terry Fenwick equalised and it needed a Hoddle penalty in the replay five days later for Spurs to retain the Cup. So, for the second year in a row, I'd failed to see the Cup presentation. There was still more football to come, but you'll have to wait for details of that.

Notts started the 1982/83 season minus Don Masson but with Nigel Worthington now first choice left back. With two draws and a 5-3 defeat away to Luton, the mood around Meadow Lane was a bit pessimistic – yes, I accept that there's nothing unusual in that – before a couple of 1-0 home wins over Manchester City and Everton took Notts into the top half of the table. The team were however extremely consistent in their inconsistency with the next home game being a 6-0 defeat to Ipswich. Suddenly the 'gloom' switch had once again been turned on.

A good League Cup run in which Aston Villa were defeated over both legs and Chelsea by 2-0 at home was ended after a 3-3 home draw with West Ham and the Londoners winning the replay 3-0.

The year ended on a high with Stoke City hammered 4-0 at Meadow Lane between Christmas and New Year. However, the main reason for Notts fans good cheer that festive period had been the outcome of the home game on 4th December when Forest made the short trip across the River Trent. The visitors were doing well and sitting third in the table, and although our record at the City Ground was good, the expectation was that, once again, our neighbours would 'rise to the occasion'.

As it happens, I'd become quite friendly with the owner of the business that was, at that time, the principal supplier of stationery to the Selston based organisation I was still working for. Brian Lightbody of LEP (Long Eaton Printers), was a committed Nottingham Forest supporter and this gave rise to a fair amount of good natured banter between the two of us.

Brian had booked a box at Meadow Lane for the derby game and had kindly invited members of our management team. I was blessed to be among them and had further luck when our MD said that he'd bring his Jaguar round to our house to pick me up and return me home after the game. Let's face it, it's not quite the done thing to accept an offer of hospitality with the proviso, "I've just got to check the bus times."

Including Brian himself, there were eight in total of whom I was the only fan of the home team. There were a couple of Forest fans, and at least one who was going to his first ever game. *NB – I'm not a real fan of hospitality packages. I'm not that bothered about the food in the first place and find it frustrating when you get talking to fellow attendees and discover that they haven't a clue what's going on.* I'm there for the sport and on this particular day, I was to enjoy myself immensely.

The Meadow Lane boxes are located behind one of the goals and from above, I was in the perfect position to demonstrate what these occasions mean to true fans when Iain McCulloch headed Notts into a 2nd minute lead. Four minutes later, it was 1-1 as another Scot, Ian Wallace, netted the equaliser. This was one of those rarities, a local derby that lived up to the pre-match hype and was entertaining.

Notts were having the better of the play and deservedly took the lead with the goal of the match when a flowing move and cross from the right saw Paul Hooks head home. Unfortunately (for me at any rate), yet another Scot, Willie Young this time, scrambled home an equaliser just before half-time. During the break, the consensus was that Notts may well have missed their chance.

What did we know?

Notts continued on the front foot in the second half and Trevor Christie scored what proved to be the winner when, from what the highlights package the next day suggested looked like an offside position, slipped the ball past Steve Sutton. TV coverage also confirmed what most in the crowd, and all bar one in our box were thinking, that Iain McCulloch was very lucky to be only booked for a reckless challenge on Steve Sutton, the goalkeeper. In truth, he should have been sent off, and we'll never know what difference that might have made.

Incidentally, I have a well-worn DVD package which features, amongst others, the highlights of this game. You're welcome to borrow it any time you like!

Amongst the eight in the box that day was a colleague and true follower of the game. As an Aldershot fan, he like me in footballing terms, 'knew his place'. That season, I went with him to Scunthorpe and York City to see the Shots, and over the years have been to a number of other footballing outposts across the country to see the Hampshire side.

Well, I couldn't leave 1982 without recalling my part in the *Tartan Army* invasion of Andalusia. Having booked a package holiday incorporating flights and accommodation in Torremolinos, four adults, three very young children and an embryo (don't forget Heather was on her way) set off in Dick Scott's car for Birmingham airport and our flight to Malaga. In addition to our respective wives, six year old Kirsty, twenty one month old Callum and seventeen month old Ailsa, plus baggage for two families and all the paraphernalia required for a fortnight away with a couple of infants, Dick and I squeezed into a vehicle designed for four.

We made it, and like many before us making this type of journey for the first time, couldn't believe the heat as we left the plane. Up to that time, I'd never been further south than Jersey. Despite leaving from Birmingham, probably half of the passengers were Scottish, or at least accompanying those who were. When the reps directed us to the various buses waiting to take us to our respective hotels, it was clear from the accents that our two weeks would be like having a 1950's type holiday in Dunoon, Rothesay or even Arbroath. The only difference being that it was perhaps just a little bit warmer.

Having checked in and got our bearings, we decided that we'd travel into Malaga the following day to get tickets for the Scotland games. Yes, I know this may seem bizarre now, but the SFA had only been allocated a limited number of tickets and we'd been advised to go to the stadium on arrival in Spain to buy them.

So it was then that the following day, all seven of us (not forgetting Heather!) travelled into Malaga on the local train and walked up to the ground where Scotland were to play twice. Other than the fact that we had to purchase tickets for all three games scheduled for that venue – in addition to our games v USSR & New Zealand, the game between those two nations was also taking place at La Rosaleda – there were no problems and they were very affordable. I can't remember exactly how many pesetas, but I reckon they were about the equivalent of a £1 each. Even allowing for inflation, that is very cheap.

Brazil, like all the top nations, had been given the advantage of playing all three group games in the one location and we were told that we'd have to go to Seville to buy a ticket for Scotland's game there. Well, that was out of the question and Dick and I resolved to keep our eyes and ears open for any spares when we headed back to Torremolinos.

That night, we took the kids for a stroll along the main beach promenade at the resort. There were Scots everywhere, but the lasting memory, and one that I'm sure has remained with Helen to this day, was of hearing bagpipes in the distance and then realising that they were coming from a double decker bus as it slowly passed down this sea front road. The bus, which had travelled over from Glasgow, had all sort of patriotic messages plastered over the outside and was crammed with Scots of all shapes and sizes. We later found out that most had just jumped aboard as it made its way through the town, but about a dozen or so had actually come all the way in it taking three days to make it.

Scotland's first game, against New Zealand, was held on Saturday 15th June. Dick and I travelled over to Malaga on one of the football 'specials' that were picking up Scots from various hotels. Scotland scored three goals (Kenny Dalglish and a couple from John Wark) to be in complete control at half time. However, after the Kiwis pulled back a couple early in the second half, nerves began to jangle a bit. Not to worry, John Robertson and Steve Archibald ensured that the Scots had got off to a winning start. We were happy. Even happier when Dick and I made friends with a gang who were staying at another hotel and took up their offer to have a drink with them when we got back.

That was a mistake, and Helen tells the tale of how, when I eventually got back to our hotel, I entered quietly enough but then leant over the cot where Ailsa was sleeping soundly to give her a blow by blow account of how Scotland had just won a famous victory. Boy, was I feeling rough in the morning. Dick was in better health than me and didn't exactly help my recovery when he told me later in the day that he'd managed to get a ticket for the game v Brazil in Seville. There were only a couple of days to go and it looked as if I was going to miss out.

We spent the Monday by the hotel pool, and in between introducing Ailsa to the joys of splashing about under a clear blue sky, I listened and watched, ever alert for any 'transactions' that might be taking place. I also asked around but it seemed as if the only way I could accompany Dick the following night would be on the basis of trying to get a ticket outside the ground. It was a possibility, but not one I fancied.

Well, I overheard a conversation the following morning suggesting that there was a guy in our hotel who had got some spares. I went over to find out more and was told that 'Wullie', in room no whatever, was the man to see. I found him, and yes he'd got a ticket I could have. He told me that it was one of the SFA allocation and I could have it for a certain price. Seven times face value! I wasn't in a position to quibble, and as by modern day standards it was still relatively cheap, I told him I'd be back in a few minutes.

I went to see Helen, told her of my good fortune (but not the apparent fortune it was costing and this is probably the first she knows of that!)

and got the 'green light'. Clutching my pesetas I went back to see 'Wullie' and gave the greedy bastard what he had asked for before going to reception to put my name down for the bus. We were leaving in about three hours' time.

You'll be aware that Scotland totally outplayed the Brazilians for much of the first half and took the lead through a David Narey thunderbolt. That was about as good as it got however, as firstly Zico equalised to leave the teams level at half time, before three second half goals gave the Brazilians a 4 -1 victory.

We got back to Torremolinos about 4.00am – there was no intimate whispered conversation between me and my daughter this time – with another game to pull in later that night. Despite having a ticket, Dick decided not to go to Malaga to see the USSR v New Zealand game so I was on my own as I travelled over on the train. There were however a number of fellow Scots who, like me, were hoping to see New Zealand do Scotland a favour and provide a shock by at least drawing this game.

USSR had lost to Brazil in their opening game, but only by 2-1 which suggested that if Scotland were to progress, they would probably have to beat USSR in the final group game. New Zealand could do us a big favour. Despite raucous vocal encouragement from the many Scots who were present, they didn't, with USSR winning by 3-0. That was it then, Scotland had to win that final game.

Despite using the train to get to Malaga, I'd decided to walk back to Torremolinos after the game. It was only about eight miles and still pleasantly warm. Besides, if I cracked on, I'd probably get back to the Principe Sol Hotel around the same time as was likely if I'd gone back by train.

After about a mile I was joined by a couple of young Spanish guys who engaged in conversation. Their English was very good and they seemed really interested in my story and were impressed when I told them I was walking back. After a few minutes and a chat between themselves in Spanish, one of them said that we would soon be passing a bar where they knew someone who could give me a lift. I said that sounded like a good idea to me and followed them into the bar. As a favour, I bought them a drink but immediately began to feel a bit uneasy.

I don't know what it was, but I just gained the impression that I was being set up and began thinking of how I might extricate myself from what was looking increasingly like a dodgy situation. My two friends went off with their drinks to talk to someone, when I heard English being spoken further down the bar. It was an American voice.

I sidled up to him, apologised to the lady he had been talking to, and quietly explained that I thought I was being set up for something like a mugging and asked did he know this pub. He didn't, but said he was leaving soon and his car was just down the road. He'd be happy for me to leave with him and his wife and he could drop me off somewhere well away.

I took him up on his offer, and when safely inside his car he said they were travelling back to their hotel in Torremolinos and when asked where I wanted to be dropped off, I said "That'll do nicely." I'll never know if my fears were unfounded or not, but do think I possibly had a lucky escape that night.

If you've got this far, I'm assuming that you really do know your football and will already know the outcome of the USSR game. Even if you're not a big fan, you'll have noticed a pattern developing and can probably guess what happened. You'd be right. The nation that gave the world the likes of Don Masson, Iain McCulloch, Ian Scanlon and later Gary McSwegan and Stuart Garden were destined not to be World Champions.

NB – as Scotland now seem to have temporarily forgotten how to qualify, I guess it's not going to happen any time soon either.

Joe Jordan scored (the first player to do so in three consecutive World Cup Final tournaments) and Scotland were good value for their half-time lead and likely to progress to the knock-out stages. When USSR equalised however, and then scored what looked like the winner in the 84th minute we thought our fate had been sealed. Not yet!

Within two minutes, Graeme Souness scored. A draw was not good enough and with USSR on the defensive, Scotland threw the kitchen sink – funny phrase that and I've never quite understood why it became so common in sporting reportage – at them, but to no avail. After a less than generous period of 'added time', the referee blew his whistle, the disconsolate players took the applause of the *Tartan Army*, and the groundsman and his staff went onto the pitch to remove the kitchen sink. This left Scotland, and especially their supporters, to think of what might have been, before preparing for the journey home. Once again, their team had been eliminated on goal difference!

The Scott and Gyles contingent had a couple of days left before flying home. Helen, Ailsa and myself used one of those to take a bus trip and headed over to Morocco for a day, where, amongst other things, we took the obligatory camel ride and visited the souk in Tetouan. We had earlier gone on an excursion to Granada to see the Alhambra. All very interesting and I'm making a point of recording that this fortnight was not just about football.

Helen, going on six months pregnant, coped reasonably well with the heat. However, our baby daughter, who as a result of her bright red hair was fussed over wherever she went, failed to acclimatise. She was never ill, but struggled to eat and survived almost exclusively on a diet of Wotsits and yoghurt. It's fair to say, that she's never looked back.

As for Helen and myself, as you'll eventually find out, we'd got a taste for this kind of holiday. There's more to come!

1983

This was the year that my Mum died on Christmas Day. She had suffered a stroke in April, which she survived and seemed to be recovering from. However, there were other issues which resulted in her being hospitalised for the last six months of her life. I went up to Scotland a few times, and I'll come to that in due course, but suffice to say at this point that it was a difficult time for us being so far away, with no transport of our own, and two young daughters to care for.

In the meantime, the first game of 1983 saw Notts County travel to Anfield. I took my brother-in-law, Ian, who had married Helen's sister in December 1980. He was not really a football fan, much more into motor sport, especially bikes, but did have a soft spot for Liverpool. Well, I was going anyway, and with Ken giving us use of his car, off we set with one of us in expectation and the other in trepidation. Liverpool, were current Champions and runaway leaders. No shock then when the final score was 5-1 to the home side, with recent signing Justin Fashanu, scoring the consolation.

With family commitments, and no transport, my away trips were limited to Leicester for a 3rd Round FA Cup tie where a 3-2 victory saw me subsequently travelling to Middlesbrough for the next round. A football special went up to Teesside which, fortunately for me, stopped at Alfreton. In what was regarded as a bit of a shock at the time, Notts lost 2-0.

As the season came to a close, following good home wins over the likes of Arsenal, Coventry City, Tottenham Hotspur and West Brom, we could look forward to a third consecutive season in the 1st Division. Although finishing in 15th place again, the final total of 52 points was three more than the year before. It wasn't much, but it was progress.

Sadly, we were to lose Howard Wilkinson. He had been made manager, with Jimmy Sirrel 'moving upstairs', at the beginning of the season, but to use a cliché often used he had 'taken the team as far as he could'. He dropped down a division (although undoubtedly increased his salary) and took over at 2nd Division Sheffield Wednesday. He was a Sheffield lad and lifelong 'Owl', and on that basis, I'm assuming there was very little Notts could do. He left with the best wishes of all associated with the Club, and as all football fans know, he went on to bigger and better things. As I write, he is the last Englishman to manage a team that went on to be Champions.

Notts replaced him with Larry Lloyd. The former Forest centre half had enjoyed a couple of successful years managing Wigan Athletic and, particularly with him having connections both local and national, he looked to be a good acquisition. The early signs were encouraging. He replaced the departing Raddy Avramovic with the experienced Irish international goalkeeper Seamus (Jim) McDonagh, and persuaded Martin O'Neill to leave Norwich City.

On the evening of Tuesday 30th August Notts were top of the 1st Division and stayed there for............ one whole day! Sadly, it was downhill after that.

Notts had travelled to Leicester on opening day, and courtesy of a Trevor Christie hat-trick and O'Neill's first goal for the Club, won 4-0. Two goals from Rachid Harkouk the following Tuesday night, saw Birmingham City beaten 2-1. They had to wait until November for their next league win, and despite home victories over Aston Villa (5-2) and Sunderland (6-1) as the old year ended, most supporters were resigned to a relegation battle in the coming months.

Those fears had been magnified when Notts failed to sign Glenn Roeder who had been on a month long loan from Queens Park Rangers. He played in all four league games in November and was a significant contributor to the much improved return of seven points from the twelve on offer in that month. If we were to sign him on a permanent basis – and most fans hoped that we would – QPR had put a price of, from memory, £150,000 for the deal to proceed. Given some of the fees being demanded at the time, this seemed reasonable enough. He was a class act.

Chairman, Jack Dunnett had made it clear that the Club could not afford that. He did however say that if fans could contribute one half of that sum i.e. £75k, he would personally match it. I don't know how much was raised – they certainly got my £25 cheque – but in the end, the appeal failed to raise sufficient money and Glenn Roeder never returned.

There followed an unedifying episode when Notts offered to return all monies sent in by the various contributors to the fund. The alternative was to allow the Club to retain the contribution and have it effectively treated as a donation. As a result of the administrative effort and cost required to process 'refunds', and with the best interests of the club at heart, I naively assumed that almost all fans would have been happy for the Club to keep the money. Sadly, not so. There was a lot of mumbling and grumbling, which in my opinion, didn't reflect well on those who were doing it.

With six games played, it could be argued that the League Cup was a welcome distraction. To put things into context however, they played just two teams in that 'run'. Aldershot were defeated 8-3 over the two legs of the 2nd round and Notts were then drawn away to Birmingham City. Following a 2-2 draw at St Andrews, the Blues were brought back to Meadow Lane a fortnight later. This game finished 0-0 after extra time. Back to St Andrews the following week where, after 120 minutes we witnessed another goalless stalemate. Seven days later, Birmingham finally progressed after a 3-1 Meadow Lane win. It was fun while it lasted.

One notable development took place on Saturday 17th September when I took Ailsa to her first ever game. It wasn't a particularly cold day, but we have a photograph taken outside the house before we set off where she's wearing a thick anorak and scarf (black and white of course) and looking as if she was about to cross the Antarctic rather than getting on a bus to go to Meadow Lane. Notts lost 4-0 that day to an Arsenal side that included the recently signed Charlie Nicholas. Following a couple of 1-1 draws (Stoke City and Norwich City) she saw her first win, that 6-1 thrashing of Sunderland, on 10th December.

The night after the first 0-0 League Cup draw with Birmingham City, I saw another scoreless draw. Nottingham Forest had been drawn against Celtic in the 3rd round of the UEFA Cup, with the 1st Leg at the City Ground. The level of support for the Glasgow side, whilst no surprise to me, came as a shock to the good burghers of Nottingham.

Young (& not so young) men and women wearing hooped replica shirts swamped the city. Although largely good natured, the alcohol induced anti-social (as opposed to hostile) behaviour of the Bhoys was an eye opener. It seemed as if half the crowd of 32,017 were supporting Celtic, and despite dominating much of the game played on an icy cold evening, they would have been happy to go back to Glasgow with the draw. I didn't go to the second leg – Notts were still trying to get past Birmingham! – but Forest shocked the Scottish footballing world when goals from Steve Hodge and Colin Walsh saw them win the tie 2-1 on aggregate.

Another game from this year that I didn't attend took place on 11th May in Gothenburg. Aberdeen had reached the final of the European Cup Winners Cup and were playing Real Madrid. I watched the game at home on television, and for purely patriotic reasons, wanted the Scottish League team to win. The fact that they were neither Rangers nor Celtic made me even keener that they do.

Eric Black opened the scoring early on, but a Real Madrid penalty soon levelled things. In a tense game there were no more goals until well into the second half of extra time, when John Hewitt threw himself at a Mark McGhee cross and headed what proved to be the winner. Aberdeen comfortably held on for their shock win.

Within a minute of the final whistle, and before the presentations, our phone rang. It was Dick Scott, who knew I'd be in a similar mood to himself, and simply asked "Fancy a pint?" Ten minutes later, with me walking along Church Lane and he having come down Commonside, we were both in the Horse & Jockey. We bought our drinks, stood in the bar area and instantaneously and without prompting burst into a loud and melodic (OK, that may be stretching things a little) rendition of *The Northern Lights of old Aberdeen.*

The usual Wednesday night regulars were in there, and once we had finished, there was a smattering of applause followed by some ill-informed questions about the quality of Scottish footballers. "Well", responded the two jubilant latecomers, "how many teams have won European trophies where every member of the squad, including manager, are from the country that the club plays in?"

They couldn't answer of course, but when we told them it was three, with Celtic in 1967, Rangers in 1972 and now Aberdeen in 1983, they soon went back to talking about real ales and the like and ignored us. *NB – to be absolutely fair, the Rangers reserve goalkeeper sitting on the bench in the 1972 ECWC Final in Barcelona, was Gerry Neef, a German.* Still, why quibble, we'd made our point.

I reckon we had three pints at the Horse & Jockey. Not bad considering it must have been after 10.00pm when we'd arrived, and headed back up to our house for a couple of home brewed ales by way of further celebration. That leads to another story but it's been well covered in my first book.

Finally, and in truth this was the highlight of 1983. I went up to Scotland three times to see Mum whilst she was in Ninewells Hospital in Dundee. The understanding was that once she was ready to be released, she spend time with family to ensure the right conditions for convalescence. Things subsequently got very complicated and messy but the initial plan was that we would have her with us in Selston for a period and then Alan would take her up to York to where he had recently moved.

Anyway, my three weekends in Dundee coincided with games at both Dens and Tannadice Parks. Dundee were in mid table whilst their near neighbours were in a tight three way fight for the title with Aberdeen and Celtic.

The first game I saw was a dull 0-0 draw at Dens, but the other two were 4-0 victories for United over Kilmarnock and Motherwell. This meant that if United won the last game of the season, taking place the following week across the road at their rival's ground, they would win the Scottish League title for the first time in their history. On Saturday 14th May, with goals from Ralph Milne and Eamonn Bannon, Dundee United won 2-0 and secured the Championship, finishing one point ahead of both Celtic and Aberdeen. I may not have been there in person, but I certainly was in spirit.

Aberdeen were to win the title in the next two seasons, but since then (1985) – and, as I type, unlikely to change any time soon – only two clubs have been Scottish Champions. If you need me to tell you who they are, you're reading the wrong book.

To finish off, Mum's funeral, especially given the time of year, was very quickly arranged for Friday 30th December. We made arrangements for Helen's parents to look after our two girls and headed north on the Tuesday. I'd seen Notts lose 3-0 to Luton on Boxing Day, and with our next game away at Old Trafford, we went north-west to begin with and witnessed John Fashanu score twice as Notts came back from 3-1 down to gain a surprise 3-3 draw.

We reckoned that, from Manchester, we'd be in Arbroath around 11.00pm. Sadly, we didn't make it. Not that night anyway. We'd not long crossed the Border when I began to lose power, and eventually the car shuddered to a halt. We were a few miles from Lockerbie on a cold and very dark night with no means of communication. Luckily, we'd just passed an emergency services phone point, and even more fortunately, once I'd asked for AA assistance, a very nice man got to the car within minutes.

His analysis was both quick and brutal. The 'big ends' had gone and he could do nothing other than get us off the A74 and to a garage in Lockerbie. That was closed of course, but having found somewhere to spend the night, we saw the owner in the morning and he confirmed that there were two options. Either a new engine or he'd see what he could get in terms of scrap value. I explained the circumstances and we agreed that he'd store the vehicle for up to a week to give me the chance to discuss the situation with Ken.

Helen and I then caught a train from Lockerbie to Glasgow and then over to Edinburgh for an Arbroath bound service. Whilst in the town, we were able to book an overnight bus back to England for Friday, the day of the funeral. This got us into Mansfield at about 7.00am on Hogmanay, and after another bus journey, back home in Selston an hour or so later.

After freshening up a bit, we walked over to Kirkby to a) collect the two girls and b) to spill the beans. Ken was fine about it and agreed that, whatever the cost, I should ask my man in Lockerbie to fit a new engine. We got the girls home on the bus, and remarkably, I went back to Mansfield in the afternoon to see the Stags draw 3-3 with Crewe

Alexandra. I just don't know how I do it/get away with it. Take your pick.

1984

It may have been the previous year, although it's more likely to have been this one, when I started something that has proved indispensable and invaluable as I collect and collate my memories.

Within six months of Heather being born, Helen had become a part-time barmaid at the local pub, the Bull & Butcher. Money was tight and with two additional mouths to feed, she worked three/four nights a week. Fortunately for me, she was not required on either Tuesdays, which meant that I could still get down to Meadow Lane for any mid-week matches, or on Thursdays, allowing me to continue collecting Littlewoods Pools coupons.

On the nights that she was working we'd get the two girls into bed, and while I read (although I generally made up) a story, Helen got changed and went off down the pub. Once she'd gone, I usually cracked on with some work that I'd brought home and would often still be working away when Helen got back. It was a tiring arrangement for us both, but it worked.

Well, on one of my baby sitting nights, I had no work to be getting on with so to amuse myself, decided to make a record of my accumulated football programmes. Initially, in hand written form, I listed them by date showing the two teams, competition and ground. It took me a few nights to do this – I probably had between 700 and 800 by this time – checking various football reference books for missing information as I did it, and then thought, "What next?"

Well, through a combination of checking back where I'd got more than one programme for a club in the same season, and again checking the many and various football reference books that I'd gathered over the years, I added the score and attendance. This left a number of gaps, some of which still exist, but through ongoing research, including a one-off trip to the Newspaper Library at Colindale in north London, I've whittled them down.

Since the initial exercise, I've diligently maintained and updated my records. I had thought about incorporating the full list at the end of this book, but changed my mind when I saw how many additional pages this would require. Recording the up to nearly 3,000 games that I know I've attended takes up a lot of space. That's ignoring of course, the likely couple of hundred more games that I attended in my youth for which programmes were not issued.

Once we had a home computer, the hand written record was consigned to history as I set up a database allowing me easy and quick analysis of the data. *NB – should anyone want a copy of the list (perhaps e.g. looking for a specific programme?) they should get in touch and I'll forward one.*

I should just point out to any ladies who might be reading this and asking themselves "Why?", that this entire exercise can best be categorised as 'it's a man thing!' For example who in your house puts the books/CD's/ DVD's in order? See what I mean?

Once again, where was I?

The year started with Notts in a relegation battle. Despite Trevor Christie's nineteen goals, and the occasional victory giving rise to the hope that they might stay up, our three year stay in the top division came to a limp end. The Club were not helped by injuries to key players including Aki Lahtinen, Justin Fashanu and Brian Kilcline. The most crucial however, came in a 1-0 victory over Manchester United in April when Iain McCulloch, who had missed a number of games earlier in the season, was to break his leg in an accidental collision with Gary Bailey. That not only ended his season, he never fully recovered, at the age of 29 it effectively ended his career.

Liverpool were to clinch the title in the penultimate game at Meadow Lane. The highest attendance of the season, 18,745, in windy conditions and on a bumpy pitch, watched a 0-0 draw. Still, a point was enough for the Scousers, and most of that crowd went home happy.

It was not all gloom however and Notts had a good FA Cup run overcoming Bristol City in a replay, Huddersfield Town and

Middlesbrough. *NB – I missed the last one as Mrs Gyles went off to enjoy a spot of shopping, leaving me to look after the two girls. I'd been disgracefully drunk the night before and this was my punishment!*

In the home quarter final tie against Everton, Kevin Richardson gave the away side the lead but John Chiedozie equalised, and Notts remained optimistic of getting a second chance in a replay at Goodison Park, until Andy Gray headed the winner. It was hardly one of the classic towering headers for which the former Dundee United player is associated. In fact, he was almost crawling along the ground when his head made contact with the ball.

Everton went on to win the Cup. I took Eric Fenn, a stalwart of Selston FC, to the Wembley game where we saw Andy Gray score again (a hotly disputed goal), in a 2-0 win over Watford.

There was an expectation at the beginning of the 1984/85 season that Notts would do well now that they were back in the 2nd Division. In addition to Iain McCulloch though, they would have to do without Trevor Christie, and John Chiedozie with both opting to stay in the 1st Division having respectively moved to Nottingham Forest and Tottenham Hotspur.

Larry Lloyd – he never managed another club – had been replaced by Richie Barker, but Martin O'Neill, Rachid Harkouk and Justin Fashanu remained. There were also a number of youth team players, regarded as good prospects, who were expected to do well. These included Simeon Hodson, David Clarke, Tony Daws, Darren Davis and Dean Yates.

Supporters' hopes were quickly re-appraised however, when, following seven defeats from the first eight league games, it looked as if we might be leaving the 2nd Division after all, but in the wrong direction. Experienced replacements like Steve Sims, Dave Watson and Alan Young were brought in. They didn't make a great deal of difference however, and as the old year came to a close, Notts had only gained fourteen points from the first twenty one games. They'd have to improve dramatically in the second half of the season to escape the drop.

There was some good news, of a purely personal nature, however. With the help of a £1,000 windfall courtesy of Helen's late grandma, we were able to buy our first car. That Mini Mayfair, VRN B666 HRB, may have been red, but it didn't half make life easier. Instead of taking Ailsa (plus pushchair) to Meadow Lane on the bus, we could now leave later, arrive back earlier and have much less walking to do whilst in Nottingham.

It also meant that the logistics of getting to away games had been made much simpler, and with an immediate requirement to road test the Mini, I was soon on the road to Norwich for a mid-week League Cup defeat, Maine Road, and Oakwell (Barnsley). The car was fine, but on each of those three return journeys I was unable to describe any of the goals that Notts had scored. There hadn't been any!

Nonetheless, I was grateful for the opportunities that having my own car created, even though away trips on a Saturday were restricted to locations within two hours driving time. I had to make sure that I could get back by 7.00pm to relieve Helen and let her spend Saturday night in the pub. OK, out of context, that probably doesn't read very well, but I've already explained the arrangement!

1985

Of the first four league games of the New Year, three were scoreless draws (as was the final game of 1984) and the other a 5-0 defeat at Elland Road. It was against this background that Heather first experienced live football. On 26th January, she attended the fourth of those games, a 0-0 draw at home to Charlton Athletic in front of 3,409 downhearted spectators. Not that either Heather or her sister were too miserable. I'm sure they enjoyed it!

The seemingly inevitable slide towards a second successive relegation saw Richie Barker relieved of his duties with Jimmy Sirrel once more taking over as manager. There was no immediate improvement until, with five games left, it looked as if Notts would have to win them all, to stay up.

The first of these was away at Huddersfield, a 2-1 victory. Next up, Carlisle came to Meadow Lane and were beaten 3-0. Could something remarkable be about to happen? On Saturday 4th May, a family of four set off in their little Mini Mayfair for Oxford. While Helen and the two girls had a picnic and gambolled around the river Isis, I went to the Manor Ground and saw Justin Fashanu score in what ended as a 1-1 draw. Failure to get three points was disappointing, but as I met up with Helen and the girls and listened to Sports Report on the way home, I realised that we could still do it. Depending upon results elsewhere, winning the last two games might be enough.

On Bank Holiday Monday, Notts were at home to Manchester City who, if they won, would be promoted back to the First Division. In front of a crowd of over 17,000, most of whom had crossed the Pennines, Notts had a 3-0 lead at half-time. Sadly, whilst we were joyous, believing that what now looked like a win would mean we'd go into the final game with a chance of survival, many of the Manchester City fans were unhappy. Distinctly so.

With a real fear that they might not now secure the third spot, and with it promotion, some of them who were massed on the Kop began to tear at the fences behind that goal. It was in effect a riot with the desired outcome being abandonment. Following appeals for calm over the tannoy system from both managers (Billy McNeill was in charge of City), the re-start was delayed by thirty minutes to allow repairs to be carried out. Throughout this time, I was trying to explain what was going on to a wide eyed four year old girl. Not easy!

The second half was played in an almost surreal atmosphere, made even more so when City pulled two goals back. Notts held on though, and with the final whistle blown at around 5.20pm, we knew that if we bettered Middlesbrough's result on the last day of the season, we would stay up. I had a problem however. Notts County's last game was at Fulham, and I'd be unable to get to that game and return early enough to allow Helen to get to work. This required some creative thinking.

I came up with a solution that, whilst not perfect, meant that in some small way, I could perhaps help Notts from afar. Middlesbrough were playing at Shrewsbury. If they were to lose, Notts County could control their own destiny. That was it, I'd go to Gay Meadow and be a Shrewsbury Town fan for a day. As I couldn't guarantee getting back to Selston for 7.00pm, I suggested taking both girls with me. That way, it wouldn't matter if I was delayed. With Helen having no objection, I contacted Shrewsbury, explained my circumstances and got three tickets for the game.

To make it more of a day out for the girls, we stopped off for lunch en route before arriving at the ground. There were plenty of 'Boro fans – a win and they were definitely safe – and they were in boisterous mood. I had a bit more explaining, this time to a pair of young girls, to deal with their questions. Middlesbrough were 2-0 winners, and as we left the ground, I knew that I'd be taking the two girls to Third Division football in a few weeks' time.

It was all academic, as when I got into the car, I heard that Notts had lost 1-0 at Craven Cottage. Still, with Jimmy Sirrel back in charge, and all those youngsters beginning to emerge, perhaps we could bounce back straight away. Those thoughts were put on hold however, as I drove back listening to harrowing tales of what had happened that afternoon at Valley Parade. This was 11th May 1985, the day of the Bradford fire!

I had tears in my eyes as reports of what had happened came in. The disaster had only just occurred and the detail was sketchy. However, the fact that many men, women, and for me most poignantly, children had perished when an old wooden stand had gone up in flames, became personal. This could have been the County Road Stand at Meadow Lane, and with two young kids constantly wanting to go to the toilet, I could easily relate to how some of those poor people had ended up trapped. A sad day all round, making Notts County's relegation take on a new perspective.

When football returned in August, Jimmy Sirrel had decided that Dean Yates was now a confirmed first team player, and as was his way, appeared to have made up his mind what his best side was, and tended to stick with it. Alongside Yates, were Mick Leonard, David Clarke, Steve Sims, Ian McParland, Mark Goodwin, Rachid Harkouk, David Hunt, and latterly, Mick Waitt.

The team got off to a reasonable start, with McParland scoring regularly, and by Christmas were well enough placed to suggest that with a bit more consistency in the second half of the season, they might be in a position to challenge for promotion.

Back in August, having lost the opener to Cardiff City, 4-1 at Meadow Lane, I headed off to Blackpool for the first away game, fearing the worst. Nonetheless, all four of us travelled up in the Mini, and whilst Helen entertained the two girls on the Blackpool sands, I made my way to Bloomfield Road.

Blackpool had been promoted from the 4th Division, and buoyed by the success of last season, and with it being a Bank Holiday weekend, there was a good crowd. A new stand had been built on the south side of the ground since my only previous visit and I decided to see what this was like. It was behind the goal, so not my preferred viewing spot, but it was fine enough. Meanwhile, any Notts fans there were stood on the open terrace at the other end.

Blackpool took an early lead with the goal scored right in front of myself, and probably 500 jubilant home supporters. I was relatively unmoved, as indeed as I was when Notts quickly went up to the other end and equalised. I may just have grinned, ever so slightly however!

Notts then took the lead and I reckon I emitted a barely heard squeal. However, when the third goal went in, I only just prevented myself from allowing a full 'arms in the air' celebration. However, to the alert observer, I was probably just a little too happy with the way things were going and my true allegiance, especially for an unhappy Blackpool fan, would have been questioned.

Well, my barely concealed delight had been noticed by a young Blackpool supporter and I could hear him whispering to his girlfriend. The gist of the conversation as he looked in my direction was, "That bloke there, he's a Notts County fan and he shouldn't be in here. I'm going to get him thrown out."

I neither said nor did anything, other than try, with some difficulty, to suppress the grin, and continued to watch the game.

At half time, the guy who had sussed me, left the stand and came back a couple of minutes later with a policeman in full uniform.

"There he is. It's him constable", said the young fan pointing to me as I innocently read my programme.

The policeman came over, looked me dead in the eye and asked, "Are you from Nottingham sir?"

"No", says I, in as broad a Scottish accent as I could muster, "I'm frae Arbroath an' a'hm jist doon here fir the hoaliday."

Satisfied with that response, the policemen left me and the seething, but sadly disillusioned Tangerine fan. Now, had he re-phrased the question, and asked if I was a Notts County supporter, who knows whether or not I'd have confessed. Whatever, I resisted the temptation at the end of the game to whisper to the girl that her boyfriend had been right all along.

In the meantime, you may recall that I'd given advance notice of how a couple of Wales fans would gain some measure of revenge for Scotland's deserved (my words)/unjust (their words) World Cup Qualifying victory at Anfield in 1977.

18th May 1985 was the day of the FA Cup Final. I'd managed once again to get a ticket, and set off for Wembley expecting to see a bit of history. Everton, were playing Manchester United, and a win would secure a rare 'treble' of Championship, European Cup Winners Cup (having just defeated Rapid Vienna in Rotterdam on the Wednesday night) and FA Cup in the same season.

Everton were the better side and with Kevin Moran of United, late on in the second half being the first man ever to be sent off in an FA Cup Final, as the game remained goalless after ninety minutes it looked as if Everton would surely go on to win. They didn't. Norman Whiteside scored in the second half of extra time and it was Manchester United who could look forward to their own open top bus parade. NB – win or lose, Everton already had one arranged.

Now then, if you're keeping up, you should be asking yourself what all this has got to do with Welshmen gaining revenge.

Before the game, as is my want, I was enjoying a drink in a north London bar, unsurprisingly full of people going to the Cup Final. I got talking to a few people and ended up with a couple of guys who had come over from Wales. They were Newport County supporters who, like me, had managed to get tickets through their club. During our conversation, I told them of how I'd been at Anfield for that 'infamous' game and was desperately trying to get a ticket for the forthcoming qualifier between the same two countries, scheduled for Ninian Park in Cardiff in September. It was a game that Wales needed to win and Scotland only draw to qualify for the 1986 tournament in Mexico.

"We should be able to get you a ticket for that," they said, "we have good contacts at Somerton Park" i.e. Newport's old ground. Well, these two had suddenly become my best friends and I gave them my details and bought them a drink each. Here I was, having a pleasant drink or two, looking forward to going to the FA Cup Final and now I'd got a good chance of being at the game that would see Scotland qualify for the World Cup, for the fourth consecutive time. I couldn't have been happier.

I got talking to a few others and then, just before leaving and heading to the ground, I went back to my bosom buddies and gave them a £1. "Here," says naïve me, "take this to cover any expenses you may incur." *NB – this was 1985. You could buy a lot with a pound back then!* "Oh thanks boyo", came the grateful reply, "we'll be in touch."

I'm still waiting!

I reckon there are two guys in south Wales who, for years, have 'dined out' on their story of how easy it is to get money out of a Scotsman. The postscript of course, is that courtesy of a Davie Cooper penalty,

Scotland got the draw they needed and it was they, and not Wales, who were to cross the Atlantic the following summer. Sadly, Jock Stein would not be joining them as manager as he collapsed towards the end of the game and died shortly after the final whistle.

Finally, having gone to her first home game earlier in the year, Heather had her first experience of seeing Notts away from home before the year was out. Five of us piled into the Mini on Saturday 2nd November and headed for Birmingham. I dropped Helen and her Mum off there as their plan was to enjoy a bit of self-indulgent early Christmas shopping. Meanwhile, the two girls and myself (it was Ailsa's first away game as well) went up the A34 to Fellows Park to see a 0-0 draw with Walsall.

Although only 4 and 3 years of age at the time, I managed to keep them both amused during the dullest of dull games on a very cold afternoon. I doubt if they have any memories of this day – unless it's of the freezing conditions – and they can just be thankful that I haven't managed to find any coverage of the game on YouTube!

1986

Notts managed to negotiate rounds 1 and 2 of the FA Cup prior to the turn of the year and were in the draw for the 3rd round. They'd overcome Scarborough (6-1) and Wrexham 3-0 in a replay after a home 2-2 draw. Being drawn away to 2nd Division Stoke City was not what the Club had hoped for. The tie was postponed for weather related reasons on the original date and re-scheduled for nine days later, a Monday night.

NB – Notts had a home Freight Rover Trophy tie with Doncaster Rovers subsequently re-arranged for the Thursday night. This, of course, seriously disadvantaged Pools Collectors everywhere. Don't panic – I somehow managed to sort something out and ended up seeing four games in eight days.

Notts caused a minor shock in beating the Potters 2-0 and were already aware that the reward was a home tie against Tottenham Hotspur. Clive Allen gave Spurs an early lead but an Ian McParland equaliser led to a White Hart Lane replay. Eric Fenn joined me on the trip to London the following Wednesday night. Former Notts player (from better days), John Chiedozie, opened the scoring and helped Spurs sweep Notts aside. The final score was a painful 5-0.

Despite the Cup run, the 1985/86 season drifted to a close. Without seriously threatening a promotion challenge, Notts finished a comfortable 7th in the table. Ian McParland had continued to do well and finished as top scorer with 21 goals in all competitions. He had been well supported by Mick Waitt who managed 18.

With youngsters like Paul Barnes, Mark Harbottle, David Kevan, Paul Smalley and Wayne Fairclough making the occasional appearance, there was just a glimmer of hope that the Club could improve on 8th position the following year. It was clear from attendances (2,245 at the final league game of 85/86), that Notts were never going to be able to buy their way to success and finding and nurturing their own talent had to be the way forward.

Before then, there was a big change in our domestic situation. Helen had continued to supplement family income by working as a part-time barmaid. She was no longer at the Bull & Butcher but had moved up to the White Lion at the other end of Selston. She enjoyed the work, could get up there in the Mini so had no long walk home late at night, and had become good friends with David & Moira Barclay who ran the pub. The arrangement was working, but was far from perfect in terms of conventional family life, so we decided to do something about it.

With Ailsa turning five and starting school, it would be difficult for Helen to work in a day time job until Heather reached the same stage. The answer was to find something that would allow her to work from home and be there for both girls. We started looking around for a small general grocery store with living accommodation that we could afford. We had fun looking and eventually agreed a deal with the then current owners of a shop in Newton. We moved to 90 Main Street in the village on Thursday 8th May 1986.

It was an exciting time for us all and within a couple of days a new sign went up above the shop frontage. It told everyone in the village, and those who passed by, that this was now *Helen's Stores*. The Gyles family were now business people and were about to become an entrepreneurial success story. I had visions of, in a couple of years' time, Notts County players running onto the Meadow Lane pitch with *Helen's Stores* emblazoned across their chests as our expanding business became shirt sponsors. Don't get ahead of yourselves here. Despite our best efforts to promote the shop as the 'must visit retail outlet' of east Derbyshire, we gave it four years before closing down.

Now then, those of you who know your stuff are probably wondering how I managed to get to that summer's World Cup Finals in Mexico. After all, it wasn't so far to travel as Argentina in 1978, and now that we were on the verge of becoming food retailing millionaires, finances shouldn't have been an issue. Besides, Scotland, managed by Alex Ferguson on a temporary basis, were once again thinking that this could be their year.

Well, I just had a feeling that this optimism was a bit over the top so, with Helen's full approval...... ....we decided to give this one a miss! Just as well. Scotland couldn't even claim that they were unluckily eliminated on goal difference and finished bottom of their group with one point gained from a 0-0 draw with Uruguay. They were lucky to get even the draw despite the fact that the South Americans had been playing with only ten men for eighty nine minutes. Glad we didn't go!

The 1986/87 season got off to a good start. McParland and Waitt, but particularly the former, continued where they had left off in the previous campaign. They were receiving good service from new signing David Thompson, a tricky red haired right winger, who had arrived from Rochdale. Fans were anticipating promotion at the turn of the year with Notts lying in second place.

It was a good job that the league form was so encouraging, as the Club had no cup football to look forward to in the later stages of the season. Knocked out in the first round of the League Cup and then the qualifying round of the Freight Rover Trophy, they had at least beaten Carlisle

United in an away replay before losing at home to Middlesbrough in the 2nd round of the FA Cup. Promotion it had to be then!

The Club's finances were a constant source of worry however, and it was in October that I joined many other concerned supporters at a meeting in Nottingham. This had been arranged to explain the rationale behind a new fund raising venture. That night Steve Sims, who was still at the Club, took my application form, and with number 73, I remain a member of *Lifeline* to this day. There is no doubt that this initiative helped to save the Club back then, and in subsequent periods of crisis has also come to the rescue. I now willingly and happily fund seven different family memberships.

1987

Sadly, Notts fell away in the second half of the season. Too many draws, eight in total, were the problem and they eventually finished seventh, one place and five points better off than the previous year. There were very few highlights, as once again, early season promise failed to deliver on expectations. Play-offs had been introduced to English football in this year, and to qualify, Notts had to finish no lower than fifth. With four games to go, this looked almost certain, but one point from the last four games, including two disappointing home defeats (Swindon and Bury) meant they ended up two points short of achieving even that limited objective.

Having seen Ipswich Town become FA Cup winners for the first time in 1978, I was lucky enough to get a ticket for the 1987 Final and be present at Coventry City's greatest ever day as, led by joint managers, John Sillett and George Curtis, they defeated hot favourites Tottenham Hotspur 3-2 after extra time. I've never yet had the opportunity to drop into a conversation with a Sky Blue fan of a certain age, the statement, "I reckon I know what you were doing on Saturday 16th May 1987", but I'm sure my chance to impress will come.

During the close season, whilst sharing a Breton gite with old friends Tony and Ann Clewlow – a holiday that I reckon our girls can just about remember – we happened to chance upon a small bar/restaurant whilst on a day trip to the local salt marshes. Just what we were looking for to sustain us for the rest of the day.

In the bar I noticed pictures of a football team and made enquiries. They were of the local French 1st Division side, Nantes, and many of the regulars were fans. Well, I was in my element now and gave a brief outline of my own interest in the game of football. When they found out that I was raised in Scotland, some of them got quite excited. I could have a go at what they were saying, but to prevent you trying to remember long forgotten French from schooldays, a simple summary was that the current top player for Nantes................ "Il est Ecossais!"

Mo Johnston, established Scottish International, had joined from Celtic before controversially later signing for Rangers. I could have stayed there all afternoon were it not for domestic responsibilities. Anyway, the upshot was that Tony and myself were invited to join some of 'nos nouveaux amis' on a supporters' bus leaving from the pub the following Saturday night for the game v Matra RC Paris. Well, it would have been rude to refuse!

We were well looked after that night. There was plenty of French beer on the bus which they managed to force down our throats and not once did we have to put our hands in our pockets. Moreover, the game itself was quite entertaining ending as a 1-1 draw with, and you could have scripted this, Mo Johnston getting the Nantes goal.

For the record, Mo Johnston stayed in France for two years, scoring 22 goals before he became a pariah in parts of east Glasgow.

Back home, there had been some big changes at Meadow Lane. Jack Dunnett had left, having sold the Club to a Nottingham businessman (and former director at Nottingham Forest) called Derek Pavis. Having made his money in plumbing, he was no Arab sheikh, but he promised to turn the Club's fortunes around.

That summer there were regular press conferences as new personnel were introduced. Jimmy Sirrel was once more 'moved upstairs' and John Barnwell installed as manager. He had enjoyed a good playing career in the top division with both Arsenal and Nottingham Forest.

Becoming a coach and then manager he had some success, particularly at Wolves, but in that summer of 1987 was available.

He brought in a number of new players. In addition to Gary Lund who had come from Lincoln City with Mick Waitt going the other way, there was Geoff Pike (ex West Ham) and three who had previously played with Nottingham Forest, viz. Gary Mills, Paul Hart and Garry Birtles. In the coming months both Chris Withe and Adrian Thorpe arrived at Meadow Lane. These were exciting times!

Initially, he also brought in the much travelled Andy Gray, a former signing of his from his days at Wolves. This was a loan signing but was intended as permanent as the official team photograph pre 1987/88 season clearly demonstrates. As it happens, Gray played just the six games, scoring once, ironically against Wolves in a League Cup tie, before going back to his then parent club, Aston Villa. They promptly sold him to West Brom where, one assumes, he would earn far more than he was likely to at little Notts County.

The early part of the season featured some high scoring games including a 4-4 draw with Wigan Athletic (I missed that – still in Brittany), a 5-3 away win (York City) and 6-2 (Southend) at Meadow Lane. There were also some disappointing set-backs but a run of nine unbeaten games up to the end of December, which had begun with a home win over Sunderland, saw Notts sitting second in the table behind the Roker Park side. Once more, expectations were high that promotion back to the 2nd Division would be achieved.

1988

Notts took on Sunderland on 19th March, now ahead of their rivals on goal difference at the top of the 3rd Division table. After a 1-1 draw, positions remained unchanged and it looked as if both sides would be celebrating promotion in May. Once again however, there was a bit of a wobble and three consecutive defeats saw Notts slip to third.

However, an away win at Bury, followed by a 4-0 home win over Rotherham, saw me travel to Fellows Park where Notts, back in second place, were to take on Walsall who were third. After a 2-1 defeat, it was the Saddlers who moved into the automatic promotion spot, with Notts slipping to 4th.

A defeat at home to Port Vale the following Saturday meant that if Notts were to be promoted, it would almost certainly have to be via the play-offs. As our fate was out of our hands, I gave the away game at Preston a miss (Notts won 2-1) and travelled to Grimsby with Alan Baldwin to see Aldershot gain a point and avoid relegation. Unfortunately, for the large contingent of home fans, that result consigned Grimsby to relegation themselves. Fortunately for us, as Alan has reminded me, we managed to get out of Cleethorpes unscathed.

Walsall were the opponents in the play-offs. Despite taking an early lead through Dean Yates, Notts lost the 1st (home) leg 3-1 with David Kelly scoring a couple. It was more out of loyalty and duty that I travelled west three days later. Once more Dean Yates scored to give hope that Notts might progress. However, a second half goal from Trevor Christie (yes him!) settled the nerves for Walsall and they finished as 4-2 aggregate winners. They went on to beat Bristol City in a two legged final to win the promotion that Notts County had in their grasp up until the final three weeks.

There was double disappointment for Notts as, having overcome Northampton Town, Brentford, Cardiff City, Colchester United and Brighton, they had reached the final (Southern area) of the Sherpa Van Trophy. Wolves stood between them and the Club's first ever trip to Wembley, where they'd play Burnley who had won the Northern area final. It wasn't to be for Notts as Steve Bull scored three goals in helping Wolves to a 4-1 aggregate win. A few weeks later, over 80,000 saw Wolves lift the Trophy.

Just to keep you up to date on the domestic front, having gained a Ford Escort Estate as a company vehicle, we were emotional as we said goodbye to the Mini Mayfair. There will always be a place in our hearts for B666 HRB. Meanwhile, the new car (E27 ENN), made its maiden visit to Meadow Lane for the first of those two games with Walsall. This was

Sunday 15th May, the day after Wimbledon's FA Cup victory over Liverpool.

Having gone so close, John Barnwell added a few new names during the close season. With Ian McParland and Gary Lund each scoring in excess of twenty goals, only Sunderland had managed to score more than Notts. In an attempt to tighten up, he brought in David Norton and Nicky Law as defenders and Don O'Riordan as combative midfielder.

However, following a home defeat (2-1) to Gillingham, and with Notts only five places off the bottom of the 3rd Division table, Barnwell was asked to 'clear his desk' in December, and assistant John Newman put in temporary charge. I don't know for a fact, but I reckon that the £200,000 signing of Stuart Rimmer, who made four league appearances (one off the bench) for the 'Pies, may have been the straw that broke the camel's back for Derek Pavis. To be fair to Mr Barnwell, when he took over as manager of Walsall in 1989, he gave the Chairman some of his money back, buying Rimmer for his new club.

Results did improve slightly after the sacking, but despite a 2-0 win over Bolton Wanderers on the last day of the year, Notts were still 18th and faced a struggle to retain their status as the New Year dawned. Although we were unaware of it at the time, things were about to change.

1989

Notts suffered a 1-0 away defeat to Port Vale on Monday 2nd January. With that, the Club dropped to nineteenth, and it was announced later that week that Neil Warnock was to take over with the simple brief, 'make sure we don't drop into the 4th Division.' John Newman remained in caretaker charge for the following Saturday's game away at Swansea. I took Heather with me that day, and travelled back knowing that a 2-0 defeat had seen the Club slip another place.

Still, travelling to South Wales (and all the way back) I had the pleasure of listening to how Heather's hero, Danger Mouse, saved not only his assistant Penfold, but the whole world. By the time we got back to Newton, the cassette tape may have been almost worn out, but at least

I could impress my work colleagues on the Monday as I was almost word perfect.

This was the day before the Kegworth Air Disaster, not that this little contemporary snippet is in any way relevant. I did recall afterwards however, that had it been twenty four hours earlier, we may just have been travelling up that stretch of the M1 at about that time. Whatever?

The one significant change in Neil Warnock's first team selection, was the dropping of Garry Birtles who had been playing as sweeper, to be replaced by Nicky Law as a conventional centre half. This home game against Blackpool ended as a 1-1 draw.

After five games in charge, and following a 3-0 defeat away to Chesterfield, the new manager made changes. This was Mick Leonard's last game in goal for Notts, as during the week he was replaced by Steve Cherry. Charlie Palmer arrived at Meadow Lane at the same time. The changes seemed to have an effect as, although the next game was an away defeat at Chester City, the following four were victories lifting Notts to a much more comfortable 12th in the table.

Phil Turner was signed during this run and fans were seeing more of youngsters Mark Draper and Tommy Johnson. There was renewed optimism, and whilst it was too late for the 88/89 season, there were signs that a team was being put together that might be serious contenders in the near future.

Ailsa and Heather were by now joining me at almost every game, home or away. Helen had to stay at home however in the hope that there be busloads of shoppers arriving at *Helen's Stores* to spend lots of money. She'd have been better off coming with us!

There were a few memorable games that we enjoyed as the season came to a close. A 4-0 hammering of Bristol City at Ashton Gate comes to mind as does a 3-3 draw with Bolton Wanderers at Burnden Park. In that latter game, Notts were 3-0 up at half time. Not only that, as we listened to the tannoy during the break, we heard that Little Polvier had won the Grand National at odds of 28/1. This was Heather's choice and she was excited, although a little less so when I suggested that we use the winnings to take Mum for an Indian meal when we got back. After all, we'd have double cause for a celebration.

Well, Bolton Wanderers scored three second half goals to slightly dampen the expected celebration, but as a family, we did enjoy our curry later that evening. Heather, even now, occasionally questions who it was that made the decision that we all go out for a meal, paid for by **HER** winnings, claiming that we took advantage of a naïve six year old girl!

The following week, I had only Ailsa for company (Heather was at a birthday party somewhere) as we headed north-west again. Notts were at Preston. I can't remember why Steve Cherry didn't play that day (suspect it was through injury), but it did give Aidan Davison the chance to play in goal. The team lost and this proved to be Davison's only game for the Club.

Memorable though that fact might be (well to him anyway), the day is best remembered for events that were simultaneously taking place in Sheffield. It was Saturday 15th April 1989 and the FA Cup semi-final between Liverpool and Nottingham Forest had been abandoned. You won't need to be a football fan to know what happened at Hillsborough on that day. Even though I was wary of allowing Ailsa to hear the graphic details, I couldn't turn off the radio on the way home. It made for sombre listening!

Notts finished the season strongly, and despite real concerns from only a few weeks previously over whether or not they could avoid relegation, they ended up in ninth position, remarkably only five points off a play-off place.

Both girls were now *Junior Magpies*, an organisation set up to encourage young supporters. The key people in this organisation were Steve and Annette Chantrey. I reckon that Annette was actually employed by the Club and that co-ordinating the activities for the youngsters was just one of her responsibilities. There were a number of benefits like parties, quizzes, match-day giveaways etc. There was also a raffle at the end of the season for all signed up young 'Pies. This was free to members, with the prizes having been supplied by local businesses that had been won over by Annette's charm.

The raffle was drawn at half time at the last home game (a 4-1 defeat of Aldershot in 88/89) and the winner of the first prize, a brand new Raleigh bike, was Heather Gyles of Newton. A photograph of a smiling and pig-tailed Heather sitting on her prize was taken and printed in the *Football Post,* the last of the season, the following week. Sadly, the bike was too big for her and was passed on to her sister. Don't panic, she didn't miss out again. By way of compensation, we went out and bought her one that was better suited to her size.

There was one final treat for the girls, although I do accept that they might question that, when I took them to Wembley for the first time. Bolton Wanderers played Torquay United in the final of the Sherpa Van Trophy. Both girls were each given a fiver spending money which they 'blew' immediately upon arrival at the ground. They were more attracted to the yellow of Torquay and spent the lot on 'tat' from merchandise sellers. Their £5 bought them a yellow flag each plus a flat cap for Ailsa and something else (who knows?) for Heather. For the record, Bolton won 4-1.

Neil Warnock was busy during the summer, adding Nicky Platnauer, Phil Stant, Phil Robinson and Craig Short to his squad. Out went Chris Withe, Garry Birtles, Geoff Pike and Ian McParland. This was now his team.

Stant was a bit of an enigma. His story was well known at the time. As a veteran of the Falklands War, Hereford United had paid £600 to buy him out of the Army. He did well at Edgar Street and a number of clubs were apparently keen to sign him. Neil Warnock's charm must have worked because, with Hereford United receiving £175,000, he joined Notts. He appeared only thirty times (many as sub) scoring seven goals for Notts before being allowed to go out on loan. He did however get off to a good start, with the only goal of the opening game away to Leyton Orient. That was about as good as it got for him at Notts, although he did go on to have a successful time at other clubs, most notably Cardiff City.

Early season results were a bit inconsistent, and after a 2-0 defeat at Bristol City on 17th October, which I didn't attend, Notts were lying 12th in the table. Gary Chapman, a pacy forward, had been brought to the Club on loan from Bradford City. Three goals in his first two games were promising, but he scored just the one more and increasingly gave the impression of being a 'flash in the pan'.

Still, after that defeat at Ashton Gate, Notts went on an unbeaten run, and following a 3-2 win over Birmingham City on 30th December, had taken 26 points out of a possible 30 and sat top of the Division.

Having been knocked out of the FA Cup at the first opportunity (1-0 away to Doncaster), Notts didn't have a game on 9th December. As a result, I went to Rochdale that day as Spotland was a ground I'd yet to visit. The home team defeated Lincoln City 3-0 to progress to the 3rd Round. The key memory from that day however, is of hearing on the radio on the return journey that Scotland had been drawn with Sweden, Costa Rica and Brazil (again) in the group stages of the 1990 World Cup Finals to be held in Italy. As I drove back, it seemed as if there was much to look forward to as the year/decade drew to a close.

Chapter 9

1980's – some new sporting experiences

What with working long hours, pools collection, responsibilities with Selston FC and not forgetting having two young girls to entertain for much of this decade, other than for football, my sport watching was almost exclusively limited to listening to the radio or whatever was on the television.

I did however have my one, and to date only experience, of watching top golfers in action when, with Helen having just discovered that she was pregnant, we had a week's holiday in Jersey at the end of May.

The Jersey Open Championship began on Thursday 29th May. Some of the game's big European players competed in this on an annual basis and I thought it was too good an opportunity to miss. We made our way to the La Moye course, found a good spot where we could see two greens and settled down for a few hours.

We just went on the first day and saw most of the top players as they came through. The first two days were played in good weather and scoring was relatively low. However, come the Saturday, the day of our return ferry journey, the golfers will have been cursing as the wind began to blow a gale. *NB – that boat trip back to Portsmouth is the only time I've been sea sick. Fortunately, I'd booked a cabin for Helen, but it was me that was in more need of it than her*

Back to the golf, the conditions deteriorated to such a degree that in the seventeen Open championships held on the island before it was discontinued, no winner ever exceeded the one over par score of 281 that Jose Maria Canizares required to win by two strokes from Steve Martin, the Dundee golfer who never quite made it on the Tour.

I honestly cannot remember seeing Jose Maria Canizares on that opening day of the tournament, but given where Helen and I had stationed ourselves, I must have done.

On late May Bank Holiday Monday in 1989, I took the girls and their friends from across the street, to Long Eaton Stadium to watch what I thought was going to be an afternoon of stock car racing. Sadly it wasn't, although that didn't stop the girls opening their eyes wide open in amazement at a 'demolition derby' type meeting. I think they enjoyed the spectacle although it wasn't for me. Yes, there is skill involved, but it all seems so senseless.

We probably saw a couple of Sunday League games down at Trent Bridge during 1980. Other than that, my live cricket watching during the 1980's was largely limited to Test Matches. I kept up to date with Nottinghamshire's progress and was as pleased as anyone with the success that the Club achieved in that period. With Clive Rice joined by Richard Hadlee, and the further development of Derek Randall, they were becoming more competitive towards the end of the 1970's. However, with the emergence of Tim Robinson and Paul Johnson and acquisition of Chris Broad and Eddie Hemmings, they became a force in both Championship and one day cricket winning four trophies in the decade. It's just a shame that I couldn't fully embrace this success.

On summer weekends, in both Selston and later Newton, I used to spend whatever time I could spare in the garden with the radio tuned to Test Match Special. If I was lucky, I'd then have time for a shower and watch the BBC highlights. John Arlott had retired in 1980 but Don Mosey, Brian Johnston, Henry Blofeld, Christopher Martin-Jenkins, and latterly, Jack Bannister kept me informed and entertained throughout the decade. Fred Trueman and Trevor Bailey, in curmudgeonly fashion, would make their contribution as summarisers.

Having treated Dad to his first taste of international cricket in 1977, like me, he had to wait another eight years. David Gower captained England against Australia in 1985, a series in which England were looking to regain the Ashes. Six Tests were to be played, and with England victorious at Headingley and Australia (as was their custom) winning at Lord's, the Third Test at Trent Bridge was nicely set up.

I missed the first day as it just got too complicated to re-arrange my Thursday pools collection, but Dad saw England have a comfortable day with David Gower's 107* the highlight as his side reached 279/2 by close of play.

I joined Dad for the next three days and after being bowled out for 456 (Gower went on to 166), England struggled to make headway when the Aussies replied. At close of play on the Friday evening, with Australia on 94/1, it looked as if a draw was the only realistic outcome. So it proved to be. I did however finally get to see a batsman start his innings and go on to score a century. In fact I saw two and they were both Australian. Graeme Wood made 172 and Greg Ritchie 146.

The Australians had a first innings lead of 83 and Graham Gooch and Tim Robinson had reduced that by 8 runs as I left Trent Bridge on the Monday evening and the game drifted to the inevitable draw the following day.

Dad had now got the bug and the unsaid arrangement was that I now try to get tickets for all five days of any future Trent Bridge Test matches. Well, that was a real bugbear. Just what was a man supposed to do? Fortunately, Helen was happy enough to accommodate her father-in-law for a week and it gave our two girls the chance to get to know Grandad Paddy.

In 1986, both India and New Zealand toured England with Trent Bridge hosting the Kiwis in the second of a three Test series. Again I missed the first day when, having been put in, England struggled to 240/9 with Richard Hadlee taking six wickets.

England having added 16 runs on the Friday morning, New Zealand were 45 runs behind with five wickets in hand at close of play on the Friday. It became New Zealand's Test to lose on the Saturday, when Hadlee converted his overnight 53* to 68, but more importantly, John Bracewell came in at the fall of the sixth wicket and made 110 before being last man out. New Zealand had a lead of 157 and it looked as if only the weather could save England. It nearly did with much of the fourth day lost to rain.

However, on the Tuesday, with Hadlee taking another four wickets and only John Embury providing any sustained resistance, New Zealand's target was a mere 74. They reached that for the loss of two wickets to gain only their second ever Test victory in England, and with both the 1st and 3rd Tests being drawn, their second consecutive series triumph over their old colonial masters.

Much to Dad's disgust, Trent Bridge was not allocated a Test for the 1987 home series v Pakistan. I wasn't too happy about it either so we had to miss a year and wait for the West Indies to visit in 1988. At that time, with their feared pace attack, the *Windies* were unofficial World Champions in the longer format of the game, and the 1st Test in Nottingham was to be a real test for Mike Gatting's men.

On the Wednesday before the Test there was a 'gentleman's dinner' held in Nottingham. This was hosted by Colin Slater of Radio Nottingham. It wasn't cheap, but as it included a three course meal, entertainment and an after dinner speech by guest of honour, Fred Trueman, I reckoned this would be something that Dad would enjoy. He did, but my lasting memory is of Fiery Fred's openly racist views. OK – he was of a previous generation to myself, and many older members of the audience would have had no objections to his observations, but they shocked me. His material would not have been out of place had it been delivered by Bernard Manning.

I managed to make the first day this time, and for a while, all seemed to be going well for England. Chris Broad and Graham Gooch put on 125 for the first wicket before Gooch went for 73, the first of six wickets for Malcolm Marshall. On the second morning, England lost five wickets for 22 runs and were all out for 245. In reply, in a rain interrupted innings, the West Indians had a lead of 19 with six wickets remaining at close of play on the Saturday.

When they declared with a lead of 203 on the Monday, it looked as if England were facing defeat. However a dogged 146 from Graham Gooch and uncharacteristically restrained 88* from David Gower saw England bat out the final day to salvage a draw.

Things went downhill from here however as England lost the final four Tests. Not only that but they lost Mike Gatting as captain after he was found to have 'entertained' a chambermaid at the Loughborough hotel where the England team were based. "Behaviour most unbefitting of a man charged with leading the troops. What! What!" was the considered view from Lord's. John Embury took on the captaincy for the next two Tests before being replaced by Chris Cowdrey, who lasted just the one before Graham Gooch took over for the last Test. Not a glorious summer for English cricket!

Australia, captained by Allan Border, arrived in England in 1989 with the simple objective of regaining the Ashes in a six Test series. By the time they arrived in Nottingham for the fifth Test, they had all but achieved that having won two and drawn two of the first four. However, England had Mike Atherton and Devon Malcolm making their debuts. Might this be the Test when England's fortunes, albeit late in the Series, took a turn for the better?

Sadly, no it wasn't, and on the evidence of Australia's first innings, it looked as if Malcolm would be a one Test wonder as he sprayed the ball all over the place. Allan Border won the toss and decided to bat. At close of play on the first day, David Boon, due to go in at the fall of the first wicket, had sat with his pads on all day. Australia were 301/0 with Geoff Marsh on 125* and future captain, Mark Taylor also unbeaten on 141.

The first wicket went down on the second morning with the score at 329 (Marsh 138) and the second at 430 (Taylor 230). There was then a bit of a 'collapse', if that's the right term for losing four wickets in proceeding from 500 to 600? Australia declared on the third morning at 602/6 with Malcolm taking 1/166.

England promptly lost Martyn Moxon for a three ball duck, then Michael Atherton for a two ball duck, followed by Tim Curtis for a sixteen ball two runs. They were 14/3 and Terry Alderman had taken all three. Robin Smith counterattacked and made 101 and there were contributions from the lower order as England closed on the Saturday night on 246/9. The rest day gave them a chance to re-group, although whether or not they made the most of that opportunity is open to question.

Following on 347 runs behind on the Monday morning, they were all out for 167 to lose by an innings and 180 runs. To be fair, injury meant that Ian Botham was unable to bat in the second innings, but even Beefy in his pomp would have failed to change this result. The sixth Test at the Oval was drawn but that was of little consolation. The Ashes were to remain in Australian hands for a very long time.

Chapter 10

1990's – roller coaster ride (Part 2)

1990

Things were looking up at the start of the decade. Not only were the 'Pies top of their Division and looking good for promotion, but Helen had concluded that *Helen's Stores* was unlikely to ever achieve an annual turnover in the millions, and had decided to look for alternative employment. With both girls now well established at school, she found a part-time job in South Normanton, and we promoted a GRAND CLOSING DOWN SALE. By May, everything that could be sold had gone. This of course meant that Helen could also now join the three of us on future exotic trips to the likes of Bury, Shrewsbury and Burslem.

Not forgetting of course, that in addition to all this excitement in our lives, there was the very real prospect, later in the year, of seeing Scotland prove once and for all that they were the greatest footballing nation on the planet. Let's not get ahead of ourselves though.

Notts scored just the one league goal in January and by the end of the month, had lost top spot. They would never get that high again. In fact, a series of inconsistent results saw them slip to 4th and the pessimists amongst us were concerned that securing even a play-off place was now problematical.

Kevin Bartlett and Dean Thomas were signed in March and almost immediately made a difference. Following a 2-0 away defeat to Tranmere Rovers, Notts had twelve games in which to turn things round. They made full use of them and with eight victories and four draws they were to remain unbeaten. As the season ended, only the two Bristol teams were ahead of them as they finished third, a full eighteen points ahead of the final play-off spot.

The nearest Notts came to a loss during this run was at Gay Meadow for a mid-week match at Shrewsbury Town. With eight minutes remaining, they were 2-0 down when Tommy Johnson pulled back a goal. A minute later, Kevin Bartlett scored an equaliser. This was the night that the now famous *Wheelbarrow Song* was first sung. This must have been during the Easter holidays as Ailsa came with me and she is one of a now rapidly reducing number of fans who can honestly say that "I was there on the night when................."

Kevin Bartlett scored eight goals and Tommy Johnson seven in that run, and Notts were the form team as the regular season came to a close. They were a two legged tie away from their first ever trip to Wembley, although Notts fans to this day think they should have already booked a place at the national stadium.

I'd seen them get the better of Fulham, Peterborough, Bristol City, Hereford United and Maidstone United to reach the Southern Area Final of the Leyland-DAF Cup. They were to face promotion rivals Bristol Rovers with the first leg at Twerton Park. They lost this 1-0 but remained confident of winning the home leg the following week and of meeting Tranmere Rovers in the Final.

Nearly 11,000 made it to Meadow Lane for the return leg. Notts were on top for much of the game but couldn't find a way through, at least not until the 89th minute, when substitute Phil Stant scored with a header. At the very least, this was likely to mean extra-time, something that the home side's performance deserved. The celebrations were short lived however, as the referee disallowed the goal for an offence that only he amongst the majority of those on the ground saw. Sad to say, although not that any Notts supporters shed any tears over it, but Mr Brian Hill of Kettering, was never again to officiate at the home of the World's Oldest Football League Club!

The run in that competition had taken in five lengthy mid-week trips. In fact, for me it was six, as the original tie away at Maidstone, scheduled for 28th February, was postponed at 7.15pm. I was just parking up when I spotted some chaps in Notts County colours walking away from the direction of the Stonebridge Road Ground (Maidstone were then playing in Dartford). They shouted across to me "You're wasting your time. The pitch is under water and the ref has just called it off!"

There was no time left to think about seeing if there was another game on in the area, so I just jumped back into the car and headed for home accepting that I'd have to come back on the re-arranged date. That was two weeks later and Phil Turner scored the only goal of the game in extra-time to set up the tie with Bristol Rovers.

One other sad feature of that aborted trip relates to the Dartford Crossing. Back then, the charge was £1 and there were a number of lanes where you could save time by simply dropping a £1 coin into a basket at the side of an unmanned booth. Unfortunately, I missed the basket and despite getting out of the car to have a look, I couldn't find it. With a queue of increasingly impatient drivers behind me, I had no alternative but to use another coin. That did little to help my mood on the return journey!

If any of you notice a £1 coin at any time when you cross the Bridge, can you please somehow get hold of it and arrange for it to be returned to me.

Back to the 1989/90 Third Division Play-offs. Bolton Wanderers were the opponents, and having finished lower than Notts, staged the first leg. They took an early lead through a contested penalty, but a Gary Lund header from a corner saw parity and the game ended as a 1-1 draw. With no 'away goal' advantage applicable, it simply meant that whoever won at Meadow Lane three days later would be going to Wembley.

Despite a Tommy Johnson goal after two minutes, most of the 15,197 present that night remained tense until Kevin Bartlett scored midway through the second half. Whilst this didn't exactly settle the nerves, it helped smooth them just a little as the minutes were counted down. There was no further scoring and history had been made. Notts County would be playing Tranmere Rovers in eleven days' time for a place in the 2nd Division.

On Sunday 27th May, all four of us travelled down the M1. As with their first visit the year before, both Ailsa and Heather decided to invest their spending money on top quality merchandise from the various Cockney barra boys outside the Stadium. Whatever did happen to that tat?

Notts had the better of the game and took the lead via a Tommy Johnson goal, his twentieth of the season, after half an hour. A second goal for the 'Pies, courtesy of a Craig Short header with about thirty minutes remaining, was enough to seal victory. We were happy - Heather can be clearly seen on the end of season video, joyously waving her very expensive flag on footage of the celebrations - and treated ourselves to a takeaway Indian meal when we got back. We'd had a good day out and there was a second trip to France to look forward to in a few weeks' time. Life couldn't get much better.

Friday 8th June was the day that the Gyles family packed themselves into the Estate and headed for their pre-booked Dover ferry and the long road to the Cote D'Azur. The day before had been an absolute nightmare. For those who want to know why, the full unabridged story can be found in *Processed Peas, Macaroon Bars, Warm Pork Pies and Well Made Bras*. Let's just say that for all sorts of reasons, I had difficulty sleeping the night before setting off.

Tired or not, the driver's adrenalin was flowing, the journey was smooth, the ferry departed on time and la famille Gyles enjoyed an overnight stay in Arras. The next day, the near 680 miles to our Eurocamp destination at Saint-Martin-du-Var seemed to pass by in a flash as we listened to a cassette of Rod Stewart's Greatest Hits on constant loop. If you don't believe me, just ask any of my fellow passengers.

We got to the camp around 7.00pm, and having checked in and sorted out the sleeping arrangements in our caravan, went exploring our surroundings. It was clear, within a couple of minutes, that many of the 'campers' had the same thought as myself, viz. wouldn't this be a good base for travelling over the border into Italy. In fact, it looked as if a whole platoon of the *Tartan Army* had decamped. Next door were a family from Wishaw, and over the next fortnight, Ailsa and Heather became good friends with wee Rosa, a happy-go-lucky girl of similar age.

We'd arrived with tickets for just the one game (Costa Rica) in our possession. My brother and his family were camping further down on the Coast to the west of us near Antibes, and he had the tickets for the Sweden game. As for the final game (Brazil) my boss had made contact with an Italian based supplier who, as a favour, had procured four tickets. I just had to pick them up from............Milan!

Having spent the Sunday making good use of the on-camp facilities - and they were just ideal for the likes of us - we joined the convoy travelling over to Italy for the opening game. There was disappointment when we arrived in Genoa as all vehicles carrying Scottish fans were directed by the Carabanieri to an enormous car park near the docks. There was a tense atmosphere as we were told quite forcefully that we had to stay there in the red hot late afternoon heat, and could only leave when the humourless police said so.

Looking back, I can understand that there were concerns about the possibility of violence, but c'mon, they clearly hadn't done their research. This was the *Tartan Army,* more likely to smother both locals and opposition fans with good humour than look for a fight. We were just there for a good time. After what seemed like ages, we were allowed to leave but only via a prescribed route. As we marched the couple of miles or so to the ground, there were police officers to the front, side and rear. It was dehumanising and not something we were used to.

Costa Rica had qualified for the tournament for the first time in their history and all the pundits reckoned they were only there to make up the numbers. As far as the Group was concerned, it looked as if it had to be a straight shoot-out between Scotland and Sweden to finish behind Brazil and qualify for the knock-out stages. What followed will however, be forever remembered by those with an interest in how the Scotland international team performs.

The four of us had excellent seats at Stadio Luigi Ferraris (home ground for both Genoa FC and Sampdoria FC), and so they should have been. I paid the equivalent of £250 for them. Yes, back in 1990 that was £62.50 each. Whatever, that was the price and I suppose we did get value for money of a sort, as we watched Costa Rica's first ever goal and first ever victory at a World Cup. Scotland didn't play too badly, but they couldn't really complain. They just hadn't done enough.

Given the heavy and hostile police presence before the game, you would have thought that after that result, the Scottish fans would have been given an even more regimented escort back to our vehicles. Not so, with heavy hearts and drooping shoulders, we just wandered back occasionally engaging in good natured banter with the local ragazze who had never seen so many men in skirts before.

We got back to the camp at about 1.00am, and along with other returning fans, were shocked to find that we were locked out. After we'd summoned an irate Frenchman from his bed we were eventually allowed in, but only after he'd muttered a few profanities directed at 'Ecossais stupides' and told that we should have asked for the security code from reception. "Aye. A' right. Nae bather me sewer" was the collective reply.

After a lie-in the following morning, we enjoyed four relaxed days of holiday, combining trips to Nice and Monaco with time in camp and getting to know Rosa and some of the other youngsters who were there.

The Sweden game came next. As Alan had only the two spare tickets for this one, Heather stayed back at the camp with her Mum. In the early afternoon, Ailsa and I travelled across to meet up with her uncle and cousin (Scott) and Alan's pal Bill, and his lad. The six of us, with four squeezed in the back, headed over the Italian border.

It looked as if the Carabanieri had learnt lessons from the first game and had revised their strategy. We were not treated like vermin, allowed to park where we liked and could make our own way to the ground. Much more civilised!

Stuart McCall scored an early goal but it needed Mo Johnston to convert a penalty in the 81st minute before victory seemed assured. Even then, we had a nervous last five minutes as the Swedes scored late on. We held out and the joyous celebrations as the *Tartan Army* headed back into town will live long in the memory. We knew that Brazil had defeated Costa Rica earlier that night and were confident that a draw in our final game would see Scotland finally remove the monkey from the nation's back. Surely Sweden would get the better of Costa Rica in four days' time and with our anticipated point in Turin, at long last, the Scots would not be heading home after just the two weeks. We'd got it all worked out.

Firstly though, I had to fetch my tickets. With Helen and girls having been offered a lift by Rosa's mum and dad to a nearby water park that we'd visited earlier in our stay, I knew they'd not miss me for a day, and for the third time in a week I headed over the border. It was about a 550 mile round trip from camp to Milan.

I found the design studio that I'd been asked to contact and entered somewhat apprehensively. After all, if this was some sort of scam and the guy I was to meet was either not there, had forgotten to bring the tickets, or simply didn't exist, how was I now supposed to see Scotland get that expected draw against Brazil? I needn't have worried as I was welcomed with open arms, the only downside being the disappointment on their faces when they saw I wasn't wearing a kilt.

I handed over the cash - a lot less than £250! - and received my four tickets for Brazil v Scotland at the Stadio Delle Alpi in Turin. After some refreshment with my short lived Italian friends, I headed back to France singing along to Rod Stewart.

The good weather that we had been enjoying broke as we travelled over to Turin. We arrived early and sat in the car for a while hoping for the rain to cease, or at least relent. It did, but it was rather cold and miserable as we made our way to the stadium and, depressingly, we had not dressed accordingly. Still, we'd be comfortable enough once we were inside.

The scenario was simple, Sweden had to win and we had to make sure that we didn't lose. At half-time all was going to plan. We heard over the tannoy that the Swedes were winning and Scotland, whilst not in complete control, had not looked in any serious danger against the Brazilians.

Into the second half and with each minute that passed Scotland were getting closer to achieving their objective. We didn't know what was happening in Genoa in the other game but had to assume that Sweden were more likely to add to their lead than lose it. All was going well, until the 81st minute when the Brazilians scored. This made things very complicated but the consensus was that if Sweden had gained a wider lead they would progress on goal difference. Ach well, that's the way it always worked for Scotland. We were used to it!

Still, there was only one goal in it and if we scored an equaliser that would put us back to square one and we'd surely get the bare minimum required to get out of the group. In those last few minutes Scotland threw caution to the wind and finally made the opportunity they required. Mo Johnston was unmarked in the six yard box when the ball came to him. We rose in anticipation as he kicked and .... the ball flew over the bar. The next sound was that of a collective 30,000 heads hitting hands and a few minutes later we were on our way back to our cars.

As it happens, Costa Rica scored two late goals to beat Sweden. In reality, Scotland would have had to have beaten Brazil by at least two clear goals to have won through. That should help all of us who were there to put things into perspective, but I don't think we'll ever forgive Mo Johnston for not taking a chance that most of our grannies could have put away.

Arriving back at camp in the wee small hours of Thursday morning, we had another couple of days before heading back. Once again the Scotland team would be home before the *Tartan Army*! We made the most of that time. Regardless of the football, it had been a good holiday. Probably the first that Ailsa and Heather have really vivid memories of.

Early on the Saturday morning we left the camp and drove throughout the day reaching Amiens, and our pre-booked overnight stop, in the early evening. I may have got this wrong but a Rod Stewart cassette might just have mysteriously flown out of the window as we drove north. Whatever, I've no idea where it is and even now whenever I mention it, I'm sure I detect some sheepish looking faces.

Back in 1990, fuel was much more expensive on the Continent than in the UK. As a result, I planned to run the tank down and fill up when we came off the ferry. Our return crossing was via Boulogne, and when prompted by Helen, I assured her that we had enough to get from Amiens to the port. I was right, but only just.

Those who have used Boulogne will know that there is a long, almost two mile drop into the town when coming from the south. Well, as we headed up the hill on the other side, the engine began to cut out and Helen made some unladylike remarks which might best be summarised as "I told you so!"

I've got out of a few scrapes in my time and this was certainly one. There were just enough fumes to get us to the brow of that hill before silence. I'm referring to the engine here, not Helen! I kept my foot on the clutch, and at about ten mph we got over the top and slowly picked up speed on the descent. We were still in trouble though and would probably require a bit of a push to get to a garage - but at least it would be shorter and we did have three pushers! - when, just as the road flattened, I could see some petrol pumps ahead on the other side of the road. Fortunately, there was nothing coming the other way, so I crossed over and glided to a stop, directly alongside a pump dispensing 'essence sans plomb'. I calmly filled up and not another word was said.

We got back late on Sunday afternoon, and after clearing everything out of the car, I went up to Tibshelf to get the Indian takeaway that the girls had been salivating over for the previous three hours. I was back ten minutes later having to break the difficult news that the Tibshelf Tandoori had closed down. We'd only been out of the country for sixteen days!

147

Notts County's first game back in the 2nd Division was away to Hull City on Saturday 25th August. Goals from Gary Lund and Charlie Palmer in a 2-1 win got them off to a good start. Phil Turner was injured, which gave Mark Draper the chance to stake an ultimately successful claim for a regular first team place. Essentially then, it was the team that had won promotion a few weeks earlier.

Notts surprised many by winning six of their first eight league games before hitting a bit of a blip. Neil Warnock took action with Nicky Platnauer (permanently) and Gary Lund (temporarily) discarded and Paul Harding and Dave Regis brought in from Barnet. These changes helped to stop the rot and by the end of the year, with four straight wins including away victories at Blackburn Rovers and Newcastle United, there was just a hint that they might be contenders for a second successive promotion. This was just as well as they had made little progress in either the League Cup or Zenith Data Systems Cup.

With Helen now in a more conventional, albeit part-time job, school holidays became an issue. For the October half-term week I made a suggestion to help with the child care arrangements. The plan was that I'd look after the two girls for three days, Helen herself for one and they'd have one day with their grandparents over in Kirkby.

In practice I was to take them into work with me on the Tuesday morning, keep them busy in a corner of my office, and then all three of us would travel down to Plymouth for the mid-week league game. Surprisingly, everyone bought into my suggestion and so it was that, with blankets and pillows in the back of the Estate ready for the long drive home, after a good lunch and a bit of fussing of the girls in the works canteen, we set off for Home Park.

The game itself was scoreless but I saw a sign of things to come. Paul Harding made his debut that night and it was clear that here was a player who may have lacked a bit of finesse, but who was a midfield battler. He had replaced Nicky Platnauer, who had his strong points, but didn't have the 'bite' that Harding provided. That was encouraging. Having said that, it required a Steve Cherry penalty save to secure the draw.

The girls settled down in the back and managed to get some sleep as Dad drove back very carefully. They were in their own beds by 3.00am and enjoyed a fun filled Wednesday and Thursday as I took them swimming and then into the Peak District where we enjoyed a night at the Hartington Hall Youth Hostel. We had a family room, on the door of which was a plaque which declared that 'It was in this very room that Bonnie Prince Charlie slept as he (& his forces) marched south in 1745'. Happy memories!

1991

Following a 2-1 win over Brighton on New Year's Day, a victory that kept the good run going, Notts headed to Boothferry Park for a 3rd Round FA Cup tie. They were to win 5-2 and were then drawn against fellow second division side Oldham Athletic in the next round.

Before that game I had a memorable, although extremely short conversation with Graham Taylor. As a family, we were walking up behind the Main Stand to get to the Junior Magpies section, when I spotted the manager of the England team going the other way. In an attempt to impress the girls, I whipped out my programme and shouted across, "Excuse me Mr Taylor, but can I have your autograph?" He looked across, and very reasonably asked, "Have you got a pen?" When I said that I hadn't, he just carried on his way. OK – it was short, but as I've never forgotten it, that surely makes it 'memorable'!

Oldham were defeated 2-0, a result that saw Manchester City arrive at Meadow Lane for the 5th Round tie on 16th February. The weather in the week before had been very wintry, and up until the day itself, it looked as if there would be a postponement. However, the efforts of the ground staff and volunteers to clear the snow paid off, and after a fantastic double save from Steve Cherry, a late Gary Lund 'bobbler' somehow sneaked into the Manchester City net for the only goal of the game. Notts had reached the quarter finals of the FA Cup.

They were drawn away to Tottenham Hotspur, a team managed by Terry Venables that included the likes of Gary Lineker and Paul Gascoigne amongst other established internationals. The match was chosen by BBC1 for live coverage and took place on Sunday 10th March with an early kick-off.

It was a frenetic affair with Notts more than holding their own when, just before half-time, Don O'Riordan hit a shot that went like the proverbial bullet to beat Norwegian international goalkeeper, Erik Thorstvedt, low to his left. Sadly, the shock that probably most TV viewers (and Gooners) wanted, failed to materialise as two second half goals sent Spurs through to a semi-final with Arsenal. They won that and then defeated Nottingham Forest in the Final.

I'm a fairly phlegmatic guy at the best of times, but that defeat set me back a bit. It came at a time when our league form was suffering (only one point from nine) and this was further compounded by a drab 1-1 draw with Port Vale the following Tuesday. I try not to let football get the better of me, but for a few days, I have to admit that it did. I was feeling low.

Things got better, very quickly. There were sixteen league games remaining after the Q/F defeat and Notts won eleven (including the last seven in a row), drew three and lost just two. They finished just two points off automatic promotion and had to overcome Middlesbrough in a two legged play-off semi-final to secure a second consecutive visit to Wembley.

I missed the last of those final seven victories, a 2-1 away win at Upton Park that meant Oldham Athletic, and not West Ham, were promoted as champions. I was a bit disappointed to have missed that - the date clashed with the Selston FC end of season presentations - as I was now beginning to note the number of grounds on which I'd seen Notts win. As it happened, I didn't have to wait long.

By way of consolation, I travelled up to Halifax with Alan Baldwin that Saturday. If Aldershot were to win that afternoon they would have finished 90th in the Football League. Sadly for Alan and all 'Shots fans, in front of 1,428, they were well beaten 3-0, and the season ended with only the one team, Wrexham, below them. *NB – the Welsh side would ordinarily have lost League status but were saved as a result of Maidstone United folding.*

Over 22,000 were at Ayresome Park for the first play-off game. Just like twelve months earlier, a 1-1 draw set up a 'winner takes all' second leg three days later. It could have been better for Notts as Phil Turner had given them an early advantage which they held until conceding the equaliser late on.

The second leg saw the highest crowd of the season attend Meadow Lane, and all of them endured a very nervous 79 minutes. At that point Paul Harding scored his first ever senior goal, and for most there on the night, the last eleven minutes just dragged and dragged. When the final whistle went, the euphoria (amongst Notts fans anyway!) was probably greater than the year before. Such was my joy, that when I got back to Newton at around 10.30pm, I was pleased to see the pub next door was still open. I'd never done this before (or since) but I called in for a celebratory pint. As a game, football can certainly play with the emotions. It was only a few weeks before when, after the defeat at White Hart Lane, I'd fleetingly considered never going to another game. *NB – I suppose a few seconds can be summarised as 'fleetingly'!*

For the Wembley trip, I found requests from many to a) get tickets and b) arrange transport. There would be many more than just the four of us this time. In fact, with the help of Ian Wilson, we hired two mini buses and twenty six of us headed down the M1 on Sunday 2nd June. As an old hand at Wembley visits, I led the way and we parked up on a car park just off the top of Ealing Road. It was free on a Sunday and only fifteen minutes away from the Stadium. What could possibly go wrong?

Opponents Brighton, who had accumulated ten fewer points than Notts County during the season, were better supported. There were around 25,000 following the 'Pies in a crowd of 59,940. In the early stages, it was those from the south coast who were in better voice. They were outplaying Notts, and came close to scoring a few times. However, in the 29th minute, Tommy Johnson headed the opening goal and although they needed the intervention of a post to prevent Brighton from equalising, managed to survive to half-time.

It remained tight at the start of the second half before another Tommy Johnson goal (that was three from two Wembley appearances), followed by one from Dave Regis, enabled us to relax. Dean Wilkins scored a late consolation but we weren't bothered. Neil Warnock had led Notts back to the 1st Division.

Our group's joy was tarnished a little when we got back to the car park. You'll remember, this was the one that I'd recommended! One of the mini-buses had been broken into. Fortunately none of the passengers had left anything of value although a jacket was missing. However, according to its owner it was the most precious and expensive jacket that had ever been made. Fortunately, the owner, Ron Peat, was able to claim off his insurance, but that didn't stop him moaning for months. Luckily for me, this was not the bus I'd been driving and I felt for those travelling back as they not only had to put up with a broken window but listening to his grumbles. They weren't to know it at the time, but they were the lucky ones.

I pulled into Watford Gap to fill up. With a big tank it took something like £50 worth of diesel, and whilst I was seeing to that, my passengers had a short comfort break. All back on board, I headed out onto the Motorway but had only just cleared the slip road when I noticed what looked like black smoke in my rear view mirror and a loss of power. I pulled over to the hard shoulder and apologised profusely to the rest of them. I'd only just discovered that I'd filled a petrol driven vehicle with..... ....diesel!

Well, undaunted, and led by the likes of John Olney, a few passengers jumped out and pushed me back into the Service Station. Fortunately, there is a bit of an incline as you leave Watford Gap and this helped. *NB - we couldn't do it now as this stretch of the M1 has been upgraded to 'smart' and there is no hard shoulder.*

There is a garage unit at Watford Gap which, at that time, was manned during daytime hours. It was now around 8.00pm and the on-site mechanic was still there. When I explained the problem he said he might have time to help before he left at 10.00pm. All my passengers then decamped inside.

To cut a long story (and it was) short, we managed to remove the diesel between us and then a few of the guys pushed me back to a pump to fill up again, this time with petrol. At last, we thought, we'll be on our way. Our hopes were dashed however when I just couldn't get the engine to fire. I tried and tried, and probably as a result, the starter motor went. We were in deep trouble now, especially as the mechanic to whom I'd 'slipped' a tenner for his help, had gone home, and the joy of a few hours before had all but evaporated.

I noticed an RAC van and mechanic nearby with his head under the bonnet of another vehicle. I explained our dilemma and the fact that although I was with the AA we had got a passenger who was a member of his organisation. He agreed to come over when he'd finished that particular job.

It was about 11pm when he shook his head and said he couldn't do anything with the starter motor and suggested the only thing he could do was tow me around the almost empty car park in the hope that we'd be able to kick start the engine. We tried for about half an hour, but to no avail. We weren't now just in trouble, the entire group, who to their credit had been very supportive, were now getting desperate. Would we ever get home?

Our very patient RAC man made one last suggestion. As we were limited in the speed we could travel at in the car park, we might just succeed in kick starting the engine if we went out onto the Motorway. If that didn't work, he'd tow us back down the other side and leave us at the service station on the south bound carriageway. I put this to the group, and as there was no alternative, they agreed to give it a chance. They all piled back into the mini-bus. It was, by now, after midnight.

We got out onto the Motorway and over the incline and were travelling at about 50 mph when I let out the clutch. There was a bit of coughing and spluttering, but thankfully and miraculously, the engine burst into life. It sounded a bit sick but it was running. I flashed the RAC man to pull over and as he uncoupled us, I kept revving the engine to make sure I didn't stall. After thanking him profusely I set off, conscious that at all costs, I had to keep that engine running.

I had various drops around the Underwood, Brinsley and Selston area, and with all passengers safely home, took Helen to Ian Wilson's house, where I'd left my car in the morning *(NB – the previous morning of course!)*. She then followed me to the top of Victoria Road in Selston, where I parked up the mini-bus. My hope was that, when I returned, I'd get sufficient speed rolling down that hill to bump start the engine. The Gyles family then went back to Newton and were in bed by 3.00am.

I didn't sleep at all and was on my way again three hours later. Fortunately, I managed to get the mini-bus started, and while making sure I kept the engine running, joined up with Ian Wilson to get both vehicles back no later than the pre-agreed 7.00am. We were just to leave them and push the keys through the letter box. He had contacted the hire company the night before to tell them about the broken window and we quickly knocked up a note to explain about the starter motor to leave in mine. We dropped the vehicles off, and in Ian's car, headed back to Selston where I went to work, a bit later than normal, but still in plenty of time.

I thought there might be further disappointment, but to the credit of the hire company, they didn't come chasing for more money and I've got to be thankful for that. I'd wasted enough on diesel and the like as it was!

As a family, we had booked a week in a caravan park near Filey for August. This proved to be a little inconvenient as the first Saturday of the week coincided with the start of the 1990/91 football season. As it happened, it wasn't too bad as Notts first game was in Manchester, at Old Trafford, and we decided to head north-west and then east from there after the game.

Manchester United, with Peter Schmeichel and Andrei Kanchelkis making their debuts, won 2-0. There were no new names in the Notts

County line-up - the only close season signing being defender, Richard Dryden - and the biggest disappointment for us was an injury to Don O'Riordan. He was substituted in the 51st minute and was not to play again that season. I reckon that was a bigger blow than we realised at the time.

We missed the first home game, a 1-0 win over Southampton, but were back from holiday in time to see us lose 4-0 to Nottingham Forest. Things did pick up a bit after that, and with away wins at West Ham (see, I hadn't had to wait too long after all!) and Sheffield United, plus a home win over Sheffield Wednesday, after nine games back in the 1st Division, Notts were in 9th position. That was as good as it got however.

Paul Rideout had been signed from Southampton and scored on his debut at Bramall Lane. He looked a class act, but played only a further ten games (two as substitute) before being sold to Rangers. At the time, Club owner Derek Pavis, said that this was good business for Notts County as he had been sold for twice the fee required to bring him from Southampton. That's as may be, but at the time, it smacked of a lack of ambition.

With Dave Regis also leaving, Tony Agana was brought in from Sheffield United for a record fee - one that stands to this day and is unlikely to be beaten - and worked very hard but failed to find the back of the net as frequently as he had done when paired with Brian Deane. In thirteen appearances, he netted just the once and there were wild celebrations when he finally scored in a 3-0 win over West Ham in the last game of the year. That, and a home 2-0 defeat of Chelsea on Boxing Day had seen the Club move four points clear of a relegation spot. There was an air of optimism then around Meadow Lane as the old year drew to a close.

Before I move on to 1992 though, with Notts having been up and down all four divisions during the previous twenty years, I was aware that I was getting close to qualifying for the '92 Club'. I only had a few grounds to 'tick off' to complete the set. On 9th November, with Notts having no game because of the international break, I headed down to Underhill to see Barnet, a new entrant to the League, defeat Halifax 3-

0. It was just something I had to do, although little did I suspect that I'd be watching Notts there before the decade ended.

At the next international break, in February of the following year, I made it to Scarborough to see them lose 3-0 to Rotherham United. At that stage, there were only three clubs remaining to complete the '92', although I'd have to revisit some that had moved to new stadia.

1992

In defeating Wigan Athletic and Blackburn Rovers in home FA Cup ties, Notts headed off to Carrow Road for a 5th Round tie with Norwich City. A 3-0 defeat in East Anglia meant that, having dropped into the bottom three, survival in the 1st Division was now the Club's only priority.

Despite bringing in experienced players like Andy Williams and Kevin Wilson on a permanent basis, plus John McClelland (loan) and blooding youngsters Michael Johnson, Steve Slawson and Mark Wells, the highly probable became inevitable and was confirmed in a 2-0 defeat at Maine Road on 25th April. I guess that the writing was on the wall as early as March when Derek Pavis decided to cash in on one of the Club's assets and Tommy Johnson was sold to Derby County.

They did defeat Luton Town (and effectively relegate the Hatters) in the final game at Meadow Lane, but it was too late. Notts finished four points adrift of safety with West Ham United finishing bottom, thereby becoming the third club leaving the 1st Division to bizarrely play football the following season in.................the 1st Division!

A majority of the 22 clubs in the top division (including Notts) had that year decided to form a breakaway league (the English Premier League) for the start of 1992/93. What was the 2nd Division was, as a result, subsequently re-named the 1st Division of the English Football League. As we all know now, the football that we loved and had grown up with, had changed for ever.

At the end of that final home game, Steve Cherry gave the impression that he had played his last game for the Club as he threw his goalkeeping gloves into the crowd. I managed to get one and it's been slowly deteriorating in an upstairs drawer ever since.

That one season in the top division, the last that Notts County and clubs like them can realistically hope to enjoy, was memorable for many reasons. Notts had played a total of 50 competitive games and I missed just the one, the home game v Southampton back in August. I'd made it to every away game and in addition to taking the objective view that Leeds United were worthy champions, took pride in Liverpool fans' comments that Notts County had the most philosophic (& noisy) fans as, with John Olney alongside me, we out sang the Kop as we watched our team being walloped 4-0.

The period between dropping out of the 1st Division and starting the 1992/93 season in the ......1st Division, saw major changes at Meadow Lane. In fifteen weeks, three sides of the ground were demolished and rebuilt. This was to comply with the recommendations of the Taylor Report into the 1989 Hillsborough Disaster. One of these was that spectators at games played in the top two divisions should be 'all seated'. There was a phase-in period for this to happen, but as Derby County fans never fail to remind me, their club underwrote the cost of the re-development of Meadow Lane through the purchase of first Tommy Johnson and then, after five games of the new season, Craig Short.

In addition to these two, Paul Harding had also left the Club during the close season. The newcomers, Shaun Murphy, Dave Smith and Meindert Dijkstra joined Paul Devlin who had signed at the back end of 91/92, as key squad members.

The opening game of the season was away to Birmingham City, and as it had been selected by ATV for live coverage, was played on a Sunday. There was only the one goal in it. Sadly, for the Gyles family, it was not scored by the away team!

As I'm sure you've gathered, football can sometimes play havoc with my emotions. I try to keep a lid on them but I have to admit that my eyes were on the point of 'leaking' when the four of us took our seats in the newly created Family Stand for the first home game of the season. To witness how Meadow Lane had been almost totally (the old Main Stand remained) transformed in such a short space of time, was a joyous experience.

Despite success over Wolverhampton Wanderers in the League Cup - Notts lost at home to Cambridge United in the next round - the first half of the season was a disaster. With only four wins from the opening 23 games, the year ended with Notts in the bottom three. Early away wins at Peterborough and Watford were more than balanced by hammerings at Millwall (6-0) and Swindon Town (5-1). The trip to London, for the first of those big defeats, was made in the latest car, another Ford Escort Estate (K974 GNU) and was the first time that I had found myself acting as an impromptu traffic policeman to make sure we got to the ground on time.

We found ourselves at a T Junction with about twenty cars in front, most of whom were turning right, across the flow of traffic. We waited and waited until I could stand it no more. I pulled the hand brake, went up to the main road, and walked into the middle with arms stretched out wide stopping traffic from both directions. Once I'd let the twenty cars (I may be exaggerating a little here) exit the junction, I strode back to our car and didn't hang about when it was my turn to exit. We missed the first few minutes but not any of the goals. Shame really.

Although we saw West Ham win 2-0, Helen and I had the opportunity of watching from the Directors Box at Upton Park. I'd contacted Derek Pavis to advise him that my wife was to reach a momentous birthday the day before this game, and was there any way in which the Club could recognise this. I rather helpfully added that, whatever he thought, we'd be at Upton Park. To his credit, two free passes duly arrived.

I'd booked overnight accommodation, and after the game, when we got back to the hotel and had showered and changed ready for a visit to the theatre, we went into the bar for a pre-show aperitif. There, hidden away in a corner, were Ailsa and Heather. I'd arranged to have them secretly transported down from Kirkby where they were supposed to be staying with their grandparents. See, it's not all just about the football!

So, as the year ended, and just like eight years earlier, Notts were facing the possibility of a second successive relegation. Fans were becoming mutinous, Neil Warnock was becoming bad tempered, and perhaps more significantly, knives were being sharpened!

1993

Notts County's 3rd Round FA Cup tie at home to Sunderland was postponed, so the first game of the New Year was a home game v Millwall. Dean Thomas scored in a 2-1 defeat, and at the end of the game, I swear I could hear the sound of something metallic being rubbed up against stone from somewhere at the back of the old Main Stand. You couldn't hear much else as even the few fans who had stayed to the end had given up on moaning.

Sure enough, the 2-0 defeat to Sunderland in the re-arranged cup tie the following Tuesday night was Neil Warnock's last game in charge. Now I don't know whether or not this turned out to be the right move, and in truth, we'll never know. Looking at his record over the following near thirty years just has me wondering whether or not the Club would have slipped as far as history shows it eventually did, had we retained the rumbustious Sheffielder.

Clearly results were not good and crowds were falling, but my theory is that the relationship between Chairman and Manager suffered following the sale of Paul Rideout and was exacerbated by the poor return from the heavy investment in Tony Agana. Despite his wholehearted commitment, three goals from his first 42 league appearances did not do him any favours.

With Mick Jones, assistant manager, leaving the Club as well, the Chairman asked youth team coach, Mick Walker, to take temporary charge. His first two games were away to Luton Town (0-0) and Leicester City (1-1). The two points gained in those games suggested that, with Michael Johnson recalled, and Paul Cox making his debut at

Filbert Street, the defence had been tightened up. Paul Devlin was also brought back into the side.

Now these changes did make a difference but I noticed something that was to have a profound effect on the rest of the team and on one player in particular. Mark Draper appeared to have been given more of a free role and not only looked much more assured as a result, but he was 'shooting on sight' and it was his goal that secured the point at Leicester.

Three days later, Notts played their first home game under Mick Walker and the change in personnel and style was now evident for all to see. Tranmere Rovers, who were challenging for promotion, were beaten 5-1, with the rejuvenated (bit unfair that as he was still only 22!) Draper running the show. His performances over the next eighteen months would eventually lead to bigger and better things for the local lad.

Although the next game, away to Charlton was lost, and results remained inconsistent, Notts, especially after the introduction of another youth team product, Richard Walker, and the acquisition of David Reeves from Bolton Wanderers, now looked as if they would avoid relegation. However, having picked up only three points from the five previous games, there was still a chance that they would go down if they failed to beat Sunderland (& other results went against them) in the final game of the season.

To add to the pressure, Sunderland, a point ahead of Notts, needed a win themselves to guarantee staying up. Notts did what they had to do, and a 3-1 victory with goals from David Reeves, Dave Smith and Draper (the pick of the lot) ensured that they would not be relegated. Results elsewhere meant that Sunderland also retained their status and so it was that all 14,417 at Meadow Lane that day, if not deliriously happy, went home relieved.

There were a couple of games in the second half of the 92/93 season that remain in the memory for non-footballing reasons. The first was in late February, when the four of us headed up to Grimsby, a ground that I'd visited many times, but where I'd yet to see Notts win. It was a

160

very cold but clear afternoon, and as we took our seats at the back of what was then known as the Findus Stand, we had a superb view of Spurn Head in the distance and of the steady flow of transport ships entering and leaving the Humber Estuary.

Notts took a 3-1 lead in the second half and I was hopeful that my Blundell Park jinx was about to end. However, Helen pointed out over the Estuary at what looked like an endless black cloud coming in off the North Sea. Within five minutes it had enveloped the ships and crept up to the shore. We could no longer see anything out at sea, and as the cloud released a snow storm, we could barely see the other side of the ground. With some difficulty, play continued, which is a bit of a shame, as Grimsby scored two goals and escaped with a 3-3 draw. I'd enjoyed the eerie weather experience but was disappointed with the result. My wait for a win at Grimsby would have to continue.

As for the second game, rather than re-invent the wheel so to speak, the following was published in Paul Mace's *One Flew Over The Magpie's Nest,* an excellent account of fifty years of following Notts County.

Charlton Athletic v Notts County – 30th January 1993

It's a match that I recall with mixed emotions, a combination of deep pride and embarrassment verging on shame. Charlton had returned to the Valley the previous month following their six year exile to Selhurst Park. I had driven down on my own, parked up and gone for some pre-match refreshment in a local pub. I got to the ground about 20 minutes before kick-off and came across some fellow 'Pies who were angry that they were not being allowed in.

Apparently Charlton had been expecting a relatively small number of visitors, possibly following advice from Meadow Lane, and with The Valley still undergoing reconstruction, the small section allocated to travelling fans had already filled up.

Amongst those fans who were now effectively locked out, some were resigned to going home, while others were looking for a vantage point from where they might get a limited view of the action and others, in an angry mood, were just wandering around and clearly a cause for concern for those overseeing security.

As for myself, having travelled all that way, I was determined to see the game. After all, I'd already paid for my programme! I walked around the perimeter of the ground until I came across a burger van behind which was a fence and a view of the rear of the recently re-opened main stand. Seeing my chance, I slipped behind the back of the van, gained a bit of leverage from some gas cylinders, and in a highly undignified manner 'went over the top'.

I was now inside the ground and appeared not to have been spotted, but still had to cross 'no man's land' to the apparent security of the Charlton supporters congregating under the stand. That's when some of my fellow disappointed 'Pies did me a favour. They began creating a bit of a commotion at one of the entrances, and although I was not immediately aware of the reason, I could see a number of yellow-jacketed stewards running, initially I thought towards me, but they veered off. I could hear one of them shouting on his walkie-talkie that 'some fans are trying to break in.' The coast was clear and I wandered, unchallenged, up to the stand.

Given that all home seats had been sold (the capacity was restricted to 8,500) I still had the problem of finding somewhere to watch the game. I waited until I could hear that the teams had come out and then nonchalantly and self-confidently went to the bottom of an aisle with steps leading upwards. I spotted an empty seat and went and sat down. Within seconds a guy came up and looked at me as if to say 'You're in my seat.' I simply mumbled an apology and continued on upwards. I found another seat, but just as the game was kicking off, another latecomer arrived and I had to move on again.

Fortunately, I did come across a third vacant seat, and from this one was able to watch Notts lose 2-1 (Mark Draper got the consolation goal) without further interruption. As I've said, I have mixed emotions when I recall this. I'm not particularly pleased with my actions on that day. I was a 42 year old Human Resources Manager at the time, with responsibility for something like 1,000 employees, and I'm not sure how my company would have responded had my escapade become public knowledge. Yet, deep down, I'm proud of how I kept cool under pressure, showed initiative, put no-one at risk other than myself and can say............ 'I was there.'

Given the encouraging second half of the previous season, Mick Walker became manager on a permanent basis and was given some cash by the Chairman to help improve the squad. Whether or not the Club got true value for the £675,000 they spent in bringing Andy Legg and Gary McSwegan to Nottingham is up for debate. What cannot be questioned, is the fact that they certainly brought a bit of quality.

Before the season started, I made a trip up to Arbroath to see Dad. He'd had a minor operation and the visit was primarily to make sure he was all right. I needn't have worried. A very independent chap who had been coping fine on his own for effectively twenty years whilst working away, and then following retirement, he was fine. It did give me the opportunity though for a nostalgic visit to Gayfield for the first time in seventeen years. The 5-2 defeat to Queen of the South was a reminder of less happy times and had me looking forward to the following week's first game of the season at Meadow Lane. That wasn't much better though, despite Notts scoring two late goals. Unfortunately Middlesbrough were already 3-0 up by the time that happened.

In the League Cup, Hull City were overcome on away goals in a two legged tie. For some reason I was unable to get to either the home or away games against Newcastle United in the next round. Probably just as well as both were lost with a final aggregate score of 11-2. Ouch!

There was some cup success in the Anglo-Italian Cup however. There was a complicated set up with a preliminary group to reduce the number of English teams. Notts came through that and were then the best placed English team in their group at the International stage. The details are irrelevant. All you need to know is that their efforts saw them reach the semi-final scheduled for the New Year.

League form was inconsistent. A stirring 4-0 home win over Derby County (Gary McSwegan hat-trick) was more than balanced by a 5-1 away defeat to Charlton Athletic. Still, as being in 15th position at the end of December suggested, this was a big improvement on where the Club had found itself twelve months before. The optimists amongst the fan base, and there were a few, thought that with a good run in the second half of the season, they might just challenge for a play-off place.

1994

Southend United were the opponents in the English semi-final of the Anglo-Italian Cup. I didn't make the away leg which was lost 1-0. The 2nd Leg was scheduled for Tuesday 15th Feb but was postponed (frozen pitch) and hastily re-arranged for the following night. Paul Devlin levelled the aggregate scores mid-way through the second half, but despite extra-time, there was to be no more scoring. Steve Cherry (he hadn't left after all) was the hero in goal however, as Notts prevailed 4-3 on penalties. Having waited 68 years for their first ever visit to Wembley, the Club were going back for the third time in less than three years.

The Final, on Sunday 20th March, perhaps befitting the level of interest in the competition, was a forgettable affair. Just over 17,000 attended with barely 1,000 of them supporters of the Italian opponents, Brescia. One goal was enough for the trophy to return to Italy (Cremonese had thumped Derby County in the 1993 final), and although Notts played well in patches, no-one could seriously argue against the fact that the better side had won. Still, it was a privilege to see Gheorghe Hagi, Romanian international and former Real Madrid (& future Barcelona) player, demonstrate his class.

Although the first league game of the New Year was an away defeat at Bolton Wanderers, Notts had a good run, losing just one of the next nine games. The optimists were gaining in confidence as a gradual climb up the table saw the Club rise to 8th. They had become serious play-off contenders.

By the night of the away game at the Baseball Ground on Wednesday 20th April, Notts were in sixth place and a win would see them overtake their opponents. What's more, depending upon results elsewhere, they could even climb to third. With eleven minutes remaining, Mark Draper scored and most spectators in the ground groaned. The Rams looked like blowing it. However, in the 90th minute, in an episode for which he'll always be remembered, Meindert Dijkstra inexplicably headed over Steve Cherry as the goalkeeper came out to gather a hopeful punt forward.

Notts didn't win any of the three remaining league games and finished 7th, one place and three points behind Derby County, the last of the play-off contenders. That own goal at the Baseball Ground was crucial in so many ways. It may have denied Notts the chance of extending the season, but it also gave Derby the opportunity to get to the play-off Final where, despite an inevitable Tommy Johnson goal, they lost to Leicester City.

The season may have ended in disappointment then for Notts County - they've never finished as high since, nor realistically, will they ever again - but there were highlights. They held West Ham United to a home draw in the FA Cup. I took John Olney with me to the replay at Upton Park. There had been no goals and with just two minutes of extra time remaining, and the tie looking as if it would be settled by penalties, Lee Chapman scored for the Hammers. We may have been tired when we got back but our sympathies were with the players. They had just played a full 120 minutes, and in less than 72 hours would be facing promotion chasing Nottingham Forest.

Forest were sitting third in the table on the morning of Saturday 12th February. By 5.00pm they were sixth. In an exhibition that surprised everyone, Notts more than held their own against their rivals, and with on loan Peter Reid inspired in midfield, looked a threat throughout. A 55th minute goal from Gary McSwegan put Notts in front and it stayed that way until, with six minutes remaining, David Phillips equalised.

Notts were not to be denied however, and a couple of minutes later, Mark Draper floated over a free kick which was headed into the net by Charlie Palmer. His run down the touchline in celebration was the fastest I, or anyone else for that matter, had ever seen him move. Paul Devlin, who was no slouch himself, couldn't catch him and the moment was captured for posterity in a photograph. I have a framed copy of this. It is a reminder of the last ever league meeting between the two clubs. A day, the anniversary of which is now called 'Sir Charlie Palmer Day' by Notts fans across the world.

The last home league game of the season, a 3-3 draw against Charlton Athletic, was played on a ground where the old Main Stand, built in 1910, was being demolished. We had been promised that when we returned in August, the stadium re-development would be complete. We'd have to wait though, as there was a World Cup to enjoy that summer.

Even though Scotland had failed to qualify for the first time in twenty years, the 1994 World Cup tournament to be staged in USA had been on the radar from, well, 1990 actually. Towards the end of our holiday on the Cote D'Azur, I can remember sitting outside our caravan in Saint Martin-du-Var and suggesting that we go to America in four years' time. As there were no objections from Helen or either of the girls, I took that as a fait accompli (see what I did there?) and began mentally planning.

In some respects, Scotland not qualifying made my job of getting tickets easier. I'd initially written to the only Americans that I was aware of who were playing in England, asking them if they knew how I could get tickets. John Harkes, who had just moved to Derby County, and Tim Howard, then at Manchester United failed to reply.

However, Kasey Keller from Millwall wrote to say that he personally was unable to help, but provided information which proved useful. He gave me not only contact details for a ticket selling agency, but suggested that as we were not planning on seeing Scotland - he was sympathetic - I wait until the draw was made and then try to buy tickets for games in which one of the nations was likely to be poorly supported. As a result, he suggested, demand would likely be lower. Top man!

That is why we decided to become honorary Cameroonians and fly in and out of Los Angeles. Cameroon had qualified in 1982 and again in 1990, when England needed extra-time to eliminate them in a quarter final tie. They were regarded as one of the emerging African nations who could pose a threat in the near future. However, they would not have great travelling support and the ex-pat community in the States was small in number.

Kasey's theory came up trumps and his contact suggestion delivered. I managed to get four tickets for the games v Sweden and USSR and two for Brazil. As a bonus, I got one ticket for the Colombia v Switzerland game.

Ailsa was in her second year at secondary school, so there were no crucial exams in the pipeline, and with Heather in her final year at Newton Primary, the timing of the tournament was, from an educational viewpoint, not seen to be an issue and we had the blessing of both Heads. As a result, on Thursday 16th June, we flew from Manchester Airport. John Wallis, husband of Margaret, who worked for me, took us up in my car. The idea was that the car would then be available for work purposes while we were away, on the understanding that John would pick us up on our return.

In an effort to have us identified as 'Cameroonians' I had visited numerous sportswear retail outlets in advance, but only succeeded in drawing strange looks when I asked where they displayed their Cameroon stock. I got round this by contacting the Cameroon Embassy in London. They could supply sweatshirts and baseball caps with the Cameroonian flag as a motif. I sent off my cheque and the stylish (that's stretching it!) produce arrived in plenty of time.

On our first full day in Los Angeles, we became aware of a developing news story that appeared to have the entire nation gripped. There was live footage on television of a convoy of cars slowly travelling along the LA freeway system. We'd no idea what was happening. I went out to the motel reception, and sure enough, the lady there was watching her small TV intently. When I asked, she told me that the police were following OJ, as they wanted to question him. That didn't help a great deal, and it was only later that we found out that this was OJ Simpson. Like most people outside America, we had no idea who he was.

Our first game (Sweden) was at the Rose Bowl, Pasadena, where there was no cover and we watched a 2-2 draw in baking heat. There was a sizeable number of Swedes in the crowd but very few obviously supporting Cameroon. However, when they took the lead early in the second half, it was clear that the neutrals, many of whom were Hispanic, favoured the apparent underdog.

The other three games were to be played at Stanford University in Palo Alto, just south of San Francisco, with a six day gap before the next. That gave us the opportunity to do a bit of exploring and after a couple of days in San Diego and two more in Las Vegas, we headed up through Nevada and over the Donner Pass back into California. After one night in Sacramento, we had four more in the 'City by the Bay'. This was all very exciting, and as a family, we all agreed that it had a bit more going for it than that caravan park in Filey, a few years before.

In between doing all the things that a first time visitor to San Francisco must do, there were three more games of football. Ailsa accompanied me to the Brazil game. At 1-0, with Romario the scorer at half-time, there remained a chance that Cameroon might spring a shock, but two goals (Marcio Santos and Bebeto) sealed what was eventually a comfortable win for the pre-tournament favourites.

A couple of days later, before carrying on to the game, I left Helen and the girls at a place called Half Moon Bay and they pottered around at this pleasant spot where the Pacific Ocean breakers kept up a constant hum.

Colombia, who were highly rated with the likes of Carlos Valderrama, Freddy Rincon and Faustino Asprilla in their side, were 2-0 winners. However, as they had already lost to Romania (Gheorghe Hagi was captain) and the USA, they were eliminated. Six days later, the Colombian full back, Andres Escobar was dead. He had been murdered, apparently for the own goal he had scored in the earlier 2-1 defeat to the United States.

Two days later, we checked out of our motel in the city and headed to Palo Alto, the plan being that we drive down to Los Angeles straight after the Cameroon v USSR game. The Russians, with no points, were already eliminated. The Cameroonians had to win and hope that the Swedes lost to Brazil to give them a chance of advancing to the knock out stages on goal difference. It was to be an historic game, but not in the way that Cameroonian supporters had hoped.

USSR were 3-0 up at half time with Oleg Salenko scoring all three. Roger Milla scored straight after the restart to give Cameroon some hope, but a further three goals (two from Salenko) gave the Russians an ultimately worthless, in terms of the tournament, 6-1 victory.

This game was historic for two reasons. Firstly, Oleg Salenko, who played briefly for Rangers the following year, is the only player (and remains so) to have scored five goals in a single World Cup Finals match. Secondly, at 42 years of age, Roger Milla was (and also remains) the oldest player to have scored in such a game.

It's a long drive south (approx. 360 miles) from Palo Alto to Los Angeles. Back in the car for 3.30pm, I reckoned it would take around six hours. It was however, nearer midnight when we pulled into our Redondo Beach motel. On the way south, I'd been stopped by the police for speeding.

The limit on Route 1 is 55mph and I, plus the three other vehicles I'd been following in a sort of informal convoy, had been clocked at 74mph, apparently from a spotter plane above. Once the patrol car driver had persuaded me that, yes, he wanted me to stop, he took pity on me when he read my licence and saw that I was 'fromoutatown'. "Go on your way sir," were his parting words, having earlier cautioned me that I may be allowed to drive at up to 70 mph where I came from, but not in California.

It may have been late, but we made it back without any further incident and our first long haul adventure was almost complete. We headed back on 30th June with many happy memories and a plan formulating in our heads (well it may just have been the one) that we do it all again in four years' time in France.

Notts first league game of the 1994/95 season was away to Portsmouth. Substitute Paul Sherlock, on for the injured Michael Johnson, scored an equaliser and looked to have salvaged a draw. An 89th minute goal for the home team resulted in a 2-1 defeat however, and a long journey home in which to reflect on whether or not things would improve.

Other than Michael Emenalo, the Nigerian international who, a few weeks before had played against Greece, Argentina and Italy in the World Cup, there had been no major signings during the close season. Understandably, Mick Walker had been impressed with how his team had improved towards the end of 93/94 and was prepared to give his squad the chance to build on the previous season's seventh place finish. There was never any threat of that and after fifteen games they had won just the once and Mick Walker had been relieved of his duties after only seven of them.

His replacement, Russell Slade, took charge on a temporary basis, but other than the odd result, the league form continued to disappoint, and by Christmas, the unthinkable, i.e. a drop down to the old third division, was looking highly probable. Notts were bottom of the division and in danger of being cut off.

There was some respite however, in cup football. The Anglo Italian Cup had a slightly different format which, if anything, was even more complicated than the year before. There were eight Italian clubs and eight English clubs with four from each nation split into two different groups. The English teams would play each of the Italian clubs in their group once, and after all four games had been completed, the highest placed team from each of the two countries in either group would compete against the similarly placed club in a semi-final. Hope you're keeping up!

Suffice to say that in a group which included Swindon Town, Tranmere Rovers and Wolves, Notts had the best record having beaten Lecce, and drawn with Ascoli, Atalanta and Venezia. Once again, they were one tie away from a Wembley final.

In the League Cup, Notts defeated Bristol City home and away to win 4-0 on aggregate, and as a reward, gained a home draw against Tottenham Hotspur in the 3rd Round. This was the team, now managed by Ossie Ardiles, containing plenty of internationals like Gica Popescu, Ilie Dumitrescu, Jurgen Klinsmann, Nick Barmby, and future Notts star (?) Sol Campbell.

Just under 17,000 saw the shock of the round as Notts went 2-0 up after 20 minutes through Tony Agana and Gary McSwegan, and then witnessed Ilie Dumitrescu being sent off just before half-time. When McSwegan scored a third midway through the second half, the outcome was all but certain, and with no more scoring, Notts County were briefly featured on the back pages. In truth, the content was more about 'under pressure manager, Ardiles' than on how brilliantly Notts had played.

For the 4th Round tie many expectant fans travelled to Carrow Road to see the 'Pies take on Norwich City. Notts conceded a goal in the 1st minute, and although they played well and created a number of chances, none of them were taken and one route to Wembley was eliminated.

1995

The first fixture, away to Grimsby Town, was postponed because of icy weather and we had to wait until 8th January before Notts were in action. They were at home to Manchester City in the 3rd Round of the FA Cup. After Notts had twice taken the lead, City forced a replay at Maine Road, with a goal from David Bracewell. This took place ten days later when City went on to comfortably win 5-2.

This was Russell Slade's last game in charge. A number of players had been taken on loan to try to arrest the slide. These included, Nigel Jemson, John Williams, Chris Marsden and Ray Daniel. In addition, Peter Butler (from West Ham), Devon White (QPR) and Gary Mills (Leicester City) had been signed/resigned on a permanent basis. These measures made no difference and the Chairman reckoned that a change of manager was required. He appointed Howard Kendall, but on condition that Russell Slade be retained as his deputy.

The change had a short term effect as wins over Burnley and then away at Roker Park, gave fans hope that relegation might, even now, be avoided. Howard Kendall brought in Steve Nicol from Liverpool and Graeme Hogg from Hearts, and Notts travelled to Grimsby on 28th January knowing that a win would see them move off the bottom of the table. They lost 2-1, and other than a brief spell of four weeks, were to remain at the foot of the division for the rest of the season.

After ten weeks in charge, Howard Kendall became the latest manager to be asked to clear his Meadow Lane desk. This time with the accompanying instruction.............'and take that Russell Slade with you!'

Wayne Jones and Steve Nicol took charge of team affairs for the remaining seven games of the season. A Devon White goal against Watford gave them their only victory, and by the time this happened, relegation had been confirmed. The entire Gyles family were at Millwall on Wednesday 19th April when failure to win - they did though gain a creditable 0-0 draw - meant that there was no possible escape.

There were apparently 100 Notts supporters hemmed into a small section of the New Den that night and a photographer managed to capture them all in one shot. This was printed in the following evening's Nottingham Post with a promise from Derek Pavis that he would ensure that all 100 of us would receive a free ticket for a future match. From memory, the accompanying headline was 'Chairman Derek Pavis, wants to reward the loyal 100'. We never took up the offer.

We drove home that night listening to accounts of the horrendous events in Oklahoma City. 168 people died as a lorry load of explosives destroyed a federal building. Timothy McVeigh, who was responsible for the bombing, had that day inflicted the deadliest domestic terrorist attack in the USA. *Just another example of 'I know exactly where I was and what I was doing when............!'* Perhaps more importantly, it is a reminder that whilst relegation is disappointing, it is by no means a disaster, and has to be put into context.

The number of players used during a season is usually a good indicator of whether or not things have gone smoothly. Jimmy Sirrel was a guy who looked to create consistency and would generally get through an entire season with less than 20 players making appearances for the first team. Notts County had used 36 players in this season.

There was however, something else to look back on fondly from the 1994/95 season. Notts had a two legged tie with Stoke City to decide who would go through to the final of the Anglo-Italian Cup to face Ascoli. Following a scoreless draw at Stoke City's Victoria Ground, on 24th January, the second leg at Meadow Lane seven days later, went to penalties after a further 120 minutes without a goal. In the shoot-out that followed, on loan goalkeeper Jason Kearton was the hero as Notts won 3-2.

Less than 12,000 squeezed (perhaps not the most appropriate choice of language!) into Wembley for the Final. Within that number there may have been around 200 supporters hoping for an Ascoli win. They were supporting a team whose starting line-up contained 10 Italians and one German, Oliver Bierhoff. He was little known at this time of course, but sixteen months later would be back at Wembley to score the two goals that enabled Germany to win the final of the 1996 European Championships. It would be interesting to hear which of the two games he enjoyed the better.

Notts took the lead when Tony Agana touched home an Andy Legg long throw but were quickly pulled back, and it required a Devon White goal just before half-time to restore the lead. It remained 2-1 to the end and Phil Turner became the first Notts captain in over 100 years to lift a major trophy.

The competition was abandoned in 1996 following Genoa's 5-2 defeat of Port Vale in a Wembley final attended by 979 more spectators than had seen Notts twelve months earlier. In effect then, Notts County, who after relegation to the third tier were not given the opportunity to take part, are the last English club to have won this prestigious (?) trophy.

Notts were to begin life in the old 3rd Division for the first time in 22 years with a new managerial pairing. Colin Murphy (as General Manager) and Steve Thompson (as Team Manager) were tasked with taking Notts back up at the first attempt. They didn't make too many changes to the squad at first with Darren Ward and Gary Strodder being the only significant newcomers. Between them, they would miss just three games all league season.

After losing just two of the first ten league games, Notts were sitting in fourth position and Devon White had become a bit of a cult figure. With James Hunt coming through from the youth team and Vinny Arkins and Ian Baraclough being brought in from Shelbourne and Mansfield Town respectively, the positive results continued, and although they had briefly climbed to second, the Club ended the year sitting third in the Division. Swindon Town were already looking good to go up as champions. As for Notts, a play-off place was the least they expected.

Earlier, in the League Cup, Notts had beaten Lincoln City 4-0 on aggregate (Devon White scoring all four) but then lost 3-2 over two legs to Leeds United. They were still in two cup competitions however, as the old year ended. They had defeated both York City and Telford United in the first two rounds of the FA Cup and had a home tie against Middlesbrough to look forward to. Equally exciting (?) they had reached the Northern Area Quarter Final stage of the Auto Windscreen Shield.

1996

The onward march in both cup competitions came to an abrupt end, losing 2-1 to Middlesbrough and going down 1-0 away to York City in the AWS. However, with Notts still in 3rd place and having apparently strengthened the squad by acquiring Ian Richardson (initially on loan), Paul Rogers, Tony Battersby and Chris Wilder and later Gary Jones and Gary Martindale before taking Steve Finnan on loan from Birmingham City, there was lots to look forward to.

174

Sadly, league results in the second half of the season were just too inconsistent, and by the time of the last game of the season, away to Chesterfield, the Club were guaranteed a play-off place, but no better.

In March, having won three games on the trot, hopes were high when Notts went to fellow promotion challengers Blackpool. Ailsa went with me and was sitting in the passenger seat when, as I turned right at a T junction close to Bloomfield Road, I failed to see a car coming past and there was a noisy crunch as the two vehicles came together. We stopped and got out to look. There was no damage to my car but a bit of work was required on the other.

I accepted responsibility - not sure what Ailsa would have said had I not - and exchanged details. The driver of the other car was a Blackpool supporter who had travelled over, as he did for every home game, from Scunthorpe that morning. I don't know whether or not it went down well when I told him that it was a good job I'd hit him at that precise spot, when it could have been at any point over the 100 or so miles that we'd been on the same road.

Notts faced Crewe Alexandra in the play-off semi-final, with the first leg at Gresty Road, and were 2-0 down at half-time. Second half goals from Steve Finnan, and then in the 90th minute from Gary Martindale, meant we were looking forward to the second leg in a better frame of mind than 45 minutes earlier. Three days later Notts County secured their fifth trip to Wembley in five years when the only goal of the game from Gary Martindale, in the 61st minute, settled the tie 3-2 on aggregate.

Bradford City were to be the opponents on Sunday 26th May. Despite losing the first leg against Blackpool 2-0, they won the away game 3-0 to go through. In events that were later to have repercussions for Notts, Sam Allardyce was fired as manager of Blackpool.

Approximately two thirds of the crowd of a little under 30,000 on Sunday 26th May were from Bradford. They went home the happier as an early goal for the Bantams from Des Hamilton, added to by another from Mark Stallard with fifteen minutes remaining, made it a very disappointing afternoon in London for the Gyles family.

On other matters, I had tried to get tickets for Scotland's three group games in the 1996 European Championships. I was unsuccessful until late in the day a business contact came up trumps and I was to be at Villa Park to see the final game against Switzerland. Prior to that, although I hadn't watched either game on television, I knew that a good win over the Swiss would be good enough for progress, providing England defeated Holland in a game that kicked off at the same time.

By all accounts, Scotland had played reasonably well in their opener to earn a draw against the Dutch. Although subsequently beaten 2-0 at Wembley by England, they may well have got something out of the game had David Seaman not fortuitously held up his arm as he fell to the ground, and in so doing, denied Gary McAllister a penalty goal which would have made the score 1-1 at that stage.

That was now history and on 18th June all four teams in the group had a chance of progressing as I headed to Villa Park. Ally McCoist put Scotland in the lead midway through the first half, and with England also winning at half-time, there was still a chance that the Scots might progress. As things stood, England were going through with Scotland and Holland tied in second place. As the Dutch had a better goal difference, they were in the better position but goals scored or conceded in the second half of either game might see that situation change.

Scotland held on to their lead without ever looking as if they might add to it. Meanwhile, England scored three times, and at that point it was Scotland and not Holland who would accompany the host nation to the knock-out stages.

That remained the case for sixteen whole minutes - and the *Tartan Army* were well aware of this in Birmingham - until, and this I have to accept is apocryphal, David Seaman shouted over to Patrick Kluivert, "Here Pat. Through my legs son. We don't want those F****** Jocks to go through, do we?"

And so it came to pass that David Seaman, one of the finest goalkeepers of his generation, allowed a tame shot from the Dutch substitute to beat him.

There was no further scoring in either game, and with Scotland and Holland tied on both same points and goal difference, the number of actual goals scored by either nation was the decider. Holland came out on top using that formula. If there was any consolation, it was that as the tournament was being held in England, individual members of the *Tartan Army* had a very good chance of getting home before the team. The first time that had ever happened!!

Next morning at work, I was first in as usual and had plenty of time to a) cordon off my work station and b) put up signage requesting that no-one discuss football with me. Not that it did me any good. One particularly lovely lady (there were a few) who shared the office, came in later, and knowing that I was really keen on football, but having no full understanding of what she was saying or indeed of where I'd been the previous night, shouted across "Did you see the football Mike? Weren't England wonderful?" She probably still doesn't understand why her colleagues went "Schhhh. Don't say another word!"

Derek Pavis still had faith in Colin Murphy and Steve Thompson and they were in charge when the 1996/97 season got underway. Other than the introduction of Shaun Derry and the return of Phil Robinson, there were no great changes to the squad.

A 2-1 victory over Preston (a game I missed as I was in Malta on a family holiday) was therefore an encouraging start. However, after elimination at the 1st Round stage of the League Cup and only five more League victories before the end of the year, Derek Pavis had a look in the Boardroom drawer for his trusty knife. Sam Allardyce, who had been 'kicking his heels' for the past eight months, would soon become the latest manager given the task of resurrecting the Club.

Two days before Christmas, it came as no surprise to - and indeed was a relief for - the majority of Notts fans that P45's had been issued to Messrs Murphy and Thompson. First team coach, Mark Smith was put in temporary charge until a new appointment was made. As a result of bad weather he was only in charge for three unbeaten games.

1997

The appointment of the new manager was confirmed on 16th January, two days after Notts had managed a creditable 0-0 draw against Aston Villa in a re-arranged home 3rd Round FA Cup Tie. In a rare shaft of light in a season of seemingly endless gloom, Newcastle Town, playing at Stoke's Victoria Ground, and Rochdale at Meadow Lane, had been eliminated to set up the tie.

The Villa game took place on a typically raw Tuesday evening in early January. In addition to Ailsa and Heather, I took a young lady called Sylvie Zockou to her first ever football match. She was French and was spending a few weeks on placement with my employer. During that time she stayed at our house. She's probably one of only a few from the crowd that night who has reason to remember the game. It was poor and almost instantly forgettable for most of us. However, Sylvie kept reminding us that she'd never experienced such cold conditions in her life!

By the time of the replay, Big Sam was in charge and had a fair idea of the problems facing him as Dwight Yorke scored a couple in a 3-0 win for Villa. With the exception of Sean Farrell and Steve Finnan who had now been signed on a permanent basis, he had inherited basically the same set of players that had taken Notts to the Play-Off Final a few months earlier. There was clearly something wrong though, as of twenty two league games played from the turn of the year, Notts won only two and it was not until his sixteenth game in charge that his team secured three points.

He tried all sorts of combinations to improve things with a succession of loan players coming and going and youngsters being given the chance to impress. It was all to no avail however and, ironically after his first win, 2-1 away at York, Notts were effectively relegated with five games of the season remaining. The Club were heading back to where, for me, I'd first found them.

During this run, Allardyce, seemingly resigned to the inevitable, either disposed of a number of players or informed others that they formed no part of his future plans. Significant developments, although we didn't know it at the time, were the signing of Ian Hendon and promotion of Matt Redmile from the youth team. Building blocks for the future were being put in place.

There was a bit of good cheer locally though. Unfortunately, we just witnessed the final game in Chesterfield's memorable run to the FA Cup Semi-Final. With Kevin Davies beginning to blossom, the Spireites had seen off Bury, Scarborough, Bristol City, Bolton Wanderers, Nottingham Forest and Wrexham to reach the last four for the first time in their history. They were to play Middlesbrough at Old Trafford.

It is well recorded that Chesterfield had a second half goal apparently wrongly disallowed. This would have made the score 3-1 in their favour. Middlesbrough came back to lead 3-2 and it needed a late equaliser in extra time to force a replay. The argument around these parts of course is that if the goal 'that never was' had been allowed to stand, Chesterfield would surely have made it to the Final.

In solidarity with fans of the club that is actually located closest to our home, as a family we went to the Hillsborough replay. Sadly, it ended in a 3-0 defeat with the international stars in the Middlesbrough line-up showing their true worth. The fact that the goals were scored by Mikkel Beck, Fabrizio Ravanelli and Emerson tells you all you need to know.

I got a ticket for the Wembley Final against Chelsea and saw Roberto Di Matteo score in the first minute. Middlesbrough never really got into the game although it required a late goal from Eddie Newton to seal the win for Ruud Gullit's side. *NB – how would the Chelsea manager's career have worked out had Jimmy Sirrel been successful in signing him for Notts County from HFC Haarlem back in 1981?* It's worth noting, that in a sign of what was increasingly happening in English football, of the twenty two players who started that Final, only eight were English.

During the summer, Notts had brought Dennis Pearce and Mark Robson from Wolves and Charlton Athletic respectively. Devon White had been re-signed and Craig Dudley, a bit part player from the back end of the previous season, was given a place in the starting line-up. I'm not sure if I speak for many, but there was no sense of optimism in the Gyles household. Season tickets had been renewed simply because 'that's just what we do!'

The opening game of Notts County's first season back in the fourth tier of English football for twenty six years took place on Saturday 9th August 1997. This coincided with the staging of the 5th Ashes Test taking place at Trent Bridge. I left the ground at about 2.45 pm and wandered across the Bridge. Helen and the girls had come down separately. By the time I slipped back into my seat at 5.00pm, I was able to report to my neighbour that Notts were 'joint top of the League'. They'd defeated Rochdale 2-1, but had required a last minute towering header from man mountain Matt Redmile, to achieve the victory.

After eliminating Darlington over two legs, the League Cup run was ended by Tranmere Rovers. Similarly, the FA Cup brought no glory. Having defeated Colwyn Bay in the 1st Round, and secured an away draw at Preston in the next round, Notts were going through to meet one of the big boys - a home tie against Stockport County actually! - in the replay, when David Moyes scored a 90th minute equaliser. Preston scored again in extra-time. The prospect of a third round tie at home to Stockport must have meant much more to them than us!

I didn't see the equaliser as I'd left a couple of minutes earlier to go and pick up my winnings. I'd won the 50/50 Draw! It was around £200 which, given the time of year, was welcome. I did get back to the ground to watch the additional thirty minutes.

Would I rather have done without the money and spent all Christmas looking forward to a game against Stockport County I hear you ask? If I'm honest, probably no. The reason being that Notts were doing so very well in the League. Up to the end of the year, they had lost only three games, and were seven points clear at the top of the Division. Normally, I'd be wanting the Club to be fighting on all fronts, but I was really hoping that this season in the bottom division would be a one-off, and a cup run might have been a distraction.

Ailsa having found other Saturday afternoon attractions - perhaps three relegations in five years had taken their toll! - it was generally Heather accompanying me to home games and the occasional away trip. It was becoming a season to remember.

1998

Notts had ended the old year with five consecutive wins and started the new one with............ five more. The 2-0 win at Field Mill meant a record ten consecutive league victories. That came to an end the following week however, when it needed a last minute equaliser from Gary Jones to salvage a point. At least the unbeaten run was maintained until, after three more wins, Heather and myself stood in a prolonged snow storm, on the open terrace at Moss Rose to see Macclesfield win 2-0. Disappointing though that was, the 16 match unbeaten run had almost certainly sealed promotion. It was not long delayed.

Three more wins and a draw meant that Notts knew that were they to win the home game against Leyton Orient on 28th March, they would be promoted. A Mark Robson goal in the 50th minute was all that was needed. Not only that, results elsewhere meant that Notts were guaranteed finishing in first place. It was the earliest that any club had secured a title since World War 1.

It all felt a bit flat the following Friday when Notts went to Peterborough in a match that had been re-arranged to accommodate the Sky TV cameras. A late goal from Steve Castle gave the Posh a win that they probably deserved.

With five league games remaining, Notts had accumulated 88 points. They could afford to lose one of those games and still reach 100 points. They were not to lose another game, but sadly drew a couple, and had to make do with a final tally of 99. I was devastated!!

Upon reflection, it was a fantastic season, especially given the doom and gloom of only twelve months before. Five league defeats in a season was the fewest that any Notts County team had suffered in their history. The front two of Gary Jones and Sean Farrell had provided over half of the league goals scored. It wasn't just those two however, as there were contributions from all over with fourteen other players scoring.

The clincher for me however, was the on-loan signing of Andy Hughes from Oldham Athletic in February. Now I accept that it may be stretching things just a little, but I remain convinced that I played a key role in bringing him to the Club on a permanent basis. In Paul Smith's comprehensive account of the season in his book *Record Breakers,* he allowed me to indulge myself in that belief with his inclusion of the following article, reproduced below.

With a bit (OK, a large chunk!) of poetic licence

My part in ensuring promotion

Having returned from a very snowy Macclesfield on Saturday 28th February 1998, and seen Notts lose for the first time since they had travelled to Colchester on 18th November 1997, I left work early the following Tuesday to make the trip to Exeter with perhaps a little less confidence than I would otherwise have done. I needn't have worried!

At a very wet and windy St James Park, I saw 20 year old Andy Hughes finally prove that he had what it takes to make it as a professional footballer. The young midfielder, had come on loan from Oldham Athletic in January, but had only made the starting line-up twice prior to that night. Sitting just behind the dug outs with the Exeter supporters, I witnessed a masterclass in energetic midfield play. Here was a guy who could replace the recently departed Shaun Derry.

Inspired by an all action display from the youngster, Notts were 2-0 up after ten minutes then 3-0 up towards the end of the first half. Exeter made a fight of things, but when Gary Jones made the score 5-2 towards the end of the game to secure the points, I decided to make an early start on the long journey home. As I came down from the stand I shouted out in my broad Scottish accent, "Sam, Sam...................yiv jist goat tae sign Andy Hughes!!"

Those Grecians with whom I'd been watching the game might have been a little surprised at this measured (my opinion, not theirs) outburst, but they were not alone. Big Sam turned to see who had proffered this excellent piece of advice and gave a look that might best be described as part admiration, part disdain.

Whatever, two days later, the Club announced that they had permanently signed Andy Hughes and the following Saturday he scored the second goal in a routine 2-0 victory over Barnet. Before the end of the month, with my hero now 'the first name on the team sheet', Notts had not only won promotion, but were crowned Champions.

People might argue otherwise - and if they do, I don't care! - but I'm convinced that having persuaded Big Sam to sign the 20 year old, who subsequently went on to score 17 goals in 117 League appearances for the Club, I was instrumental in finding the 'final piece of the jigsaw' in that memorable season.

See, I told you!

There were a couple more individual games from 1997/98 that stand out. The first of these was on 10th January, when the away win at Rochdale was the Club's 4,000[th] league fixture. They were the first English club to achieve that milestone.

The second was on 14th March when I finally qualified for membership of the 92 Club. At the beginning of the season there was only one of the 92 clubs in the four senior divisions that I had yet to visit. Well, if there was one bit of good news following relegation, it was that Notts would be visiting that club, Macclesfield Town, who had just won promotion from the Conference and replaced Hereford United.

Knowing this, I made contact with the founder of the Club, a Bristol Rovers fan called Gordon Pearce, who having visited every Football League ground in England and Wales as far back as 1966, decided to set up an organisation open to others who had achieved this feat. Not many had qualified back then, but by 1997 this exclusive club had just over 1,000 members.

Gordon wrote back to me and said that in order to qualify, members had to have seen a competitive game at all 92 grounds currently in use. This reasonable condition meant that I had not only to make my planned visit to Moss Rose, but had also to include the Deva Stadium (Chester City) and the Riverside (Middlesbrough). I'd attended games at both club's old grounds but not the more recently built stadia.

Chester was not a problem as they were also playing in the fourth tier. However, I had to look for a convenient date to get up to Teeside. Another issue was the availability of tickets. Middlesbrough, under Bryan Robson, were going for promotion and were attracting big crowds. I had luck on my side as Middlesbrough had a match v Tranmere Rovers re-arranged for mid-week, and following an explanatory phone call with their secretary, I was fixed up with a ticket. Amongst a crowd of 29,540 I saw the home team win 3-0. More importantly, I could tick off another box.

So it was then, that a late Gary Jones goal having secured a 1-0 win at the Deva Stadium, I was able to return from Chester happy with another away victory, but also in the knowledge that I had now qualified for membership of an exclusive group.

Gordon had advised me that in order to verify my claim I had to supply a list of the grounds I'd visited, adding the date, competition and score. Well, for me that was a piece of cake. I knew that the list of games attended that I'd initiated (and maintained ever since) when baby-sitting all those years ago would come in handy at some time in the future. I had more than enough detail to summarise and survive any forensic scrutiny.

So that was it then. What a year. A record breaking promotion campaign, topped off by finally becoming a member of the 92 Club. Had all of my footballing good luck been used up in the past few months? Well, possibly not, as there was still the 1998 World Cup in France to look forward to. Scotland (& their fans) were once again gracing the tournament with their brand of hopeless optimism and I was going to be one of them.

Helen and myself had now settled into a routine. Every four years we'd have a holiday in whatever part of the world was staging the World Cup Finals, and the fact that Scotland had qualified for this one was a bonus. Getting tickets might be a problem, but where there's a will................! This year however, I learned some valuable lessons.

The draw was made in December and I knew then that we'd be visiting Paris, Bordeaux and Saint Etienne. I can't remember who advised me but I was put in touch with an organisation called Portland (something or other), who were promoting the fact that they could supply tickets for any match taking place in France in the forthcoming tournament. They sent me a sheet with an accompanying properly headed letter. This was effectively a price list and all I was asked to do was select the games of my choice.

From memory, there was a limit of two tickets per game, but this was not a problem for me. I could see that the tickets were priced at more than face value but that also was not an issue. I'm a man of the world and understood that Portland would have running costs. The key thing for me was the fact that I could guarantee having them and be able to cross the Channel in a few months' time, confident that I'd be seeing Brazil, Norway and Morocco. I rang them up and paid for two tickets for each game at a total cost of £600 and was assured that tickets would be sent out to me well in advance of the opening game. This just happened to be Brazil v Scotland.

Helen and I worked out an itinerary, and with Scotland's last game in Saint Etienne, we thought we could probably pull in a visit to see Sylvia Zockou and her family at their home in nearby Lyon. We expected that she would have fully thawed out by then!

185

I got in touch and set it up. Sylvie was happy to meet up with us again and said that she'd arrange for us to both explore and spend a night in France's third largest city. Well the timing meant that we would be in that city when the USA were due to play Iran in a group game. As a result of political tensions between the two, this was an intriguing tie. I got in touch with Portland (something or other) and gave them a further £200 for a pair of tickets for this particular game. You can see where this is going can't you? Well, you'll be right!

With all travel and accommodation booked and paid for, we were looking forward to our first holiday on our own for nearly twenty years. All that was missing was the package containing the eagerly awaited tickets.

I rang a couple of times and was told to be patient and assured that there were no problems. The guy I was talking to - and I found this re-assuring as it was always the same chap - even suggested in the second call that I might be interested in some other games that had just become available. How naïve was I?

After a couple more calls in mid-May I got the distinct impression that I was being fobbed off. Something incidentally, that Helen had been thinking for a while! I was still not prepared to accept the inevitable, but on Thursday 4th June, five days before we set off, as I collected 3 x week's coupons, I heard TV news reports regarding a London based ticketing agency that had been wound up as part of a criminal investigation.

My only hope was that this was about another agency. It surely couldn't have been mine. Had that nice young fella been telling me lies all along? When I got home however, Helen broke the news to me as gently as she knew how to and I had to face up to the reality. My initial reaction was that we shouldn't go, but I soon changed my mind. We'd booked and paid for everything and would go and have a nice holiday touring parts of France we'd never visited before. Besides, if I kept my eyes and ears open, I might just hear of the odd 'spare' becoming available.

The day before the opening game we set off, crossed the Channel - there was the equivalent of a battalion of the *Tartan Army* on board the ferry - and reached Paris late that evening. After an overnight stay in a hotel to the south of the city, we used the Metro the following morning to see what was happening. If all else failed we could watch the game on a big screen at one of the fan zones we'd been promised were being set up.

We got off at Hotel du Ville, climbed up to street level and immediately came across a guy with a couple of 'spares'. Was this another of my lucky days? Well, not when he told me how much they were. "£300", I repeated, "is that for the pair?" When he told me that no, that was for each ticket, I realised that I was beaten.

We went to the big square and enjoyed the atmosphere. There was a fair bit of alcohol available and in the warm Paris sunshine everyone seemed to be enjoying themselves. Brazil took an early lead but a John Collins penalty brought the sides level, and at half time the general consensus amongst the crowd there (90% Scottish) was "Wir dain' a' right!" A Tom Boyd own goal with quarter of an hour remaining was disappointing, but we all went our separate ways at the end of the game thinking that with Norway and Morocco to come, a similar level of performance would see us progress.

After another night in Paris, Helen and I headed south west. We pulled in a couple of nights in a small farm that offered a chambres d'hotes service. We were made part of the family and it was there, on that first night, with the non-English speaking man of the house, that I watched France's first game of the tournament. They won comfortably, beating South Africa 3-0. The key memory however is of seeing Thierry Henry for the first time. He was clearly a player who would become more widely known.

Scotland's next game was in Bordeaux, and in anticipation of this we'd booked a week-long stay in a gite near to a little village called Blaye on the eastern (right) bank of the Gironde Estuary. It was perfect.

With little prospect of getting a ticket on the day of the Norway game, we made straight for the fan zone. Once again, the atmosphere was all very civilised and friendly. There weren't many Norwegians there but that didn't seem to matter. Again, Scotland had to come from behind and needed a Craig Burley second half goal to gain a draw. Still, working on the reasonable assumption that Norway would not beat Brazil, all Scotland had to do now was to defeat Morocco in a week's time and, at the eighth attempt, they would reach the knock-out stages of a World Cup.

For the next seven days we enjoyed our remaining time in and around Blaye and then headed east for, amongst other delights, a guided tour of Lyon before arriving at our last pre-booked stay in the mountains of the Massif Central overlooking Saint Etienne.

We just had the two nights in this village. Shame really - it was idyllic. On that first morning, after a spot of exploring, the plan was to head straight to the city. The rationale being that if there were any tickets going spare in Saint Etienne we had to give ourselves the best possible opportunity of getting them, and to achieve that, we had to be there.

We parked up, and just to get our bearings, headed to the ground. There were a few people hanging around the Stadium, none of whom appeared to be either Scottish or Moroccan, which seemed a bit strange. As it was still a full eight hours before kick-off, there seemed to be no logic to this. I suggested to Helen that we'd nothing to lose by having a walk round the ground with me posing the occasional question "Avez-vous des billets?" to anyone we passed.

Having completed a circuit, and had nothing but blank stares or Gallic shrugs, we began to head up the hill and into town, when we heard a shout "Allez, Monsieur!" and turned round to see a guy beckoning me back. He produced a ticket for that night's game and asked if I wanted it. Seemed like a futile question, but to be fair to him, he didn't know me. "Aye, I do. Hoo much, an' hiv yi no goat anither yin?" I asked in my best French. When he told me he'd just got the one, and he was only asking face value, I looked pleadingly at Helen and she gave her approval/permission. Not knowing who to kiss first, I chickened out and simply gave 'mon ami' his money.

I suggested that if we couldn't get another, Helen stay safe in the car whilst the game was taking place. She was having none of that and said she'd prefer to watch the game in the fan zone and I could meet up with her there once Scotland had qualified.

We spent the day in the centre of Saint Etienne as the city was gradually taken over by tartan clad 'tourists'. It was a joyous afternoon with the locals joining in. Even the gendarmerie, who were there in force, entered into the spirit of the occasion.

The central square slowly filled up with supporters, until about 6.30pm the sound of bagpipes indicated that it was time for the *'Army'* to begin the march. Before setting off, I called home from a coin box to make sure that the girls would be watching on TV - although 17 & 15 respectively, their Mama (Helen's mum) had gone over to Newton to keep an eye on them - and the sense of excitement and level of anticipation, not to mention the skirl of the pipes, travelled over 1,000 miles.

Having agreed exactly where I would meet Helen after the game, and making sure once more that she was comfortable with the situation, I gave her a kiss, bid her goodbye and joined the ranks. Normally we'd have had a thirty minute journey, but the pace was slow and it must have been near 7.30pm when we approached the ground and fans started looking to see which entrance they needed. It was then that I realised, I hadn't got my ticket. I'd given it to Helen for safe keeping and forgot to ask for it before setting off.

I'm not sure what the locals made of the lone Scotsman who appeared to be 'swimming against the tide' as I quickly ran back into town with helpful compatriots telling me "Yir gaein the wrang way son!" Helen was exactly where I'd left her and gave me a knowing look before saying coyly, "I knew you'd be back!" Clutching my precious ticket tightly, I ran all the way back.

189

As I'm sure you're aware, the game did not follow the script. Scotland were an embarrassment and lost 3-0. As it happens, even a victory would not have been enough to see them progress. Norway scored two late goals to beat Brazil and Scotland finished bottom of the group. "Ach weel", as they say in Saint Etienne, "C'est la vie!"

With thousands of other disappointed Scots, I left the ground and made my way back up to town. Helen had spent the evening with many ticketless Scots in the square and said she'd been fine. There had been a lot of drink consumed, which wouldn't have been a surprise to her, but the philosophic and resigned mood of the supporters after such a defeat did. She said that one Scot had come up to her after the game, and probably not quite sure what day it was, gave her a kiss. When Helen thanked him, he looked at her in amazement and said, "Ach, I didnae ken yi wir English!"

I have not seen Scotland play since that night, 23rd June 1998, and have vowed that I won't again until they qualify for a major tournament. On the few occasions that any of their matches have been shown on TV south of the Border, I've not watched. A couple of times I've recorded the game with a view to possibly watching later, but only if I know I'm going to enjoy it. I never have, which tells you a little about my philosophy, but probably an awful lot more about the state of Scottish international football.

It was about 1.30am when we got back to our village in the mountains. Sadly, we had to leave fairly early so didn't really get the chance to make more of that spot. It's on my list of 'we must go back sometime' places. Regardless of how the football had worked out, it was a very good holiday, and with our appetite fully whetted, on the long journey up through France, we discussed how we'd get to either Japan or South Korea in four years' time.

A few months later I just happened to notice in the local paper that a guy, originally from Derby, was looking for volunteers to correspond with any of the Japanese students that he was teaching in Fukuoka prefecture. He effectively wanted pen pals to help develop and improve their written English. Well, how could I not take advantage of that?

There were a number of changes to the Notts County squad as they begun life back in the 3rd tier on 8th August. The key departure was Phil Robinson and while Mark Robson remained, he was not to start another game for the Club. Newcomers included, Gary Owers, Shaun Murray, Chris Fairclough, Richard Liburd, Chris Billy, Fran Tierney and Duane Darby. The last named, having broken a leg, had to wait until the following season before making his debut.

The changes didn't seem to make too much difference in the opening game at Oldham Athletic. Goals from Ian Richardson and a double from Sean Farrell had Notts leading 3-0 at half time. The final score was 3-1, and we 'Pies travelled back over the Pennines wondering if we might just have another memorable nine months.

We were soon to find out that we were not, as following a 9-1 aggregate defeat (Heather joined me at Maine Road for the 7-1 mauling in the second leg) in the first round of the League Cup, Notts had gained only five further league victories by the turn of the year. At that stage, they sat only one place above the relegation quartet and the feel good factor that had enveloped Meadow Lane just five months before had evaporated.

Big Sam operated a revolving door policy during those early months, Chris Billy and Chris Fairclough were fairly quickly discarded and the Club cashed in on Steve Finnan by selling him to Fulham for £600,000. A succession of players came in on loan but it increasingly looked as if Allardyce's success of the previous season was a 'one off'.

Having become a 92 Club member in March, I had an immediate problem in strictly complying with the qualification criteria. Four clubs had moved from their crumbling old grounds into new all seater stadia, and in order to maintain true 92 Club status, these had to be visited. Fortunately, one of them, Pride Park, was just down the road and another, Stoke City's Britannia Stadium, would be visited by Notts County during the course of the season. To complete the set though, I had to make special visits to pull in the Reebok (Bolton W) and the Stadium of Light (Sunderland). Heather, and her boyfriend of the time (a Sunderland fan), joined me on that trip to the north east of England.

There was some good news as 1998 drew to a close. On 22nd December I was one of 1,109 spectators at Meadow Lane. We'd been drawn to the ground by the exciting prospect of a 1st Round match in the Auto Windscreen Trophy. The game itself, which ended as a 1-0 victory for Hull City, will live long in the memory of those who were there, as for most, it was their first chance to see the emerging talent of 15 year old Jermaine Pennant.

He came on as a substitute with twenty minutes remaining, and even in that short period, it was clear that he was a player who had far too much talent to be playing at this level. I went in to work the following day and said that I'd seen a player who would be sold for over £1,000,000 in the future. I was laughed at - no problem for me, as I was used to it - but after another substitute appearance in the FA Cup early next year, he was transferred to Arsenal for a reported £2,000,000.

He had played a total 42 minutes in a Notts shirt and should have gone on to bigger and greater things. Unfortunately for him, there were apparently character flaws, and despite further big money moves he never made full use of his undoubted talent.

In the FA Cup, after beating both Hendon and Wigan Athletic (this one on penalties) in replays, Notts were through to the 3rd Round. We had the short trip to Bramall Lane to face Sheffield United from the Division above to look forward to in the New Year.

1999

Following a draw in Sheffield, the Meadow Lane replay was twice postponed and eventually took place on what should have been 4th Round Day. Winning 3-1 with seven minutes remaining, it looked as if Notts had booked themselves a home tie with Cardiff City. It wasn't to be. The Blades scored twice in those remaining minutes, and then once more in extra-time to go through and leave Notts with the sole objective for the rest of the season of avoiding relegation.

With six defeats out of seven games played since 28th December, the team slipped to second bottom before a run of four straight wins saw them climb six places. This run broadly speaking coincided with the acquisition of Paul Bolland, Mark Warren, Peter Beadle, Kevin Rapley, Gerry Creaney and subsequently, Mark Stallard.

There were a few ups and downs before the season came to an end, but Notts managed to steer clear of the relegation spots to finish in 16th place, four points above the drop zone.

Around this time there were rumours circulating that the Club was haemorrhaging money and Derek Pavis was looking to sell. When a group of 'Pies heard from reliable sources the identity of a potential purchaser, they objected and set up the Save Notts Action Group, (SNAG) to protest. Whether or not this group was instrumental in what followed is open to conjecture. What is a fact however, is that the Club, whilst not sold on this occasion remained 'on the market' and fans had to come to terms with two decades of ongoing concern over Notts County's continuing viability.

With new signings Clayton Blackmore and Craig Ramage and Duane Darby finally making his debut, initially as substitute alongside Mark Stallard, Notts were unbeaten in their first six league games of the 1999/00 season. They had also seen off Bury in the League Cup before losing for the first time that season away at Cardiff City. They lost again the following week, at home to Bristol Rovers, and were knocked out of the League Cup by Huddersfield Town before winning five consecutive league games to reach the top of the Division. By now though, Gary Brazil was in caretaker charge.

There had been rumours circulating that Sam Allardyce was being tapped up to take on the vacant manager's position at Bolton Wanderers. There was no smoke without fire and a few days after a 3-1 away win at Bury, Big Sam resigned, stating 'personal reasons'. A few days later he was installed as manager at the Reebok. It left a bitter taste in my mouth, and I've been a bit wary about the character of the man ever since. It would appear that I'm not alone.

Whatever, life goes on. Despite the loan signings of Nick Fenton, Danny Allsopp and Brett Angell, and Gary Brazil being given the role on a permanent basis, Notts were unable to maintain their lofty position and, come the end of December, were just outside the play-off positions, in 7th place.

Chapter 11

1990's – tennis, athletics and....more cricket

With working 60+ hours a week (in addition to Pools collection of course) for the first half of the decade, and with two girls rapidly developing into young (non-driving) ladies, there wasn't an awful lot of time in the 1990's for attending live sport other than football, and whenever possible, the annual Test Match.

Having said that, it was Ailsa and Heather's growing interest in wider sporting pursuits that led me to seeing some sports for the first time. Each year, a teacher from their secondary school arranged for a bus to travel down to London for the opening day of the tournament held at the home of The All England Lawn Tennis & Croquet Club. Wimbledon to most of us! Interested pupils were invited to attend with parents encouraged to come along too to help with supervision. Ailsa and two of her mates (Lucy and Sarah) were up for it. So was I.

There was no advance purchase of tickets and the tradition was that, once dropped off, we'd all join the queue of those who were hoping to gain entry to the outside courts. This seemed a bit hit and miss to me but I needn't have worried. As we took our place on a beautiful sunny morning in June 1993, at the back of a few hundred who were already there, it was clear from overhearing conversations that this was nothing unusual.

Once inside the grounds, I suggested to the girls that we seek somewhere we could call base for the day, and I found some free seats on the back row of one of the outside courts. This had the advantage of a seat for the day and a good view of whatever games were scheduled. As a bonus, if we stood up, we could look behind us and see the scoreboard and a little of the action on an adjacent court.

We only saw two of the men's singles matches to take place that day. Wayne Ferreira (South Africa) defeated Roberto Azar (Argentina) in straight sets. Ferreira was seeded 13 and would progress to the 4th Round where he lost to Jim Courier.

The other game was closer and eventually went to five sets. Unfortunately, we had to leave at the end of the fourth to catch the bus. Well, I can now confirm to Ailsa, Lucy and Sarah, should they ever read this, that Stephane Simian (France) won that final set 6-3 to come from 2-1 behind to eliminate the American, Richey Reneberg.

Two years later, all four of us went up to Sheffield to see the Bupa International Games athletics meeting at Don Valley Stadium. In truth there weren't many internationals present and the afternoon was essentially a final competitive run out for many of the British athletes prior to the World Championships due to begin two weeks later in Gothenburg.

Many of the British stars of the day were there however, and we witnessed Jonathan Edwards win the triple jump, a young Kelly Holmes win an invitational 1,000 metres and Linford Christie the 100 metres. Three weeks later, we collectively cheered as, on television, we watched Edwards break the world record in Sweden whilst staying in a B&B in Newcastle, Co Down.

A combination of our family footballing World Cup trips and Trent Bridge not being selected as a venue, meant that Dad could only come down from Arbroath twice for his cricketing holiday.

West Indies toured England in 1991 and England were 1-0 up in the five match series when the 3rd Test took place at Trent Bridge on Thursday 4th July. I managed both the Friday and Saturday. Dad had enjoyed a good first day, watching a century opening stand between Graham Gooch and Mike Atherton. This was somewhat wasted however, and I entered Trent Bridge the following morning with the score at 269/8.

All out for 300, they had West Indies in a bit of trouble at 45/3 but they recovered to reach 262/5 by Friday evening. Although start of play was delayed on the Saturday morning following what felt like a tropical thunderstorm, West Indies took a firm grip, secured a first innings lead of 97 and then had England at 54/3 in reply at close of play.

When play resumed after the rest day, it was only spirited knocks from England's numbers 9/10/11 that took the game into a fifth day. West Indies were comfortable winners by nine wickets to level the Series which ultimately ended as a 2-2 draw.

Disappointing for Dad, but he saw every ball and appeared to enjoy himself. He did at least (as did I) see a bit of history as Richard Illingworth made his England debut, and with his first ball, bowled Phil Simmons. At the time, he was only the eleventh bowler in over 100 years of Test cricket to achieve that feat.

When Australia arrived in Nottingham for the 3rd of a six match series in 1993, they were already 2-0 up and Shane Warne had arrived on the international stage. England gave debuts to four players (Mark Lathwell, Graham Thorpe, Martin McCague and Mark Ilott) in the hope that they could win (or at least draw) this Test to retain a slim chance of regaining the Ashes.

Again, I just managed the Friday and Saturday, and was reasonably satisfied with England's 276/6 at the start of the second day. *NB – 12 year old Ailsa also attended on this day on a trip organised by her school's PE Teacher. I bought her a score book and showed her the rudiments of scoring. To this day, I don't think she's ever been back to Trent Bridge, or any other cricket ground come to think of it.*

Australia were similarly placed at 262/5 at the close and this was shaping up to be the most competitive Test of the series to date. However, with 101 from David Boon, Australia gained a first innings lead of 52 and had England at effectively 69/4 when play ended on the Saturday. It looked as if Australia could celebrate both winning the Test and retaining the Ashes at some time on Monday.

When Dad got back after the fourth day, he was anticipating an England victory as they had added a further 240 runs for the loss of only two more wickets. Graham Gooch had scored 120, and with Graham Thorpe completing a maiden century in his first Test, England declared on Tuesday morning, setting Australia an unlikely 370 to win. At 115/6 England were in the driving seat, but an unbroken seventh wicket stand of 87 between Steve Waugh and Brendon Julian ensured the draw.

England did win the final Test at the Oval but this was late consolation in a 4-1 series defeat.

1993 was the last time I was able to accompany Dad to cricket. We had planned that he come down for the first Test of the 1995 series with the West Indies. As Trent Bridge was not being used that summer, we were to go to Headingley for the first time and I booked tickets for us both for all five days. Unfortunately, Dad's own personal innings came to a close in early February.

With the exception of one day, I had no problem in getting people to accompany me to Leeds. The one day that I didn't, I sold the spare ticket to a guy outside the ground. Not long after play had started a chap came and sat next to me. We got talking and I asked if he didn't mind telling me what he'd paid for his ticket. I wasn't surprised, but he was disappointed, to hear that he'd paid £20 for a ticket I'd sold barely an hour before for a tenner.

Although West Indies won that opening Test by nine wickets, I'd achieved one of my ambitions viz. to see every ball of a Test from Day 1 through to conclusion, and England did come back later that summer to draw the Series.

England defeated India 1-0 in the three match series in 1996 with Trent Bridge staging the final match. On a pitch that may have been carefully designed to ensure such an outcome, it was a high scoring draw. In the first innings, India were 288/2 but then collapsed (?) and were all out for 521. England were 360/1, but like India, they also 'collapsed' and managed a paltry 564 to gain a lead of 43. Although Mark Ealham took four wickets in the Indian second innings, there was insufficient time to force a positive result.

The Aussies returned in 1997 and secured a 3-2 series win. It had all started so well with England winning the 1st Test at Edgbaston. By the time both teams came to Trent Bridge in August however, the Ashes had been retained by Australia and England had to win the last two Tests to salvage a drawn series. Sadly, England capitulated within four days.

In the five match series with the South Africans in 1998, Trent Bridge had been allocated the fourth Test. This took place in late July with England already 1-0 down. They needed to win both this and the final Test at Headingley to take the series.

On the Thursday, the new Radcliffe Road Stand, which had been officially opened by Sir (he had been knighted in 1975) Garry Sobers the previous day, was unveiled to a wider audience. To commemorate this momentous occasion I treated myself to a seat in this stand. It cost me an arm and a leg but WTH, for all we know, we're only on this planet once. Besides, it gave me an excellent view of Andrew Flintoff making his debut.

Alec Stewart, captaining England in his first series, asked South Africa to bat. Flintoff took just the one wicket but Darren Gough and Angus Fraser shared the other nine between them. Despite their success, as a result of Hansie Cronje's 126 and contributions from elsewhere, the South Africans made a very useful 374 in their first innings.

With an opening stand of 145 from Mike Atherton and Mark Butcher, England looked as if they might take a first innings lead. However, Allan Donald took five wickets and they fell short of that, conceding a deficit of 38.

England did make good headway when the South Africans batted again and by close of play on the Saturday, they were 92/3. With no rest day, the game was finely poised and Sunday would prove pivotal. With

Fraser taking another five wickets and Dominic Cork four (Flintoff was wicketless), the South Africans had a late order collapse and by mid-afternoon, England were batting again needing 247 to win and square the series.

The duel that followed between Allan Donald and the England top order, Mike Atherton in particular, was Test cricket at its best. Despite being clearly out, caught behind, Atherton didn't walk and the umpire was unmoved. The bowler was incensed and his mood was not improved when he later had Nasser Hussain edging behind but had to stand, hands on hips in disbelief, when the wicketkeeper, Mark Boucher, dropped the ball. At close of play, England still needed 139 to win, but with nine wickets in hand, they were now the favourites.

I was back at work on the Monday, but like most of my colleagues, was kept well informed of how the chase was progressing and of how England, for the loss of only Hussain, won by eight wickets. Atherton was there at the end, unbeaten on 98*.

For the record, England won another tight and tense Test Match up in Leeds. On the final morning, the South Africans needed a further 34 runs for victory, with two wickets in hand. They only managed ten more and England had come from behind to win 2-1. What a series!

1999, a year in which the 7th World Cup was held in England was memorable for me for three cricketing reasons.

Christmas 1998 saw Helen provide me with probably the best Christmas surprise I can recall receiving. She had purchased joint membership for the two of us for Trent Bridge for the coming summer. What a woman! This not only gave us preferential access to forthcoming World Cup games but to any domestic cricket the following summer. As I said, what a woman.

With Scotland having qualified for the tournament, I had already acquired tickets for their second group game against Pakistan, scheduled for Chester-le-Street. Now, as a Nottinghamshire member, I bought tickets for the one Group A, and two Super Six games being staged at Trent Bridge.

The World Cup meant that there was insufficient time to hold a major Test series in 1999. New Zealand were visiting however, and were scheduled to play four Tests. Trent Bridge was not to be used so I applied for tickets for Lord's, a ground I'd passed many times and even once had a mid-winter walk round, but that I'd never been in. I was lucky, and succeeded in getting tickets for the first three days of the 2nd Test. I was positively purring and eagerly looking forward to the summer of 1999. I wasn't disappointed.

Although Scotland had their moments, and had Pakistan at 92/5 in their innings, they couldn't prevent them reaching 261. Shoaib Akhtar's opening burst had the Scots reply in ruins at 19/5. They recovered slightly, but were well beaten in this game, and unlike their footballing counterparts, couldn't claim that they were eliminated from the tournament by the narrowest of margins. A record of played five, lost five, speaks for itself.

Of the games in Nottingham, England easily disposed of Zimbabwe, and New Zealand overcame India, a game that they were very much in control of whilst chasing 251. There was just the one thriller. South Africa needed 41 runs from 27 balls when they lost their seventh wicket. Lance Klusener then hit out to secure victory with a full over remaining.

England were to lose the Lord's Test allowing New Zealand to level a series they would go on to win 2-1. Yes, that was disappointing, particularly as England had got off to a good start - they were 102/2 at one stage - before six wickets from Chris Cairns saw them collapse to 186 all out. Chris Read, then 20 years of age, unquestionably the best wicketkeeper in the country and playing in only his second Test, was embarrassingly bowled without scoring as he ducked a full length ball. From that moment on, his Test future was forever clouded in doubt.

With Matthew Horne making exactly 100, the Kiwis showed more grit and built a match winning lead of 172. Although England, minus captain Nasser Hussain who had broken a finger, batted a bit better in their second innings, as we left the ground on the Saturday evening, only one result looked likely. We did witness however, some men in brightly coloured blazers in the Lord's Pavilion performing a weird form of rain dance. Their ploy didn't work, and as we drove home on the Sunday, the weather was fine and New Zealand wrapped up an easy victory by nine wickets.

Still, the experience was worth it and with Helen having enjoyed a Pimms and a salmon and cream cheese baguette, I wasn't the only one looking forward to heading back to the 'home of cricket' again in the near future. *NB – after that Christmas surprise, money was no object when it came to rewarding my wife. It's a good job it wasn't because those Lord's' treats came at eye watering prices!*

Chapter 12

Noughties - roller coaster ride (Part 3)

<u>2000</u>

The new decade/millennium began with just Helen and myself (& occasionally me on my own) travelling to games. That was no problem to me and I knew that once teenage activities and interests took precedence, Ailsa & Heather would find other things to amuse themselves.

Notts continued to flirt with the play-offs until a winless run of eight games (six defeats) ended the season. Mark Stallard and Andy Hughes (I knew he would be) were the stand out performers as the season drifted to a close. There were rumours concerning Gary Brazil's future as manager but one development was confirmed. Derek Pavis announced that he had found a buyer for the Club and that he personally would stand down as Chairman. We supporters were however, left hanging on for more news.

That last home game of the season was a particularly memorable one for me. It took place on my 50th birthday, and Helen - have I indicated what a woman she is? - had arranged for a box for the day. I was chauffeur driven down to the ground by my old mate John Olney, and met up with some old and new friends and colleagues at Meadow Lane. It was such a good afternoon, despite the 2-2 draw with Bury, that it was a shame that we had to break off from our enjoyment, to occasionally watch the game as it took place out on the pitch below us.

Cheltenham Town had been promoted to the Football League in this particular year, and in accordance with my 92 Club commitments, I'd spent the previous nine months seeing when I might be able to pull in a visit to their ground. Wycombe Wanderers' boss, Lawrie Sanchez, did me a favour when he requested that his club's home gave v Notts, scheduled for the Saturday of Easter weekend, be brought forward a day to Good Friday. A check of the fixture list confirmed that there was a home game at Whaddon Road on the Saturday. A quick chat with Helen followed and we booked a weekend stay in Cheltenham, arriving from Derbyshire via Wycombe on the Friday night. Job done!

The final game of the 99/00 season for us was the Aston Villa v Chelsea FA Cup Final on 20th May. It was the last Final to be held at the old Wembley. In truth, that was the only memorable thing about it, as in an extremely dull game, we neutrals were thankful for a Roberto Di Matteo second half goal for ensuring that we were spared extra-time. To reinforce a point I made about an earlier Cup Final, Chelsea had just one Englishman, captain Dennis Wise, in their starting eleven.

Jocky Scott was appointed Notts County manager during the close season. His new signings included Ian Hamilton, Frenchman David Joseph and Australian Andy McDermott. After three wins from the first five league games, Notts sat 4th in the table and all seemed well. It didn't last. They had slipped to 16th by November and it was only the departure of Alex Dyer, Matt Redmile and Craig Ramage, to be replaced by Nick Fenton, Anders Jacobsen and later Danny Allsopp that arrested the slide.

Mark Stallard and Danny Allsopp worked well together, and by the end of the year, following a last minute winner at Millwall, Notts were a much more comfortable 10th. In the FA Cup, they had overcome Gravesend & Northfleet and then Wigan Athletic after a replay, to earn a 3rd Round tie away at (2nd Tier) Wimbledon. Things appeared to be picking up.

Just before the end of the year, we fans became aware of a deal being agreed between Derek Pavis and Peter Storrie, formerly Chief Executive of Southend United. Partly financing the proposed deal was Albert Scardino, an American journalist who as a result of being married to Marjorie, a very successful businesswoman, described himself as her 'trailing spouse'. The apparently very complicated deal was agreed with Pavis remaining in charge in the interim until the money was forthcoming. Fans were not sure what to make of all this, but continued to turn up, albeit in reduced numbers.

I missed two of Notts away games in the early months of 00/01 as I made my first trip to the Withdean Stadium to see Brighton in their new, though still temporary home, upon their return from exile in Gillingham, and to Aggborough to see newly promoted Kidderminster Harriers. I took (& still do) my 92 Club membership seriously!

2001

Notts played two more games in that season's FA Cup. To be more precise, they played 261 minutes but still didn't reach the 4th Round. The reward for goals from Andy Hughes and Mark Stallard at Selhurst Park was a replay with Wimbledon at Meadow Lane three weeks later.

The first attempt at a replay was abandoned six minutes into the second half with the score at 1-1. Richard Liburd had given Notts a first half lead, but just as fog began to envelop Meadow Lane, and with half time approaching, Wimbledon equalised. During the break, as visibility worsened, we suspected that abandonment was highly likely. We were right, and referee Peter Walton called it off soon after the restart.

The second attempt at a replay took place on the Saturday of the 4th Round. It was scoreless in ninety minutes and again in extra-time until, with 119 minutes on the clock, Wimbledon scored. In total, from Round 1, Notts had played 531 minutes of FA Cup football. For some teams in the top two divisions, that would have been almost enough for them to have reached the Final.

There was one other abandonment at Meadow Lane before the end of the season. As I travelled down the M1, I could see the blackest of black clouds to the south of the city. That looks like rain thought I, although I hadn't realised just how right I was. The game got underway with the aforementioned cloud now directly overhead. No sooner had Wycombe (the opposition that night) kicked off, than it appeared as if someone up in the sky had opened a sluice gate and allowed the heavens to open. Within three minutes, the players were off the pitch, never to return.

This was a Wednesday night, and as it was late April, quickly rescheduled for the following night. That meant that either many devout

Littlewoods Pools clients, who for years had been telling me that 'I've been doing these since 1938 (or whatever) and never had a drag' would be disappointed, or I'd have to miss the game. I had responsibilities and couldn't/didn't let them down, and as Notts lost 2-0, I apparently didn't miss much.

You've probably guessed that as I'm spending time recalling abandonments, there was not a great deal happening on the pitch. You'd be right. Although Notts had finished in 8th place again, some punters were getting a bit disgruntled and making their views known about the style of football being played under Jocky Scott. I didn't agree with them and thought that, given the Club's resources, Notts were probably punching above their weight.

During the close season, the manager was given some money and brought in Steve Mildenhall (replacing Darren Ward who had moved to the City Ground), Darren Caskey, Marcel Cas, Kevin Nicholson and the returning Ian Baraclough.

Early season results were mixed and not helped by the rather expensive (for Notts at any rate) signing of Tony Hackworth from Leeds United. Described as an attacking midfielder, his goals return made the money spent on Tony Agana ten years earlier seem like a sound investment. The unfortunate Hackworth would go on to score one goal in fifty-four (many as substitute) appearances for the Club.

This will not have pleased the new owners and when inconsistent results were combined with a fractious relationship with the Club's owners and fans, Mr Scott's days were numbered. He packed his bags in October and Gary Brazil once more took over on a temporary basis.

The only positive thing that can be said about his second spell as caretaker, is that results did at least become consistent. Notts won only one of his first fourteen games in charge, and by the end of the year, the Club were in 21st position and heading back to the bottom division.

There was no respite in any of the cup competitions either. After a 4-3 victory away to Mansfield in the 1st Round of the League Cup, a game in which Danny Allsopp hit a hat-trick and more surprisingly, goalkeeper

Steve Mildenhall scored a goal, Notts were eliminated following a 4-2 home defeat to Manchester City. *NB – this was a game that Helen and myself questioned whether or not we should attend. It was 11th September 2001!*

Having overcome Cambridge United after a replay, Notts lost badly away to Wycombe Wanderers in the 2nd Round of the FA Cup. Yes, there was not a lot of good cheer around Meadow Lane that Christmas.

2002

Although there was no immediate lifting of the doom and gloom, the year began with the encouraging news of the permanent appointment of a replacement manager. Billy Dearden had been 'poached' from neighbours Mansfield Town. He had enjoyed some measure of success with the Stags and this had obviously attracted Notts County who were now in desperate need of something. Not only was relegation a distinct possibility, but the financial situation was a continuing cause for concern.

The change had an immediate impact as goals from Darren Caskey and the recently introduced Paul Heffernan, resulted in a 2-0 win over Cambridge United in Dearden's first game in charge. We had to wait a further ten games, eight of which were defeats, before gaining another three points. The Club were now only one place off the bottom and the situation looked hopeless.

Things turned round however, after an injury to Mark Stallard saw Paul Heffernan play alongside Danny Allsopp for the rest of the season. Although just one point was taken from the first two games, Allsopp netted all three in a 3-0 home win over Tranmere Rovers, and he and Heffernan went on to score fourteen between them before the season ended.

Remarkably, the clouds had lifted and mood changed. Nineteen points from a possible twenty seven ensured that Notts were in control of their own destiny when Huddersfield Town visited Meadow Lane for the final game of the season. A win, and the *Great Escape* as it had been promoted in the week leading up to the game, would have been achieved.

Huddersfield were guaranteed at least a play-off place, but with a win, and results going their way elsewhere, they had a slim chance of automatic promotion. However, when Danny Allsopp scored an early goal and Kevin Nicholson a second midway through the second half, the outcome seemed inevitable and there was a great outpouring of emotion. Huddersfield did score a consolation, but as we were aware that Bournemouth, the only club that could catch Notts were losing, the celebrations amongst most of the 15,618 in attendance, continued.

For eighteen months, the ongoing saga of who actually owned and ran the Club continued. The fact that Peter Storrie had resigned in February and become Chief Executive of Portsmouth FC caused alarm bells to ring. A month later it was confirmed that Albert Scardino had completed a takeover, and as a result, Derek Pavis and his wife Vivian were no longer Notts County FC board members.

It is a matter of public record that Messrs Scardino and Pavis were no longer, if indeed they ever were, friends, the suggestion being that the new owner had not fulfilled all of his financial obligations. Who knows?

Achieving the *Great Escape* was not the end of the season for Helen and myself. Southampton had moved out of the Dell and into the purpose built all seater St Mary's at the beginning of the season, and in addition to Nene Park, the home of League newcomers, Rushden & Diamonds, this just had to be visited. Well, yes it did!

We'd been to Nene Park back in September and I'd always had my eye on Southampton's last home game because, with the top division finishing a week later, and providing I could get tickets, this was a perfect opportunity to top up the '92'. Saints beat Newcastle 3-1 on the day (11th May), but more importantly for me, another box had been ticked.

Earlier in the year, we had travelled to Cardiff, for our first ever visit to the Millennium Stadium to see the LD Vans Trophy Final. For the record, Blackpool beat Cambridge United 4-1 to lift the trophy. In terms of national significance, it probably doesn't rank alongside their 1953 FA Cup Final victory, but true fans of the Seasiders won't care.

You'll by now realise that as this was World Cup year, there will have been a lot of forward planning. It had paid off, and we set off for Japan on Monday 27th May.

I had been writing to Tomoko Kasuda for over three years. It was very fragmented correspondence at times, and almost as basic as 'the cat sat on the mat' type prose, but we were understanding one another and she was a great help in advising us in advance of the trip. She was however, unable to get us any tickets!

In anticipation of Scotland qualifying, I had secured a guarantee of tickets for all of their group matches through the FIFA website. Unfortunately, a defeat in Belgium in the penultimate qualifying game meant the *Tartan Army* would be enjoying the summer of 2002 at home. *NB – had Scotland made it, I might have had a serious problem as the group matches could have been staged in South Korea and my (pen) friendship with Tomoko would have been of no tangible benefit!*

Naively, I thought that having been guaranteed tickets, I could simply transfer them to other games. I contacted FIFA to arrange this, but for reasons that I now fully appreciate, this was not possible and I was advised to re-apply for either nation or location specific tickets. When the draw for the group stages was made, I noted that Cameroon were to be based in Japan. Taking the view that there would probably be even fewer supporters from that nation travelling to Japan than the USA, I decided to assert my right as an honorary Cameroonian and applied. I came up trumps again and we could now work out an itinerary based upon where they would be playing their three games.

Tomoko helped, and although we had no real need to travel to Fukuoka on the southern island of Kyushu, after an overnight stay in an airport hotel, we found a way in our plans to get down there to meet her and family before the first game. It took just over five hours on the Shinkansen (bullet train) from Tokyo travelling at up to 200 mph at times. After about 20 minutes, we were blessed with a clear view to the west of Mount Fuji and, if not before, we now knew that we had truly arrived in the 'Land of the Rising Sun.'

The whole purpose behind this book is to record my sporting experiences, and I've no plans to deviate from that. However, I need to make the point that whilst some people might roll their eyes and question what we've done, as I'm sure Helen will confirm, sport has taken us to some fantastic parts of the world. This trip was one of them. It was just such a fantastic cultural experience especially as, in spite of Tomoko's considerable help, we were effectively on our own. It's certainly not cheap, but I'd strongly recommend everyone take a trip to Japan at least once.

After a couple of nights in Fukuoka, we headed back up to Tokyo and then north towards where the first game was taking place at the Big Swan Stadium, in Niigata. We'd booked accommodation about an hour away from the city in a place called Nagaoka. We arrived there fairly late. I was not feeling too good however, with pains in my chest and at about 1.00am whilst in bed, I was in such agony that I thought I was having a heart attack.

Well, what would have been an issue in almost any hotel in the world, was made worse as Helen tried to explain the situation to the night porter. Eventually he twigged and arranged for a taxi to take us to the local hospital. Once we got over the initial communication problems, I was seen by a very nice young man who had a basic understanding of English. After examination, he confirmed that the pain was resulting from stress induced expansion of the muscles around the heart.

NB – By way of explanation, I'd changed jobs just eight weeks before and had found myself responsible for a department on the point of collapse. It had clearly taken its toll!

He gave me some pills to help me relax and reduce the swelling plus a note to take to the chemists. He advised that it may take twenty four hours before the pills really took effect. He arranged for a taxi to take us back to the hotel where, the pills having eased the pain a little, I got a bit of sleep - not sure about Helen whose mind must have been racing – in anticipation of the busy day ahead of us.

We found the chemist and then headed for the station. When the train drew in, there were no seats available and we ended up standing in a doorway which was packed with Irishmen heading to the game. Ireland were Cameroon's opening opponents. I tried to enter into banter with these chaps, but as I was still suffering I just couldn't manage it comfortably. Shame really, as I wanted to establish where their sympathies lay. Did they sympathise with manager Mick McCarthy or support Roy Keane's rebellious behaviour?

The game itself ended in a 1-1 draw with Matt Holland equalising for Ireland in the second half. Steve Finnan made a substitute appearance and I wondered if he was the fourth ex Notts County player - after Don Masson, Nigel Worthington and Rachid Harkouk - to have appeared at a World Cup. I'm sure someone will tell me.

As the day progressed, the pain decreased and thereafter, other than the occasional sharp reminder that I'd been in such agony, the rest of the trip was fine. The pills were working. In fact, I was on quite a 'high' on the journey back to Nagaoka.

As our Shinkansen ticket allowed unlimited travel, we returned to Niigata the following day to properly explore the city. Remarkably, at the top of the escalators as we left the station, I heard someone with a Scouse accent shouting, "Tickets for tomorrow's game!" I looked at Helen and.... ....she shook her head.

Well, I went over anyway and this guy confirmed that he'd got tickets for the Croatia v Mexico game at the Big Swan the following day and he was selling them at face value. After establishing with Helen that we'd got nothing planned and explaining that it would be a shame to have come this far and miss the opportunity to see Davor Suker, Robert Prosinecki etc., she was immediately (?) won over. I bought two. Mexico won that game 1-0. The Mexican fans, who were in the majority, were a joy to share a couple of hours with.

After another night in Nagaoka we headed to Tokyo and based ourselves there for a few days. Cameroon's next game was against Saudi Arabia and took place in the Saitama Stadium just outside the capital. Germany had beaten the Saudi's 8-0 in their opening game so it was a surprise that the Cameroonians had only a Samuel Eto'o goal to thank for their win. As Ireland had drawn with the Germans the night before and had only Saudi Arabia to play, it meant that Cameroon would probably have to beat Germany to progress.

In between seeing that game - the Germans won 2-0 - in the Ecopa Stadium in Shizuoka, and returning home, we made full use of our unlimited train travel and spent time in Sendai, Nagoya, Kobe, Osaka, Kyoto and Hiroshima. As I've already indicated, if it wasn't for football, we'd probably never have enjoyed those experiences and stored away so many memories.

When we landed back in the UK, we found out that Notts County FC had gone into administration and were soon to hear, that in return for £100,000, Meadow Lane was to be renamed the Aaron Scargill Stadium. A local firm of estate agents had secured naming rights. It didn't happen, which is just as well because it would have been a waste of money. The ground would have forever be known as Meadow Lane (or the Temple of Gloom) to fans. I have no problem with new build stadia, like Arsenal's Emirates, being given a sponsor's handle, but how many people refer to Leyton Orient's ground as the Matchroom Stadium? I think I've made my point.

Back in the UK, and with me gradually getting to grips with work related issues and no more concerns about my health, given the way that the 2001/02 season had ended, there was a feeling of optimism around what might happen on the Meadow Lane pitch. This, despite the fact that there had been no major signings during the close season. Given the Club's precarious financial position, this was no surprise.

The one significant change in the Billy Dearden team was the choice of goalkeeper. I had been trying to convince fellow supporters for some time that Jocky Scott's signing of Stuart Garden had been a worthwhile legacy. The manager now agreed with me that Garden was the best goalkeeper on the books, and he replaced Steve Mildenhall as number one.

Despite this, the first half of the season was a struggle, and with only one win (away to Crewe) from the opening ten games, we loyal 'Pies were resigned to another disappointing season. There was no joy to be had from the various cup competitions either, with Oldham Athletic (League Cup), Wigan Athletic (LD Vans Trophy), and most embarrassing of all, non-League Southport (FA Cup), ensuring that Notts didn't get past the various first rounds.

There were eventually five league wins by the turn of the year, when Notts sat in 17th position, and the early season optimism had completely disappeared. The one highlight had been a 4-1 away win at Cheltenham with Mark Stallard and Danny Allsopp both scoring two goals. That was about it!

Helen had a big birthday this year, and without her being aware in advance, she had sponsored the match ball for the home game on 9th November. This was a big local derby against Mansfield Town. A number of friends and family came - we even got my sister and brother-in-law over from Northern Ireland - and they were well entertained. Richard Liburd gave Notts the lead although this was cancelled out by a Mansfield equaliser. Darren Caskey scored what we hoped would be a late winner, only for those pesky Stags to score an even later equaliser. It finished 2-2.

As for the 92 Club, I missed the 2-2 away draw at Luton to visit York Street, home of Boston United, the latest club to be promoted to the Football League. I also took advantage of Notts having lost to Southport and not having a game on 7th December, by making my first visit to the Walkers Stadium, the new home of Leicester City.

2003

Helen and I saw the New Year in at a special Hogmanay function at a hotel in Haydock. It was a good night in a hand-picked location as Notts County's first game of 2003 was at nearby Wigan Athletic. A 3-1 defeat to the eventual divisional champions was no surprise, although the day was made more tolerable by us sitting in the pub across from the JJB Stadium prior to the game, and choosing a property just north of Florence for that year's summer holiday.

The Club's early elimination from the FA Cup once again proved beneficial when, with no game on 4th January, I was able to visit the KC Stadium, Hull City's new stadium. I was back up to 92!

Although, unlike the previous season, Notts County were never in serious danger of being relegated, and did climb as high as 12th at one stage, there was an all pervading mood of apathy about the place. This despite Mark Stallard scoring 24 goals and both Danny Allsopp and Paul Heffernan contributing ten each. Whatever, it could be argued that the fact that the Club had finished four places higher than in the year of the *Great Escape*, this represented progress.

The final game of the season for us, was another visit to the Millennium Stadium to see Wolves return to the top division via a 3-0 play-off victory over Sheffield United. I'd managed to get four tickets for this game, two on behalf of Blades' fans. It was not a pleasant experience sitting next to them. They were 'canned up' and thoroughly miserable. I appreciate though that my reminding them at the end as Wolves fans celebrated, that 'it's only a game', wouldn't have helped.

Notts County remained in administration and the EFL were losing patience and threatening to kick the Club out of the League. At the eleventh hour Albert Scardino agreed a takeover deal with local business partners Raj Bhatia and Frank Strang and all looked good for the future as we set off for our Tuscan holiday.

We returned from Italy - there was no football by the way - to hear that Danny Allsopp had left Meadow Lane and been replaced by Clive Platt. Did that get the adrenaline flowing you may be tempted to ask? Well no, and neither did the signing of Steve Jenkins, Tony Barras or Simon Baldry.

It was clear that the Club's financial situation left us scrambling around for other team's cast-offs and this was exacerbated when, just before the start of the season, we heard that the deal agreed little more than two months previously, had collapsed. The EFL gave Notts five weeks to 'sort themselves out'. Thankfully, within that short time frame, Derek Pavis, by now Club President, was able to convince the League that a rescue package was imminent.

Meanwhile, on the pitch, neither Jenkins nor Platt played another game for the Club after 28th December and Mark Stallard moved on in January. A succession of players, either on loan or on short term contracts came and went. It made no difference, and following four straight defeats without scoring a goal, Notts were bottom of the Division, so I suppose the fact that they had moved up to second bottom by the end of the year was something to be thankful for.

Preston North End and Ipswich Town had been overcome in the first two rounds of the League Cup. This led to a potential money spinning away tie at Stamford Bridge in the third round. They put up a good fight but eventually lost 4-2. There was still an opportunity for glory in the FA Cup in 2004 as a home win over Shildon (7-2) and then away at Gravesend & Northfleet (2-1) gave us a trip to the Riverside Stadium, Middlesbrough to look forward to.

Perhaps, the only genuine reason for good cheer was the news in December that the Club had finally come out of administration. A combination of money from long-time supporter, Haydn Green, the recently formed Supporters Trust, and an organisation called Blenheim Trust led by Peter Joyce, had been enough to buy off Mr Scardino. As part of the deal, Steve Thompson (not the former manager and Colin Murphy's best mate) was appointed Club chairman. Perhaps things would settle down now allowing the Club to enjoy a bit of stability. Well, what do you think?

As part of an equally stressful footballing experience, in September, Wimbledon FC had re-located to Milton Keynes. In order to be a part of this historic, although largely unwelcome development, I was one of the 5,639 in attendance as they staged their first game, a 2-2 draw with Burnley, at the National Hockey Stadium.

2004

The trip north to Middlesbrough on 3rd January, followed dropping Heather off at Stansted Airport as she returned to Saint Etienne to complete the Work Placement element of her degree course. Yes, a few miles were covered that day, but it didn't make any difference to the football as Notts were beaten 2-0. I didn't go to Peterborough the following Tuesday night, where a 5-2 defeat proved to be Billy Dearden's last game in charge. He was immediately replaced by Gary Mills in what looked like an increasingly futile attempt to stave off relegation.

The new man brought in even more new players. Unfortunately, the only two who were to leave a lasting impression were David Pipe and Stefan Oakes. Whatever, despite three straight wins at the end of February/beginning of March, which briefly raised hopes of another 'great escape', it was a false dawn, and Notts finished a full nine points short of the safety line with only Wycombe Wanderers below them. Other than for Paul Heffernan, who came of age with 21 goals, the season was a disaster all round and..................the basement division beckoned once more.

Maintaining true 92 Club membership resulted in trips to Manchester (Eastlands – now Etihad Stadium), Yeovil (Huish Park) and Darlington (George Reynolds Stadium). If nothing else, Notts County's demotion meant I'd not have to make a special trip to visit the ground of whichever club had been promoted to the Football League in 2004/05. Small mercies?

The season was still not over yet. Having decided that four years was too long a wait in which to attend an international football tournament, we were now looking forward to the European Championships in Portugal.

Twelve months earlier, I'd applied for tickets via the UEFA website. With no Scotland, I didn't specify any nation on my application but looked at where the games were to be staged to try to establish which were less likely to be popular. That ruled out Lisbon and Oporto, and after a bit of research, I decided on two inland towns in the centre of Portugal. I'm not sure that I'd ever even heard of Leiria or Coimbra before, but they looked just right for me and off went my application.

I was successful and just had to wait for the December draw to see which nations would be playing in these locations. Initially I had England v France and Switzerland plus Switzerland v France. I was pleased with that, although, the organisers quickly switched the England/France game to Lisbon. The explanation was 'crowd safety', but I reckon getting approximately another 30,000 spectators into the larger stadium (and the increased income arising from that switch) was the key driving force. Whatever, I had three games guaranteed and couldn't complain.

Rather than spend a fortnight in Portugal where the nation would be football mad and prices hiked to take full advantage of the spending power of thousands of visitors, we settled on the idea of basing ourselves in Spain, and simply driving over the border for the games. That narrowed our options somewhat, but we chanced upon Salamanca. Leiria was just short of 250 miles away and Coimbra some 50 miles closer. Driving time would be around only four hours for each. Perfect! We booked a hotel in Salamanca for the fortnight, overnight ferries from Portsmouth to Santander and counted down the days.

Salamanca is an ideal destination for a relaxing holiday. Other than the three long drives over to Portugal and back, and a day trip to Madrid by train, we just pottered around the Castile and Leon region. It was bliss.

As for the football, the Switzerland v Croatia game was a dull 0-0 draw. There was no way either of these nations would win the tournament. That same night, England lost 2-1 to France - the game we initially thought we'd be seeing - with two late Zinedine Zidane goals.

A couple of days later, we were in the centre of Salamanca when we heard an English voice. As you'll know, whenever abroad, hearing voices and accents from home always stands out, but it was particularly noticeable in this city as there were very few tourists, and almost certainly no-one, apart from us, there for Euro 2004.

I got talking to this guy and he explained that he was using a fortnight's holiday to hitch hike around the Iberian Peninsula and was planning to get over to Portugal to see if he could get to any of the England games. Well says I, we can't help you with a ticket, but we can give you a lift. He was happy to take up the offer. He went off to book another night in Salamanca and met up with us later to agree the arrangements. So it was that we ferried Matt, from Birkenhead, across the border. We dropped him off, and within half an hour, while having a drink with some Swiss supporters, he sent a text to say that he'd managed to get a ticket. We were pleased for him - he was a nice lad - and I do sometimes wonder whatever happened to Matt.

He'll certainly have enjoyed the game as England won 3-0. The Swiss made it difficult, but once Wayne Rooney had scored mid-way through the first half, they were never really in trouble. The Swiss had a man sent off after an hour, and another goal from Rooney (he really arrived that night!) and a later one from Steven Gerrard, ensured a comfortable England win.

Before the game, whilst queuing up for entry, we experienced some of the less pleasant behaviour associated with a small section of England fans. There was no violence, just loud, boorish and arrogant chants that met with the silent disapproval of the majority of fans. I'd have said something - I've done it before in other similar situations - but Helen would have soon shut me up. Besides, with my accent, I'd probably just have attracted infantile abuse.

The final game was the most entertaining. France were already through, but Switzerland had to win to have any chance of qualifying. It was 1-1 at half time, with Zidane scoring for France. In the second half, class told as Thierry Henry scored twice. He was superb throughout, and based upon what I'd seen, I would have thought a France v England final, a possible outcome.

So much for that prediction. Portugal knocked out England (on penalties) in the quarter finals and France lost to Greece at the same stage. Greece of course, then went on to shock the expectant home nation in the Final.

Back home, Gary Mills prepared for his first full season as manager of Notts County making wholesale changes to the squad. In came Robert Ullathorne, Julian Baudet, Glynn Hurst, Gavin Gordon, Mike Whitlow, Matt Gill and Mike Edwards. There were also promotions from within of Shaun Harrad and Kelvin Wilson. With hindsight, only Mike Edwards and to a lesser extent Hurst and Wilson, were an improvement on the team that had been relegated a few months previously.

Statistically, the first five months were better than twelve months before if only because they won six instead of five league games. A 5-1 away defeat to Rushden & Diamonds was Gary Mills' last game in charge and he was replaced by Ian Richardson as player-manager. As it happens, a knee injury, which eventually led to his retirement, limited him to just the one game as a player whilst in the dual role.

Richardson was to have some success, and via wins over Woking and then Swindon Town after a replay, the Club made it to the third round of the FA Cup for the second successive season and were drawn to face Middlesbrough yet again. This time at Meadow Lane.

League form continued to disappoint however, and as the old year ended, Notts were in 21st position and probably thankful that only one team from the 4th Tier would be relegated and be playing non-league football the next season.

2005

Helen and I woke up in Pangbourne Berkshire on the first day of the New Year. It seems a bit bizarre now but Helen had spotted a good Hogmanay deal in an advert somewhere, and checking that the Berkshire town was not too far away from the Cotswolds - which was stretching things a bit I thought - and therefore ideal for Cheltenham, she booked it.

We had a walk along the River Thames in the morning before heading off to Whaddon Road where 2005 got off to a good start. Goals from Glynn Hurst and Chris Palmer, who had arrived in October, gave Notts a 2-0 winning start. It was another false dawn. There were to be only six further victories, more than offset by nine defeats, before the end of yet another disappointing season. The Club finished in 19th position, but were at least a comforting 22 points ahead of relegated Cambridge United.

As for that FA Cup tie against Premiership Middlesbrough, despite a goal from Tony Scully after two minutes, and holding that lead until half-time, Notts were to lose 2-1. Had they won, they would have been away to Manchester United in the 4th Round which, if nothing else, would have improved the Club's precarious financial situation. It wasn't to be. *NB – the Middlesbrough cup tie, on 8th January 2005, was the first time that Russ, my future son-in-law, visited Meadow Lane, and to the best of his memory, had seen Notts County play.*

Ian Richardson was not given the chance to continue leading the Club in 2005/06. Controversially, his playing contract was not even renewed, and so it was that Notts began the new season with the Icelandic Gudjon Thordarson in charge. He oversaw the recruitment of goalkeeper Kevin Pilkington, Stacey Long, Dan Martin, Lewis McMahon, Brian O'Callaghan and Andy White.

Whilst this was taking place, more concerns were being raised about the long term future of the Club. The Chairman of the NCFC Supporters Trust, who in his position was likely to be better informed than most, warned of 'vultures continuing to look at football clubs' and reassured fans that the Trust would ward off investors who hadn't got the best interests of the Club at heart.

In a surprise start to the season, Notts were unbeaten in their first eight games and were top of the Division when they went to Shrewsbury and lost 2-0. I missed that game, but went to Sunderland v West Brom instead as this was the day before that year's Great North Run. The defeat at Gay Meadow, saw Notts slip to 5th and begin a slide down the table. They were to win only eight (& lose eighteen) games after that encouraging start. On 31st December, after a 1-0 away defeat at Leyton Orient's Brisbane Road, Notts sat 16th in the table. It was to get worse.

First round defeats in the League Cup and Football League Trophy plus a second round FA Cup defeat (they'd surprisingly beaten Bristol City at

Ashton Gate in the first) resulted in there not being very much to look forward to as the old year ended.

Still, with three new purpose built grounds brought into use this season, I took the opportunity to make my first visits to the Ricoh (Coventry City), Liberty (Swansea City) and Kassam (Oxford United) Stadiums.

2006

A flurry of yet more loan signings failed to halt the slide, and following a defeat at Barnet on 8th April, I started to have discussions with fellow supporters about the possibility of watching non-league football in 2006/07. They disagreed, and since that time, I've been known as the 'prophet of doom'. Little were they to know that come the final game of the season, at home to Bury, with future Notts star Kasper Schmeichel in goal, relegation was a distinct possibility.

I was the programme sponsor for that game and a load of family, friends, neighbours and workmates joined us. Notts had to win to guarantee safety but were losing 2-0 with nine minutes remaining, and at that point, were likely to become the ex 'Oldest Football League Club in the World' ™. As it happens, results elsewhere, principally at Leyton Orient, were going our way, so the two late goals from Dan Martin and a Juilan Baudet penalty to secure a 2-2 draw didn't matter in the end. Notts finished three points ahead of Oxford United who were relegated to the Conference.

In February, we had a weekend away in Rome, with the Baldwins (Alan and Diane) and the first of a sequence of games in foreign leagues began. On that occasion, we saw AS Roma play Empoli at the Stadio Olympico. It was a routine 1-0 win - a record equalling tenth successive one - for the home team, but a disappointment for Italy as Francesco Totti broke an ankle that day. It was to prevent him from taking part in the coming World Cup. Talking of which.................?

With no Scotland participation to get the adrenaline flowing, and having learned from the European Championships two years earlier, I had submitted my ticket application the previous year. This time, I figured that not too many people would consider a fortnight in or around Leipzig to be their holiday destination of choice. Now whether or not that played a part in my success, I'll never know. Whatever, I secured two tickets for three of the four group games to be held in that city's Zentralstadion and waited for the draw in December. When it was made, I was happy enough as I'd be seeing Holland, France and Spain amongst others.

We drove over, and after an overnight stay near an American base outside Gelsenkirchen, carried on to Halle, 27 miles short of Leipzig and made this our initial base for the first two games.

An Arjen Robben goal was enough for Holland to see off Serbia & Montenegro in the first of those, before Spain stuffed Ukraine 4-0 with David Villa getting a couple. I was impressed with the stadium and the very efficient way in which fans were ferried to and from it via tram. Blatant stereotyping I know, but we were in Germany.

What I did have a problem with however, was a UEFA cover up regarding attendances. At our first game, this was given as being 37,216 in a stadium with a capacity of 42,960. The ground was clearly not full, and this seemed reasonably accurate. However, from that point on, official attendances were given in round figures, e.g. 43,000 for the Spain game when this was clearly a lie.

With a few days before the next game, we headed over to the Czech Republic and a couple of nights in Prague calling in at Colditz on the way. Very interesting! Returning to Germany we based ourselves in Dresden (69 miles from Leipzig) for the rest of the trip.

A Thierry Henry goal looked to be enough for France to secure victory until an 81st minute equaliser for South Korea. Having drawn with Switzerland in their opening game, the French, one of the pre-tournament favourites, had to beat Togo in their final game to guarantee qualification for the knock-out stages. They did, and then went on to the Final.

At our hotel in Dresden, I overheard a couple in reception asking how they could get to Leipzig as they were going to the football the following day. I got talking to them and found out that they came from California and had seen Mexico, their team, earlier in the competition and had tickets for the Angola v Iran game, the one Leipzig game that I'd missed out on.

Having suggested to Helen that we might take a trip back to Leipzig to see if we could pick up any spare tickets for that game, and she agreeing, we suggested giving this couple a lift. An offer, they were more than happy to accept.

All four of us met in the hotel reception area on the morning of the game. I'd taken the precaution of asking at the hotel if they could make me some sort of poster that I could hang around my neck promoting the fact that I was looking for tickets. So it was that after we got off the tram in the centre of Leipzig, I first displayed 'Alle Ersatzkarten' to the front and rear. We'd only walked about 100 yards when we heard a shout and someone was beckoning me. Two tickets at face value purchased moments later, and I was able to throw my sophisticated billboard away. The game itself, played in scorching heat, ended in a 1-1 draw, and if I'm honest, I'd probably have been better off if I'd used that money for something else!

We met up with our Californian Mexican friends after the game and headed back to Dresden. We had a couple more days there, one of which we used to travel over to Poland for no other reason than to say that we've been there, before travelling back to the UK.

The Icelandic experimentation considered a disaster, Gudjon Thordarson was relieved of his duties at the end of 2005/06 and Steve Thompson (this time it was Colin Murphy's old pal) appointed as manager in his own right. Yet again, with a change of manager we had another case of 'out with the old......etc.' New signings included Lawrie Dudfield, Stephen Hunt, Jason Lee, Austin McCann, Junior Mendes, Tcham N'Toya, Andy Parkinson, Gary Silk, Matt Somner and Alan White (not to be confused with Andy White who had left after scoring two goals in twenty six appearances). Ian Ross had also been signed on a season long loan from Sheffield United.

Meanwhile, Jeff Moore, Chief Executive of EMDA (East Midlands Development Agency) was appointed Notts County Chairman by the Trust. Being able to tap in to his expertise/business experience was generally viewed as being beneficial for the Club.

Meanwhile, only one defeat in the first fifteen games, resulting in Notts being fifth at the end of October, was considered an encouraging start. However, as in 05/06, things went downhill from there, although not quite so rapidly or dramatically.

There was no joy in either FA Cup or Johnstone's Paint Trophy losing at the first hurdle to Leyton Orient and Barnet respectively. However, surprise wins in the League Cup away at Crystal Palace and Middlesbrough followed by a home win over Southampton, which I didn't get to as we'd been to Berlin (saw Hertha beat Borussia Monchengladbach by the way) gave Notts a winnable home tie against Wycombe Wanderers in the fourth round. The visitors won 1-0 and went on to the semi-final where, despite losing, they will have been consoled by the amount of money generated from their two legged tie against Chelsea.

It was now ten years since Notts had had a season during which early promise had actually delivered success, and this was being reflected in attendances. There were very few crowds in excess of 5,000 and the few that there were, had only been achieved as a result of a good following from the visitors. The Club appeared to be inching closer to oblivion.

2007

In January, I was able to get my '92' back up to full quota as I followed Notts to Accrington and Hereford. On the same topic, in addition to my first ever visit to the Pirelli Stadium where Burton Albion were still playing in the Conference, I saw a couple of Doncaster Rovers' Johnstone's Paint Trophy games at the Keepmoat Stadium following their move from Bellevue. Rovers went on to win that competition in a thrilling extra-time victory over Bristol Rovers at Wembley. There were over 59,000 there - so don't knock it - with former Meadow Lane favourite, Paul Heffernan, and future 'Pies, Jonathan Forte and Graeme Lee getting the goals.

Later, in May, Heather and Russ joined us for our first visit to 'New Wembley' where we saw Bristol Rovers defeat Shrewsbury Town in a Play-off Final to win promotion to the third tier.

Back at Meadow Lane, Notts had a sequence of four straight wins in March/April but that was too little too late and they finished 13th. Now this was a big improvement, eight places and ten points, on the previous season, and was deemed to be enough to keep Steve Thompson in a job. It did............for the time being.

During the summer, the Club launched a business plan entitled 'Vision 2012' which set out how it was intended to get Notts County playing in the Championship (2nd tier) within the next five years. This laudable aim was somewhat undermined when Jeff Moore announced his intention to resign as Chairman, after little more than a year in the role. He was replaced by John Armstrong-Holmes, a successful local politician, businessman and supporter of the Club.

Mr Thompson got to work during the close season, and come August we were pleased (?) to welcome (?) the likes of Lee Canoville, Neil MacKenzie, Adam Tann, Paul Mayo, Richard Butcher, Hector Sam and Spencer Weir-Daley. The newcomers, plus Myles Weston, who had joined the Club the previous March, were to collectively form the nucleus of a squad that would be serious challengers in 2007/08. At least, I think that's what Mr Thompson told us.

An unbeaten four game start to the season might have been encouraging were it not for the fact that there no wins either. Three 1-1's plus a 2-2 up at Darlington, with Richard Butcher scoring four of the five goals, did have some merit, but with home crowds now regularly under 4,000 there was real concern about the future of the Club, now under the ownership of the Notts County Supporters Trust. Besides, the ominous sound of knives being sharpened could once more be heard from the back of the Main Stand.

Meanwhile, once more accompanied by Alan Baldwin, I'd visited another Olympic Stadium on a weekend away in Barcelona where we saw Espanyol beat Real Madrid in a La Liga game. I'd also followed Notts to the new StadiumMK where Wimbledon had morphed into MK Dons and to Victoria Road, to see newly promoted Dagenham & Redbridge.

Midway through a run of four straight defeats, Steve Thompson was 'shown the door'. As he was going out the back, Ian McParland was coming in through the front. As 'one of our own' Charlie was a popular choice, although he must have questioned his sanity when he saw what he had to work with. To his credit, he seemed committed from the start. Results did not improve however, and after first round defeats in both League Cup and JP Trophy, both while Steve Thompson was in charge, McParland oversaw an embarrassing 2nd Round FA Cup defeat at home to Havant & Waterlooville. In addition, at the end of the year, the Club were now four places (20th) lower in the Division that when he took over. Once more we asked "Can things get any worse?"

2008

The short answer to the earlier rhetorical question is undoubtedly yes! We were unaware when we woke up in Hereford on New Year's morning - another of Helen's excellent Hogmanay treats! - that Notts had, amongst other short term loanees, signed Guy Branston!

Mr Branston was not required for the first game of 2008, the 0-0 draw which conveniently took place at Edgar Street - what a far-sighted woman I married! - and we could see why, in the next game at home. Branston was withdrawn after 45 minutes of the game with Stockport County in what must rank as the most inept debut that probably all of the 4,120 in attendance had ever seen. He was never to wear a Notts shirt again!

Guy Branston therefore missed out on Notts County's first ever visits to Christie Park, (Morecambe) and Greenhaus Meadow (Shrewsbury's new ground). Both were draws, but at least a couple more of my boxes had been ticked without having to make a special trip. In another

226

weekend break with the Baldwins, this time in February to Lisbon, we saw Sporting Lisbon win 2-0 at the Estadio Jose Alvalade.

Back at Meadow Lane, with the odd win here and there, Notts were just managing to keep a few points and places above the drop zone. However, it needed a Richard Butcher winner in the last home game of the season (Wycombe Wanderers) to guarantee League football for at least another year. Notts finished six points and two places above relegated Mansfield Town, who joined Wrexham in dropping out of the Football League.

In the hope that - no, make that expectation - Scotland would qualify for the European Championships to be jointly staged in Austria and Switzerland, I had successfully applied for tickets for their group matches. Well, you may need reminding that in a qualifying group that contained Italy, France and near neighbours the Faroe Islands, it was only a 90th minute defeat to Italy in their final game that prevented Scotland from making it.

As I knew from the 2002 World Cup, having guaranteed tickets for a nation that ultimately fails to qualify means nothing, and my efforts to secure tickets for other games through the UEFA website failed. We'd already booked accommodation, so tickets or not, we were looking forward to a fortnight on the Continent.

After an overnight stop in Kassel, we travelled on to a pre-booked place just south of Salzburg, a delightful little village called Eben im Pongau. We were to stay there for a few nights and drove into the city on our first morning. Keeping my eyes and ears open I just happened to chance upon someone who had a spare ticket for the following day's game between Greece and Sweden. After a quick chat with Helen, she agreed what she'd be doing the following afternoon and ....the transaction was satisfactorily concluded.

So it was that on Tuesday 10th June, whilst Helen was busying herself elsewhere in Salzburg, I saw well supported Sweden defeat the then current reigning European champions 2-0, with one of the goals coming from Zlatan Ibrahimovic.

After a couple more nights back in lovely EiP we headed south and east. We'd planned to spend some time in Slovenia and had pre-booked three nights in Ljubljana. When we arrived in the Slovenian capital and found our bearings, we noted that John Fogarty, former lead singer with *Creedence Clearwater Revival*, was appearing at the local concert hall on the Saturday night. Well, we know he'd have been very disappointed to hear, that having travelled over from Derbyshire, we were 'in town' and had not taken the opportunity to see him. That's how we ended up among the 200 or so devotees who had probably been looking forward to this night for months. I've been to many better gigs, but what can you expect on a Saturday night in Ljubljana?

Being so close to the Croatian border we crossed it one day and headed over to Rijeka on the coast. Now this was not intended as a day for relaxing on the beach. It was a mission to see if one of Notts County's greatest players had a presence in the town. Radojko (Raddy) Avramovic had been the Club's record signing in 1979 and had played a key role in getting the Club into the 1st Division and then keeping them there.

He was a Yugoslavian international but had previously played for HNK Rijeka, with whom he had won the Yugoslav Cup and then subsequently appeared in the European Cup Winners Cup. Against this background, I thought I'd look up some of his old haunts and possibly meet some of his old friends. I was devastated that after numerous conversations with locals in bars and restaurants, no-one could remember him. OK, he'd left Rijeka twenty nine years before, but that was no excuse. This guy was a legend.

Putting this disappointment behind us, we crossed back over into Slovenia. After another night in Ljubljana, we carried on into Austria where we had spent a fortune in booking a two night stay at the luxurious Alpenrose Hotel, a few hundred metres above Lake Achensee. Being waited on hand and foot and sharing a dining room with people who oozed 'money', was something I wasn't comfortable with. Helen lapped it up!!

All good things come to an end however, and we'd got two nights booked in a hotel about 30 miles from Innsbruck before heading for home. On that first night, I asked if there might be a chance of getting a ticket for the Sweden v Russia game in Innsbruck the following day. The manager was not sure that I'd find one at an affordable price, but reckoned it was worth a try.

In the morning then, having made sure that Helen was comfortable in the hotel, I set off for Innsbruck with yet another hand-made cardboard billboard asking 'Alle Ersatzkarten' - I really should have kept the Leipzig prototype! - hoping to come up trumps. Well, it took some time, and with what seemed like thousands of Swedes milling around, I walked from stadium into town and back again twice, before a guy came up to me outside the ground and quietly - he was worried he'd be arrested for touting! - asked if I was serious. I said I was and he took me round a corner, away from prying eyes, and produced a ticket. He wanted a bit more than face value, but I negotiated him down a bit, and in the end, we were both happy.

I found a pub full of happy and expectant Swedes, treated myself to a stein of the local Austrian brew and sent a text to Helen telling her that I'd be at the game and not to expect me back until late.

At the Stadion Tivoli Neu, the Swedes only needed a draw to qualify for the knock-out stages and the fans were confident. I tried to tell a few that I'd been in that situation with Scotland in the past, and that though I'd be happy for Sweden were they to progress, it was dangerous to count one's chickens. Whether or not they understood that, remains a matter of debate!

My caution proved well founded. An Andrey Arshavin - I was surprised that he subsequently failed to build on his promise at Arsenal - inspired Russia went on to win 2-0. I never did see any of my new found Swedish friends from a few hours earlier, but if I had, I'd have resisted the temptation to say, "See – I did warn you!"

I got back to the hotel at about 1.00am but was up early the following morning for the drive across Switzerland and France. We had an overnight stop booked near Calais prior to taking Le Shuttle back home. On the way back, we began discussions on where we'd like to go on our South African trip in two years' time!

In some respects, I suppose the most surprising news to come out of Meadow Lane during the close season was that Ian McParland was still manager. That is not intended as a slight against him. It's just that the managerial revolving door had become such a feature of recent history that we/I had come to expect it.

Those that had been brought into the Club with the immediate task of improving fortunes this time round, included Jamie Clapham, Adam Nowland, Ricky Ravenhill, Sean Canham, Matt Hamshaw, Jason Beardsley, Delroy Facey, Jamie Forrester and later, John Thompson. Each of them had their occasional moments, but the end result remained the same. Mediocrity.

Only one (the opener at Bradford) of the first seven league games was lost. However, Notts had only accumulated six points in that period as the other games were drawn and they were already looking over their shoulder and wondering if even Luton, who had started with a thirty point deduction, could catch them. Fortunately, a couple of 2-1 wins followed, and as the season developed, it became clear that, unbelievably, some teams were actually poorer than Notts County.

The nadir for us was probably the 6-1 defeat at Dagenham & Redbridge in late November, and following a 3-0 home defeat to Rotherham United on 28th December, Notts ended the year in 17th place.

There were a few highlights, most notably a 4-0 win (all the goals in the first half) at Barnet when on loan striker Jonathan Forte scored a hat-trick. Another was me finally seeing Notts win at Grimsby (on my twelfth visit!), but happy days were few and far between. There was no cup success either. In fact, there was more ignominy in the FA Cup when, for the second year running, the Club were eliminated by non-league opponents. At least a replay was required this time before Kettering Town won the 2nd Round tie. Shame that, as we knew in advance that Eastwood Town would be the next opponents.

Still, I'd managed to get a ticket for the apparently always sold out Emirates Stadium to see Arsenal easily dispose of Wigan Athletic in a 4th Round League Cup tie. I'd also seen Aldershot win an FA Cup replay at Rotherham United's temporary home, the Don Valley Stadium. Those two trips brought me back 'up to speed' and, as a bonus, during a weekend in the French capital, we got to the Parc de Princes to see Paris Saint Germain. They were yet to acquire their wealthy backers and only finished sixth in Ligue 1 that year. Still, the night we were there, they beat Lorient 3-2 in a very entertaining game.

2009

The first game of the New Year should have been away at Aldershot. We travelled down with the Baldwin's for an overnight stay in Hampshire - we'd booked a hotel in Basingstoke - but heard at about 1.00pm that the Recreation Ground was frozen, and in the referee's opinion, unplayable. What one does in situations like that is to immediately look to see if there is another game in the area. That was good news for Wycombe Wanderers as we took a slight detour to see the home side defeat Bury 2-1. Not what we'd planned for, but at least it was a game.

The Notts County season drifted to a close, ending with an away win at Wycombe - although this had followed five straight defeats - with John Thompson scoring for the first time since joining the Club. He did it in the 30th minute and then, having discovered how easy it was, did it again in the 90th. Notts finished in 19th place, well clear of relegation. However, were it not for various points deductions, specifically for Luton Town and Bournemouth, they'd have been two places lower.

We made it to the first ever Essex derby - yes there is such a thing! - to be played at Colchester United's new Weston Homes Community Stadium. Southend United fans enjoyed the experience more than home supporters as their team were 1-0 winners.

After seeing Torquay United win the Conference Play-Off Final on 17th May, to regain their place in the Football League, we awaited publication of fixtures for the coming season. Not that we were particularly looking forward to them, but it's difficult to break the habit! Little did we know however, of what was happening behind the scenes at Meadow Lane. Notts County were about to feature on the front pages.

During the close season we were to hear that the Supporters' Trust had been made an offer to sell the Club to a company called Munto Finance. Very little was known about them but they appeared to have unlimited funds that they wished to invest in a small, unfashionable and impoverished football club. Well Notts County certainly fitted that criteria. John Armstrong-Holmes assured supporters that due diligence had been carried out and that he and fellow Trust officials were satisfied that Munto were the 'real deal'. Shares in the Club owned by NCFC Supporters Trust, were gifted to Munto Finance and a Mr Peter Trembling became Executive Chairman.

It all seemed a bit surreal and became even more so when a colleague at work, who claimed to be a football fan, but who would never lower himself to see a game at Notts County's level, came up to me and said. "Have you heard the latest? Apparently, there are rumours that Sven-Goran Eriksson is the new Notts County manager." This was news to me and I ignored his incredulous laugh at the absurdity of such a development. Well, he was certainly laughing out of the other side of his mouth the following day when, at a Meadow Lane press conference, the former England manager was introduced as the new Director of Football and announced how he could see the 'oldest football league club in the world'TM playing Premiership football within the next five years.

Now I have to say - and Helen will back me up here - that I never truly bought in to what eventually turned out to be a fantasy that could have ended in the Club folding. Having said that, I enjoyed the ride as players like Luke Rodgers, Lee Hughes, Ben Davies, Karl Hawley, Craig Westcarr and Neil Bishop joined the Club during the summer. For me, the last named was the most exciting. I'd spotted him when Barnet visited Meadow Lane the year before and was impressed. I'd even said to those who have seats near me "We must buy him!" They deny ever hearing it, but I did. I really did!

Kasper Schmeichel and Johnnie Jackson soon followed and the squad was further enhanced by the on loan signings of Brendon Moloney and Matt Ritchie. Ian McParland, for he remained as manager, appeared to be benefitting from the Club's new high profile Director of Football's influence. Not forgetting Munto Finance's millions of course!

The proof of the pudding was the opening two league games. A 5-0 home defeat (with Lee Hughes scoring a hat-trick) of Bradford City and a 4-0 away win at Macclesfield, set the tone for a never to be forgotten season. I had tears in my eyes at half-time in that opening game. Having had ten years of unremitting misery, I couldn't believe what I was seeing.

A controversial defeat at Saltergate quickly brought us all back down to earth. However, by then Sol Campbell had joined the Club, and the media attention seemed never ending. Surely this was all a dream? In early October, after a home 2-2 draw with Torquay United, Ian McParland was on his bike and alarm bells, which started when Sol Campbell had left after just the one game away at Morecambe, were now ringing loudly.

David Kevan took over on a temporary basis whilst investigative journalists were spending more time at Meadow Lane than football reporters. Kevan's two game stint was short but relatively successful - a win and a draw - as he was followed by Sven-Goran's fellow Swede, Hans Backe. He lasted a little longer, overseeing a total of seven games before resigning, claiming that he was not being paid. His mentor, the higher profile of the two Swedes, was no longer seen at Meadow Lane on match days. Those alarm bells now took on Big Ben type resonance.

David Kevan stepped up to the plate again, and results on the field seemed to be unaffected as Notts finished the year in 4th place with Lee Hughes having seventeen goals to his credit. This included three hat-tricks. Maloney and Ritchie returned to their parent clubs,

233

Nottingham Forest and Portsmouth respectively, presumably a result of Notts not meeting their financial responsibilities.

At this point we were all concerned as to what the new decade would bring. Although eliminated at the earliest opportunity from both League Cup and JP Trophy, at least the club had overcome Bradford City and Bournemouth and had a third round FA Cup tie against Forest Green Rovers to look forward to - if indeed non-League opposition for the third consecutive season was a cause for optimism! - in 2010. Whatever, Notts County would continue to be in the news for all the wrong reasons.

Chapter 13

Noughties – spreading our sporting wings

The Millennium dawned, and to all intents and purposes, Helen and I could once again do what we liked with our free time. Our parental responsibilities fulfilled, as Arthur Daley used to say, the 'world was our lobster'. That didn't mean we took on a hedonistic middle aged lifestyle, but recognising we were likely only to be 'here' just the once, we became a bit more adventurous. That in itself doesn't have any sporting significance, but we planned to celebrate surviving 25 years of marriage by going back to America and travelling down Route 66, and indirectly that trip did.

However, before I get to that, 2nd July 2000 was a momentous day. Now those of you with an excellent memory for high profile sporting occasions will immediately recall that this was the day that France defeated Italy 2-1 to win that year's European Championships. Well done if you did. However, for Mrs Gyles, it was the day that she first experienced how much fun, and indeed how profitable, 'a day at the races' could be.

Despite our two having left Tibshelf School, we were still very much involved in the PTFA - and would remain so for a while - and as a result, were happy to join in with a purely social event for parents and teachers, viz. a day out at Doncaster Racecourse.

Without a word of a lie, we each had a £5 win bet on a horse in each of the six races, and between us, had five winners. The best priced was the 16/1 (actual SP was 14/1) Style Dancer in the *Mail on Sunday Mile Handicap*. Helen, for reasons that have never been properly explained, had selected this unfancied horse. On the bus home, the hardened race goers among our group couldn't get their head round how a couple of novice punters had made a clear £85 in profit. Neither could we of course, but we just played it cool.

Helen having enjoyed that experience, later that year, we went first to York (anniversary treat) and then Wetherby (Helen's birthday) and although on those occasions the bookies had less to fear, we were hooked. So much so, that having visited three of the nine courses in Yorkshire, we (well it was more me) thought it would be fun to visit the other six. You can probably see where this is going, and you'd be right. After a trip to Redcar, the last of the nine, the target shifted to 'let's visit all sixty in the UK'. You'll just have to wait for a progress report.

One outcome from our discovering horse racing was a conscious decision to try some other sports. The first of these was Ice Hockey. We went a few times, most memorably when Dawn came over from Ulster in November 2002 (Helen's 50th), and we took her and Mark to the National Ice Centre to see Nottingham Panthers take on their team, Belfast Giants. Dawn was a real fan and found it difficult to contain her emotions. She wasn't the only one. Most of the 4,000 plus crowd could best be described as noisy and boisterous.

After approximately five visits, we gave it up. It may be a tough sport but I just find it difficult to accept some of the feigned aggression and think, just like some forms of wrestling, a lot of the action is stage managed to get the crowd going. Still, we'd tried it.

I used to watch a lot of televised snooker. I was, for example, one of the millions who stayed up until the wee small hours of Monday 29th April 1985 to see the conclusion of the famous Dennis Taylor/Steve Davis World Championship Final. The sport (OK - game if you like) probably reached peak popularity in the UK that year. To this day I still watch a little, but like many others, it is no longer a 'must watch' event.

Despite that, we vowed to visit the Crucible, conveniently just up the road from us, in 2004, to see play on the middle Sunday. I enjoyed it - Helen was less enamoured! - and to see the likes of John Higgins, Graeme Dott, David Gray and Ian McCulloch (no, not that one!) in action, in the flesh so to speak, and to sample the atmosphere, made the trip worthwhile. It was however, a 'one off'.

That visit to Sheffield for a new sport was followed the next year by a trip to Ponds Forge. In an effort to promote the sport of basketball in the UK, a work colleague had been given two free tickets to see Sheffield Sharks take on Birmingham Knights. Well, it would be a new sport and a Friday night out, so when she said she wasn't bothered and would I like to take them, it would have been rude to say no. With hindsight, I wish I had.

Basketball, very big in USA and some other parts of the world, is not for me. It just seems so tedious. Yes, there is a lot of skill involved, but the endless sequence of one team scoring points at one end, followed by the opposition going down the other end and doing the same. Repeat ad nauseam until someone makes a mistake, does not, for me, make for great spectating. Well, we gave it a go and that was one more minority sporting box ticked.

On Friday 20th April 2007, Notts County were playing at Hartlepool. I can't remember why the game was switched to Friday, but after a 1-1 draw we stayed overnight with a view to having a potter around North Yorkshire on the way back on the Saturday. The plan was to eventually drop into Headingley for our first experience of Rugby League.

Leeds beat St Helens 38-19 that night, and although it was a bit of a slow burn, I could see the entertainment value in the sport and in a few years' time would attend many more games. In fact, I'd now describe myself as a fan.

One other PTFA social event we attended was a Friday night out at the dog racing at Colwick Park, Nottingham. It was the standard 'wine & dine' type of evening with a full view of the track, and whilst that was enjoyable enough, it was another sporting experience that we'd have difficulty in recommending. I went again a few years later for a work colleague's leaving do and this just confirmed my initial impression. It was cheap and tacky and not for me.

In November 2004, a group of six of us, collectively known as the TOG's (don't ask!), made our first trip to New York City. As well as doing all the usual touristy things that first time visitors to the Big Apple just have to do, four of us visited Meadowlands, across the Hudson River in New Jersey, to see New York Giants play Philadelphia Eagles. This was a game in the 2004/05 NFL, and for the record, the visitors won 27-6.

This was not an enjoyable experience. The weather was atrocious, which didn't help, but the sport itself failed to get my (or any other of the TOG's for that matter) adrenaline flowing. Too much of a 'stop/start' sport for my liking with so many stoppages and big unrecognisable bulky men seemingly entering or leaving the field of play at random. It was another of those 'one off' and 'never again' sporting occasions.

I mentioned our plan to travel from Chicago to Los Angeles along what many Americans call the 'mother road' but which most of us in Europe call Route 66. We didn't do it on a Harley Davidson, but in a hired Chevvy which was much more to Helen's liking. In planning this adventure, one of the things I was looking forward to was sampling the 'all American' experience of going to a 'ball game'.

A work colleague in America checked the 2001 baseball schedule, compared it to our plans, and noted that we'd be in St Louis when the Cardinals were at home in a series against the Atlanta Braves. He did more than that, he got us some tickets in advance of the trip.

Cardinals won that game 4-0, with Mark McGwire, a legend in the game, scoring a home run in what was his final season. Now that fact will not mean much to a lot of people, but it will to followers of the game. That night was an introduction to a sport, much ridiculed on this side of the Atlantic, that I've followed fairy intensely ever since.

In 2007 we saw Minnesota Twins (v Detroit Tigers) in Minneapolis and two years later Colorado Rockies (v San Diego Padres) followed later on that same trip by Seattle Mariners (v Detroit Tigers again). By then, I was really getting into the sport and understanding some of the skills and nuances that I was clearly unaware of at that very first game back in 2001. I know I'd probably be wasting my time trying to convert some Brits to the game, especially when I claim that there are certain elements of it that are similar to cricket, so I won't bother. They'll just have to find out for themselves.

Talking of cricket, with Trent Bridge memberships now renewed each year without question, this was the decade when my cricket watching dreams and fantasies began to be realised. With the exception of those years when the Trent Bridge Test Match was staged whilst we were overseas, we generally saw the first four days. Failing that, other than 2005 - and what a year that was to miss out! - we'd see at least one Test at one of the other grounds.

We saw Zimbabwe at Trent Bridge in 2000 in what was only their second Test in England. England had won the 1st Test at Lord's comfortably with Ed Giddins taking 5/15 in 7 overs. That was the pinnacle of his four Test career. He played just the one more Test (Trent Bridge) and was never selected again. In addition to Giddins, this proved to be the second (& last) of Chris Schofield's short Test career.

On the opening day of the 2nd Test, Mike Atherton and Mark Ramprakash put on 121 for the first wicket and England closed at 203/3 on a day cut short by rain. The Friday was a complete wash out which was a real shame as we'd taken Graham Williams, an old pal of mine - I'd been Best Man at his second wedding - down to Nottingham. He hadn't been to Trent Bridge for years, and in a day when the umpires were carrying out inspections almost hourly as hopes of play rose and fell away again, he hid his disappointment well. In fact, I think he quite enjoyed the atmosphere. Incidentally, this was the first complete loss of a day's Test cricket in Nottingham since 1967. Just Graham's luck!

As it happens, the loss of that day's play probably saved England from an embarrassing defeat. The Zimbabweans declared their 1st Innings 89 runs behind after a career best 148* from Murray Goodwin and then dismissed England for 147. Needing 237 to win, they didn't have enough time and the game ended in a draw.

Later that summer we attended ODI's at both The Oval (Zimbabwe) and Lord's (West Indies). The first of these was the International debut for Marcus Trescothick. Despite his 79 England were to lose by five wickets. He was, of course, to go on to experience better days with England.

Even later that year we were at Old Trafford on the day that Alec Stewart scored 105 in England's 1st Innings in the 3rd Test against the West Indies. The match was drawn, but the significance of that century was that it was completed on the 100th birthday of the late Queen Mother.

We were away when the 2001 Trent Bridge Ashes Test took place. Probably a good job as it was all over in three days. We did however get over to Birmingham - we actually stayed in Kidderminster for three nights - to see the first of Usman Afzaal's three Test career. Neither he, nor England were a success as Australia won by an innings in four days. Were it not for a last wicket partnership of 103 between Alec Stewart and Andy Caddick on the first day, the match may well have finished a day earlier.

We managed the first four days of the 2002 Trent Bridge Test against India. It was the Test in which not only did Steve Harmison and Robert Key make their debuts, but Michael Vaughan made his top Test score. He had just passed 150 when we nipped over to Meadow Lane at around 2.45 pm (a 1-1 draw with Wycombe Wanderers if you must know) and were pleased to see him still there when we returned two hours later. He was soon to fall for 197 however, but with major contributions from Alec Stewart and Craig White, England gained a first innings lead of 260. Despite taking two early wickets, England were unable to force a win on the fifth day.

The Zimbabweans toured England again in 2003. The second Test of the series took place at Chester-le-Street, England's first new venue in 101 years, and we had tickets for the first three days and pre-booked accommodation in Newton Aycliffe. Those three days were all that England required for an emphatic victory. Richard Johnson made his Test debut bowling alongside Jimmy Anderson (playing just his second Test). Johnson may have been named man of the match for his 6/33 as Zimbabwe were dismissed for 94 in reply to England's 416, but he played in only two more Tests.

We missed the 2004 Trent Bridge Test against New Zealand but saw the West Indies in Birmingham. England were to win the series 4-0 and the Edgbaston Test is best remembered for Marcus Trescothick scoring a century in each innings, plus an explosive knock of 167 (his highest Test score) from Andrew Flintoff. Brian Lara, as captain of West Indies, was back at the ground where he set his world record 501*. He may have made 95 in the West Indies 1st innings (Ramnaresh Sarwan made 139) but he was leading a dispirited side.

I can't remember exactly why it was that we didn't go to the 2005 Trent Bridge Ashes Test. I had tickets for both the Friday and Saturday but passed them on to an old mate, Phil Mansfield. So it was he who saw Flintoff score 102 and Geraint Jones 85 before asking the Aussies to follow on and witness Ricky Ponting's emotional departure after being run out by Gary Pratt. I had to make do with seeing Notts beat Bristol Rovers 2-0 on the Saturday.

As a result then, I didn't get to see any of what has gone down in history as the *Greatest Ever Ashes Series*. Ach well, I've had a good run for my money, and earlier that summer, I did get to see England beat Bangladesh within three days at Chester-le-Street. In a match that started on a Friday, England had a lead of 165 with seven wickets in hand at the end of that first day.

The Bangladeshi's just couldn't cope with the conditions, and with Steve Harmison taking five wickets in the first innings and Matthew Hoggard five in the second, they managed only 420 runs (a much better 316 second time around) in total. By contrast, England needed just the one innings with Trescothick (151) and Ian Bell (162*) filling their boots. We had the pleasurable surprise of meeting up with my brother and his pal Bill Findlay on the Saturday. They had travelled down by train from Edinburgh.

Sri Lanka visited Trent Bridge in 2006. There was a Friday start to this, the last in a three Test series. England were already 1-0 up and expected to win. Jonathan Lewis made his debut, but was never re-selected.

In a tight game, Sri Lanka were leading by 288 runs with three second innings wickets remaining when we left Trent Bridge on the Sunday evening. England still had hopes of victory. However, at work next day, I was constantly interrupted by a fellow cricketing devotee who, instead of getting on with his work - as I was! – was regularly telling me that

'England have lost another one'. Muttiah Muralitharan was apparently unplayable in a spell of 8/26 from 105 balls. Sri Lanka won by 134 runs.

England's seven wicket defeat to the Indians in the second (Trent Bridge) of the three match Test series in 2007 will always be remembered for 'jellybeangate'. For reasons that were never fully explained and with no-one owning up, we'll just have to hazard a guess as to how and why Zaheer Khan found jelly beans at the crease when he came out to bat towards the end of India's first innings.

Whatever, it was one of a number of examples of bad behaviour in an ill-tempered Test and it certainly helped to 'fire up' the offended tailender. Despite Michael Vaughan's 124, Khan took five second innings wickets (including Vaughan) to leave India needing 73 to win. They reached the target with only three wickets down.

We were lucky enough to get tickets for the 2nd & 3rd days of the 2008 Lord's Test v South Africa, and by the time we left the ground on the Saturday, an England win looked certain. Kevin Pietersen (152) and Ian Bell (199) had been the main contributors in England's total of 593/8 declared and South Africa, despite an Ashwell Prince century, were asked to follow on 346 behind. However, with three century makers, they managed to bat out the final two days to salvage a draw.

When we turned up at Edgbaston for the 3rd Test, South Africa had taken a 1-0 series lead. This proved to be Michael Vaughan's last match as captain as his side lost by six wickets. In my view, Kevin Pietersen was partly responsible as he showed, as indeed he did throughout his career, that brilliant cricketer though he may have been, he was no team player.

England were battling in their second innings to build a lead with Pietersen and Paul Collingwood putting on over a hundred runs, and were inching towards setting a challenging target when, on 94, the South African went for the glory shot to bring up his century, and was caught at deep mid-on. Collingwood kept his head and managed to steer the tail, but was last man out and the 281 runs required were knocked off for the loss of only five wickets. Who knows, had Pietersen not been so selfish, the final target might just have been enough and Michael Vaughan's tenure as captain may have been extended.

Ironically, Pietersen was appointed captain in succession to Vaughan and made a big score to help secure a consolation win in the final Test. It was however, downhill from there for him.

There were other days of international cricket throughout the decade, too many to record or be of interest, but there was one ODI at Trent Bridge which is worth recalling. India were the visitors and Alex Wharf, ex Nottinghamshire but then of Glamorgan, made his England debut. He did well, taking three wickets, but it was with India at 170/7 that Steve Harmison wrote his name into the record books. He took the last three wickets in consecutive balls to become only the second Englishman - at that time - to take a hat-trick in a One Day International. England won the game comfortably.

Nottinghamshire won the County Championship in 2005 for the first time in eighteen years. Although a member, I was still working and had very few opportunities to see Stephen Fleming's successful side. I did see the odd day, but as with others who had yet to retire, my Trent Bridge attendance throughout the 'noughties' was mainly limited to one day and T20 games.

T20 had been introduced in 2003 and two of the first four 'Finals Day's' were held at Trent Bridge. I can't remember the exact price for tickets, although £20 comes to mind. Whatever, with three games played on the day, they were certainly good value for money, spoilt only by all the noise and razzamatazz that seems to be a necessary element of such sporting events.

In 2006, Nottinghamshire made it through to the Final to play Leicestershire, and under gradually heavier rain over Nottingham were still in with a chance at the start of the final over of their reply. They needed 17 but didn't make it, and it was another eleven years before they added that particular title to their long list of honours.

I can't finish off this section without making some reference to my own athletic achievements in this decade. I started running to keep fit in

1997. Rather foolishly, some might say, I'd signed up to do a half marathon in September of that year and this provided the target/incentive to keep me focussed. I'm not a natural, but I do have good staying power, and gradually increasing my distance I was almost up to 13 miles without needing to stop by the end of August. In fact, on the day of Princess Diana's funeral, a Saturday, I ran over to my in-laws in Kirkby via a route that I knew was just the right distance. A couple of weeks later, I completed the Robin Hood HM in something like 1 hours 55 minutes.

Over the next seventeen years, I gradually improved my pace and entered many other events. I peaked in 2006. I'd managed my one and only time of under 100 minutes for a half marathon in 2005 and a few weeks later heard that after four failed past applications, I had at last secured a place in the following year's London Marathon.

Other than a few wee drams in the wee small hours of 1st January 2006, no alcohol passed my lips until 7th May as I set myself a serious training programme. I did the Oakley 20 Miler three weeks before the Marathon at an eight minute/mile pace. At that rate, I thought I'd smash my London target of under four hours. Well, as those of you who have run a marathon will well know, you learn a lot on that first one. I was going well for about twenty miles on 23rd April, but then fell away to finish in 3 hours 55 minutes.

I'd have loved to have done another one, convinced that I'd benefit from the experience, but the training takes a lot out of people other than yourself, and I took Helen's advice. **"No more full marathons!"**

Two weeks later, I ran the Leeds Half Marathon with Heather. This was her first, and in wet and miserable conditions, we went round together in 2 hours 10 minutes. It was tough for her but it's not put her off as she's done a few more since and might just get a time faster than her Dad ever managed before she's finished. That Leeds race, two weeks after the London Marathon, saw me at the fittest I've probably ever been. I may have peaked too early. Whatever, it's been downhill ever since!

Chapter 14

Twenty-tens – first, the good news.....!

2010

Where were we? Ah yes, the seemingly never ending saga at Meadow Lane. David Kevan, remained in charge for twelve weeks. Of nine league games, five were victories and just two defeats. Postponements, resulting from a combination of bad weather and cup matches had seen Notts drop to seventh in the table. They did have games in hand which, if won, would have seen them climb to the fringes of the automatic promotion places, but that seemed academic. The survival of the Club, which we were hearing would soon be placed into administration, was of more immediate concern.

In the FA Cup, Forest Green Rovers were beaten 2-1 to secure a home 4th Round tie with Premiership Wigan Athletic. In that game, Notts had a 2-0 half-time lead but had to settle for a replay after a 2-2 draw. Ten days later, two goals in the last quarter of an hour at the home of the pie munchers, meant we'd have to travel to London for a 5th Round Tie with Fulham, another club from the top division. At Craven Cottage, Notts may have been outclassed in losing 4-0, but it had been fun while it lasted. Perhaps of more importance were the rumours that the Club was about to be sold.

During the following week, it was confirmed that Ray Trew, a former director of Lincoln City, had bought Notts County for the princely sum of £1. To most of us that seemed a bit overpriced, and apparently Mr Trew soon came to the same conclusion, especially when he discovered the true extent of the Club's debt. Still, the immediate prospect of administration had been averted.

During the following week, David Kevan's last two games as manager were 1-1 draws against Grimsby Town (home) & Aldershot (away). At this latter game, I went down with Alan Baldwin and met up with a few of his 'Shots supporting friends. They told me, on good authority so they said, that Steve Evans, the popular and fair minded Scot who had overseen Boston United's promotion to the Football League, and who would ultimately do the same for Crawley Town, was shortly to leave the Sussex club and take over at Meadow Lane.

On 23rd February, it was announced that Steve Cotterill, former Cheltenham Town manager, was to be the fourth (in less than six months) manager of Notts County. I think it's fair to say that 'he did all right'. He was to manage Notts for eighteen games, only two of which were lost, as the Club gained 45 of the 54 points up for grabs whilst he was in charge.

Promotion was confirmed during a run of seven consecutive wins with the Championship itself secured with a 5-0 victory up at Darlington. Such was the level of interest that the final game of the season, an away game at Plainmoor (Torquay United), was made all ticket.

This could have been a problem for me as I'd already arranged for a mini-bus to take thirteen down to the game. Accommodation in Ilfracombe had been booked and a night's entertainment in the Devon resort arranged. Fortunately, there were enough kind people in the Meadow Lane queue on the day that tickets went on sale, who were prepared to let me have the additional ticket from their limit of 'two per person'. So it was, that on Saturday 8th May, via various pick-up points in Derbyshire, Nottinghamshire and Leicestershire, we headed south.

After some pre-match anaesthetic, we got to the ground and I went on to achieve one of my ambitions. I ran out with the teams as, and perhaps I should have mentioned it before, I was one of the match-day mascots. I'd recently passed a big birthday and had organised the whole event as a way of celebrating the fact that I'd got this far.

Prior to the game I had to buy a full set of kit. Not something I'd have done normally, because I have a view that men over a certain age should not be allowed to wear replica shirts. However, needs must, and if I was going to play the part, I'd have to look it too.

At Plainmoor, I made my way round to the main stand, introduced myself, and was given a place to change and securely leave my everyday clothing. Suitably kitted up, I then lost my bearings and ended up in the away changing room. I stumbled in and there was Steve Cotterill on his own - the players were out doing their warm ups - and the look on his face was a picture. As the colour drained from his cheeks I could see that he was thinking "that must have been one helluva warm-up!" I explained what I was doing, shook him by the hand, and wished him all the best. He never said a word.

Leaving the shocked Notts manager with his own thoughts, I went out and came across the guy who co-ordinated the mascots' activities. As the other, much younger mascots were already out on the pitch having a kick around, he suggested I just go out and watch from the dugout. Once all the players came in, I went into the tunnel and waited until the two teams lined up behind the officials. Each mascot was asked to stand next to their favourite player and hold hands as they entered the pitch. I chose Ben Davies and we had a little chat, but I can assure you, we most definitely did not hold hands.

Once out on the pitch, the two teams lined up and we had the friendly pre-match hand shake of the opposition and match day officials. As I shook the hand of Steve Bratt, the West Midlands based referee, he asked me, "Is your name on the team sheet?" I think he was joking and just mumbled something like 'the warm-up took it out of me' before running off to join the Notts players as they kicked a few balls around in front of the bulk of the travelling support.

I had a general chat with Lee Hughes but a more specific one with Kasper Schmeichel. "Any chance of getting your gloves after the game?" I asked, more in hope than expectation. He shook his head and said that they were needed for whoever had sponsored him throughout the season. Fair enough thought I, but that didn't stop me from slipping a spare ball into the net when he wasn't looking. Yes, albeit from close range, I'd beaten one of the best goalkeepers to ever play for the Club!

The referee beckoned the captains to the centre circle and I joined them and the other mascots for the toss and obligatory group photograph. Once that was over, I ran back down the tunnel, got changed and made my way round the ground to join the rest of our group behind the goal. The game itself was a bit of an anti-climax - a scoreless draw - but the weekend went well. Indeed, despite all the off-field drama, the season was a great success. As I write, (August 2020), the last such season that we 'Pies have been able to enjoy.

The season may have been over for most football fans but not for us. After joining Alan Baldwin at the Don Valley Stadium to see Aldershot's play-off second leg - they lost 3-0 on aggregate - Helen and myself (but mainly Helen!) packed our bags for our near three weeks in South Africa.

I'd become a bit of an expert in using the FIFA on-line ticket application process to best advantage, and had succeeded in getting a pair of tickets for four different venues in the 2010 World Cup Finals tournament. It's a big country, but this gave us a good opportunity to see the interior.

Landing in Johannesburg, we had pre-booked airport accommodation for the first night and then, prior to picking up a car, had to go to an accredited 2010 ticketing distribution location. To limit touting activity, the decision had been made not to send out tickets in advance. It was chaotic and there were a lot of angry people in there on that morning. Eventually we got all of our tickets and could head off to our first destination, a B&B some 60 miles short of Polokwane. The couple who ran it were just fantastic. They were Afrikaners, but without some of the seemingly inbred prejudice that we were later to come across.

On the day before our first game, they invited us to join what they described as their regular Saturday night braai when a few of their friends came round. It was a very enjoyable experience although I did wonder if they'd specifically arranged this to enable some of their friends to come and have a look at 'this strange couple who have travelled thousands of miles to see....soccer!' They were all rugby union fanatics and South Africa had home tests v France and Italy while we were there. I did my best in conversation, but I guess that they quickly twigged that I knew next to nothing about that sport.

Our opening game, in Polokwane, was an instantly forgettable 1-0 victory for Slovenia over Algeria. It was however, our introduction to the infamous vuvuzela. It was not, and over the coming days continued not to be, a pleasant experience.

After another night back at the B&B, we set off for Phalaborwa, one of the gateways to the Kruger National Park. Our first full day here was spent in the Park. You can take very expensive trips with experts who guarantee that you'll get to meet the 'big five' but we decided to do our own thing. During the morning we saw nothing particularly exciting other than the big backsides of some water buffalo. The afternoon was different however, and amongst other of the native species, we came across elephants, giraffes, baboons, hippos, zebras, antelopes, vultures and lots (& lots) more water buffaloes. We even saw the front of some of them!

We had an exceptionally early start on our last morning as we had just over 300 miles to cover to get us back to Johannesburg for the 1.30pm kick-off in our second game. We made it, and saw Gonzalo Higuain score a hat-trick in Argentina's 4-1 defeat of South Korea. Although Lionel Messi didn't score, this being the first time I'd seen him, I could certainly see what all the fuss was about. The South Korean fans, especially the ladies, were just brilliant. So colourful and - I accept that this is not an adjective generally used in relation to football fans - charming.

On our way to the Soccer City Stadium, Helen spotted that alongside the vuvuzela sellers were others who were clearly entrepreneurs in the making. They were selling ear defenders, just what we (& thousands of others) wanted. I bought a couple of packs.

We used our one full day in Johannesburg to explore the city. This included a tour of the Castle Brewery and then headed northwest for Rustenburg and our next match. This was another game that failed to excite. It ended as a 1-1 draw between Australia and Ghana. In many respects the Aussies will have been the happier as they had played 66 minutes with only ten men after future Notts County boss, Harry Kewell, was sent off for his handling of the ball in the box. In addition to the dismissal, this resulted in Ghana equalising from the penalty spot.

After a tour of some of both Zulu and Boer War battlefields - this included Rorke's Drift as made famous in Michael Caine's 1964 film - we had three nights in Pretoria. It was here that we experienced arrogance and levels of disdain for the native population from Afrikaners. I won't go into detail, but having formed the view during our travels that this was most definitely a country of two societies viz. the 'haves and the have nots', we could see that one of those groups would fight long and hard **not** to change things.

Our final game was the most exciting. Whilst England were beating Slovenia to confirm their progress, Algeria were playing USA in a game that both sides had to win to have a chance of making the knock-out stages.

I was surprised by the number of Americans amongst the crowd of just over 35,000, and in pre-match conversation, just how knowledgeable they were. In our various trips to the USA I'd very rarely had a meaningful conversation with a native born American about soccer. Well, based upon our experiences that night, things are changing.

As the game went into added time with no score, it looked as if both sides would be eliminated when, in the 91st minute, Landon Donovan scored. The USA had not only won the game but they topped the group. To describe the Americans there as euphoric would be an understatement and dis-service to them. Boy, were they happy. It was a really exciting game to finish up with.

We had a couple more days in the country before flying back. Other than one instance in Pretoria when a guy tried to pick my pocket, we saw none of the crime we'd been led to believe by the doom mongers, that we could expect before we set off. It's a beautiful country, but with a lot of poverty and social problems that hold back the majority of the population. I'd go again but I'd be on my own. Helen's one trip there was enough for her.

Steve Cotterill, his short term contract having come to an end, moved off to manage Portsmouth during the close season. The new manager was Craig Short, the guy who some twenty years before had indirectly helped fund the renovation of Meadow Lane. Other than a brief spell in Hungary, he was a first time manager and it showed. He was gone by 23rd October.

Despite being in 16th position at the time of his dismissal, his record in the league of five wins and seven defeats didn't seem too bad. In addition, the Club had overcome both Plymouth Argyle and Watford to reach the 3rd Round of the League Cup - where they lost 4-2 away at Wolves - so it came as a bit of a surprise to many fans.

I reckon Craig Short's 'card was marked' after the 3-2 win away at Peterborough on 28th September. It was a good win but spoilt by the misbehaviour from players (on both sides!) and there appeared, from the touchline at any rate, to be a lack of discipline within the Notts squad. I reckon, that Craig Short was probably 'too nice' for the job of manager. To back that assertion, it's interesting to note that he has not managed another club since.

To replace Short, Paul Ince was immediately appointed on a contract running to the end of 2013/14. He didn't even last to the end of the 2010/11 season. He brought in a number of loan players, including his own young son, Tom, but there was no immediate improvement in results, and as 2010 became 2011, Notts were in 19th place.

They had however advanced in the FA Cup having beaten both Gateshead and Bournemouth at home to earn an away 3rd Round tie at Sunderland. There was then at least something to look forward to in the New Year.

From a personal viewpoint, as the year ended, I had at least managed to get back up to '92' having made my first ever visit to a) the new Cardiff City Stadium and b) the Globe Arena to see Morecambe after their move from Christie Park. On a weekend in Belgium, Helen and I had seen our first Jupiler Pro League game as we watched Club Brugge beat Lierse 2-0. Life wasn't all bad then!

2011

The excitement levels around Meadow Lane rose following the 2-1 FA Cup victory at Sunderland. Ailsa came up with us. On the day after her 30th birthday, this was indeed a treat for her. Manchester City were next, and after Neil Bishop had given Notts a 59th minute lead, a shock was on the cards. Unfortunately (for us!), Edin Dzeko equalised with ten minutes to go. The replay up at Eastlands, was much more one-sided as the Premiership big boys scored four second half goals to end up 5-0 winners. They went on to beat Stoke City in the Final.

After seven losses in eight league games, and with the Club now in a relegation battle, it was time for Mr Ince to be given his P45. Unlike Craig Short, he was to manage another club, in his case Blackpool, but he lasted less than twelve months there too. Within a week of Paul Ince leaving, Martin Allen took over with the immediate brief of keeping Notts County in the 3rd tier.

He succeeded, but not before a 9th consecutive league defeat had seen Notts fall to 22nd place. The likely prospect of the Club having just the one season in this division looked a probability rather than a possibility. Two away wins, at Tranmere Rovers and Swindon Town may have improved the situation, but relegation remained an option on the final day. A home draw against already promoted Brighton at Meadow Lane on 7th May was enough for survival.

This particular season saw two abandonments and one postponement, all away from home, and all with us having made the journey. To be factually correct, in Brighton's case, we were on the M25 and increasingly concerned that even if we made it to the Withdean Stadium through the blizzard conditions, we'd be so late that the game would probably be over, when we heard that it had been called off.

As for Hartlepool, there had been less than five minutes play when that was called off because of waterlogging. The same applied at Tranmere, when we at least got 53 minutes (and were 1-0 up) when again, because of incessant rain, the referee had to abandon.

252

There was some encouraging news during the close season. Martin Allen was not only allowed to continue in the job, but was given permission to sign Alan Sheehan, Julian Kelly, Jeff Hughes and, after a couple of league games, Alan Judge, who had spent some time on loan the previous season. Most fans thought the newcomers added a bit of welcome quality to the squad.

A 3-0 away win at Carlisle on the opening day was encouraging and after fifteen games, the Club were sitting comfortably in fourth place. Losing, on penalties, in the 1st Round of the League Cup to Nottingham Forest was a blow, particularly as Notts were leading in the 120th minute, but the team were playing in the spirit and style of their manager. Four consecutive defeats in December tempered expectations somewhat, and the Club were in 10th position after a 3-2 defeat away to Oldham on Hogmanay.

Once again, Notts had progressed past the first two rounds of the FA Cup and were due to play at the Keepmoat Stadium for the first time, as they'd been drawn away to Doncaster Rovers from the division above.

Brighton had moved to their new ground at the beginning of the season and were attracting big crowds to the Amex Stadium. Concerned that we might make the trip south and find that we couldn't get in - this was Brighton after all and I didn't want to make it an unwanted hat-trick of wasted journeys to that city - I contacted the club explaining the purpose of our visit. I was pleased with the emailed reply from the secretary who told me that he'd arrange for a pair of tickets to be left for us advising what we had to do to collect on the day. Top man!

With this, and having visited Stevenage for the first time back in February, I would be entering 2012, once more a genuine and bona fide member of the 92 Club. Strictly speaking, I still had Crawley FC and AFC Wimbledon to visit, but I had time on my side. As a bonus, Helen and myself had a weekend in Denmark in November and saw FC Copenhagen defeat Lyngby 3-0 in the Superligaen.

2012

That promising FA Cup run continued after seeing off Doncaster 2-0 with a Jeff Hughes double. This earned us a trip to Stevenage with Notts County generally regarded as favourites. Sadly, an early own goal by on loan Damion Stewart was all that was required to show how daft that pre-match assessment had been.

The day (19th February) after travelling back from a 3-0 defeat up at Hartlepool, we heard that Martin Allen had been sacked. None of the supporters really seemed to know why, and to the best of my knowledge, this has never been properly explained. Whatever, Mr Trew didn't hang around, and in an indication that this latest development had been pre-planned, on the Monday, Keith Curle was announced as the latest in an ever lengthening list of Notts County managers.

The new man oversaw four consecutive victories straight away and with ten wins from the remaining sixteen games, Notts had a remote chance of making the play-offs on the day that the last of those wins (4-1 at home to Colchester United) was achieved. As it happened, they finished in seventh place and missed out on goal difference. Things were on the up again though, and supporters were looking forward to the new season and the chance for Keith Curle to really put his stamp on the team.

Before the season came to an end, we had a weekend in London (Richmond actually) for a combined football (AFC Wimbledon) and show treat. This was our first visit to the phoenix club, and while we saw them lose to Rotherham, I was getting regular text updates that afternoon from the east (Orient in fact) where, with three second half goals, Notts were winning at Brisbane Road.

With Notts County finishing on a relative 'high', the 2012/13 season was something to look forward to. In the meantime, our summer holiday was to be another footballing adventure. We just hadn't realised how much of an adventure it would turn out to be.

I had applied through the UEFA website for tickets for the 2012 European Championships which were jointly hosted by Poland and Ukraine. Using the tried and tested approach of working out where most supporters would like to go, I figured that for ease of transport, language and EU membership, Poland would be more popular than Ukraine. On that basis I applied for six games in the former Soviet state and came up trumps with three. The December draw confirmed that we'd be seeing each of England's group games split between Donetsk and Kiev.

We had carried out some research and made plans once we knew we were guaranteed tickets. After the draw I was pleased that I'd done that. Prices would undoubtedly have increased when it became clear that England, Sweden and France, and their large travelling support, were to be visiting those cities.

We'd booked flights from Gatwick direct to Odessa and intended having a couple of days there to acclimatise. We were then to hire a car and drive over to a place that we'd make our base, as on the map, this looked convenient for both Donetsk and Kiev. Little did we know!

With all accommodation booked, about ten days before we were due to fly, Helen tried to check in on-line. When she was unable to do this, she contacted Expedia through whom we'd booked the flights, and was told that the Hungarian airline that flew that route had gone bust and...........didn't you get an email? No we hadn't and you can imagine her response. She called me and we agreed that the recriminations would have to wait, we only had a short period in which to find alternative ways of getting to and from Odessa.

It took twenty four hours but we eventually found an outward flight from Gatwick to Istanbul where we could link up with a trip over the Black Sea to Odessa. We'd arrive considerably later than we had intended but at least it would be the same day. Unfortunately, it was not possible to fit that route into the return journey unless we either curtailed or extended our stay in Ukraine. Helen found that we could leave on our planned day of departure, albeit much earlier that we'd intended, and fly from Odessa to Kiev, and from there onto Gatwick.

Whilst we were confident that our credit card would refund the cost of the initial flights, we were still going to be about £800 out of pocket. Our pre-planning nine months before when we had looked for best bargains had been a waste of time.

Our first couple of days in Odessa were lovely although, as we were to find out, didn't really prepare us for what was to follow. The city is a tourist destination, and not only is English fairly widely spoken, but there were a number of dual language signs to help us find our way around.

It came as a real culture shock then when we picked up our hire car from the airport and set off for Zaporozhye where we were to spend ten days. I had a map, but just couldn't fathom out the road signs which were no longer dual language. Without exception, they are in Cyrillic. It takes you a while, in my case about a week, to come to terms with K being L, M = N, T = R, X = U, E = F etc., with all the other letters more symbols than the standard Latin alphabet.

My problem was compounded when I tried to ask people the right direction for Zaporozhye. They could tell I was trying to find somewhere, but couldn't understand where it was I was looking for. Well, how would you pronounce it? Wrong! It is Zaproasia. Eventually, one guy twigged and we were on our way. Over the next few hours, every time I wound down the window and asked for 'Zaproasia' with a faux Russian accent, I got a positive response.

We made it by nightfall, and after driving around for an hour or so and showing the hotel booking reference to a number of people, we had still not found the place. I pulled up alongside a taxi and asked the driver thinking he should know. He shrugged his shoulders and then suddenly pointed across the road. By accident, we'd come across our base for the next ten days.

Some of the staff spoke a little English, which was a relief, and after checking in, we asked the best way to get over to Donetsk for the game the following day. For a 7.30pm kick off, they said we'd need to leave about 1.00pm. This seemed ultra-cautious to me, as it was only around

160miles. I should have known better than to doubt their word. The roads were poor and it had taken us eight hours to drive the 300 miles from Odessa.

We set off in plenty of time for the Donbass Arena and saw England take the lead through Joleon Lescott. This was later cancelled out by Samir Nasri. France probably had the better of the game, but I reckon most in attendance thought that a draw was a fair result.

The drive back was interesting and took about half an hour longer as there were very few lights and we were almost having to stop and get out of the car to check road signs.

Learning from this trip, I suggested that rather than drive up to Kiev, about 360 miles away, for the Sweden game, we have a look at trains as an alternative. We went along to the station and found someone who spoke perfect English who was keen to sell us the tickets. Unfortunately, we'd have to leave on the Thursday to get there for the Friday night game, and then stay in Kiev until Sunday to come back. We checked out buses as well and they were just as bad. We had no alternative, we'd have to drive.

On the day of the game, we set off straight after breakfast - they were excellent by the way - and after a few wrong turnings and bypassing the likes of Dnipropetrovsk (go on, you say it), we reached Kiev around 6.00pm.

We were in a part of the Olympic Stadium reserved for predominantly Swedish fans, none of whom I recognised from Austria four years before by the way. They were fine, although a bit overly boisterous. England, with Andy Carroll playing well, took the lead through one of his trademark headers. The Swedes were subdued at half time but came to life big time when they scored two early goals after the restart. We were drenched in beer and Helen had had enough. Just as we were leaving the Stadium, Theo Walcott scored an equaliser and we later heard that Danny Welbeck made it 3-2. An England draw in their final game against Ukraine, back in Donetsk, would be enough to qualify. That was in four days' time. We had more immediate problems i.e., getting back to Zaporozhye.

Travelling through the night generally doesn't bother me, but there were so many potholes and hazards on these roads that I really had to keep my wits about me. At about 2.00am I hit a pothole so hard that it knocked the air out of a tyre. There was no hard shoulder, but fortunately the offending tyre was on the nearside. Having made the car less of a target, and with some difficulty and a few choice words, I changed tyres.

There were just the first glimpses of light when we got going again, but no matter how much I tried to avoid them, I was still hitting a few potholes. It was fully daylight, and we were close to Dnipropetrovsk, when we saw a police car in a lay-by and a policeman beckoning us to pull over. One of them had a smattering of English, and whilst we tried to explain to him what we were doing at around 0500 on a Saturday morning, the other had a good look over the car.

The two of them had a chat and Ivan - yes that really was his name! - took me round to the back of the car. "Wheel – change", he said pointing to the spare that I'd put on just a couple of hours before. He graphically got the message across that there was a slow puncture. Well, you may know that I was no longer in a position to do that, but I had a job explaining why. Once I'd got this message across, the two of them walked off and made a phone call.

When they came back a few minutes later, Ivan suggested, "You – follow us". Well Helen was not having that without an explanation and I managed to establish that they had contacted a local garage owner who was going to open up his premises to get us sorted. Helen was still not sure, but we'd no other option.

We arrived before the garage owner, and while we waited, Ivan, in a convoluted way, got the message across that we should just pay for the work carried out. No more.

When he arrived, it didn't take him long to change the slow puncture tyre before telling Ivan how much he needed. I can't remember how much, but it was unbelievably cheap. I did try to give him a bit more but he turned it away and bid us goodbye. I went back to Ivan and offered to give the pair of them some reward, but he also refused to take it. We shook hands and went on our way, getting back to the hotel just as they were clearing up after breakfast.

There is a moral to this tale. All those travelling to Ukraine were warned beforehand that the locals were all 'on the make' and that the police were systemically corrupt. Well, all I can say is, from our experience, that was most definitely not the case. If you ever visit Ukraine, and I would recommend that you do although Helen wouldn't, and you find yourself in a spot of bother, just make sure that you ask to see Ivan the Policeman.

Back in Zaporozhye, we managed to get the spare tyre sorted - understandably, Helen didn't want another journey to Donetsk for the final game without one - and explored the city and immediate surrounds. This was the area where the Cossacks originated and we visited some of their traditional haunts plus I managed a swim in the River Dniepr. Yep, that's where Dnipropetrovsk gets its name.

Now much more aware of Cyrillic signage, the journey over to Donetsk, was almost a pleasure. Ukraine knew that they would qualify with a win and I expected local supporters to be fired up. Most, but not all were, and I experienced first-hand some of the division that a couple of years later was to develop into a civil war. I'd become aware that a high proportion of east Ukrainians regard themselves as Russian.

As for the game, a second half goal from Wayne Rooney secured the win for England to see them through to the quarter finals. Back in Kiev for that tie, they held Italy to a scoreless draw after extra-time, but were then eliminated on penalties. Although our adventure was over and we were back in the UK by that time, I didn't see the game on television, but by all accounts, based upon the 120 minutes of play, Italy had deserved to go through.

Meanwhile..................back at Meadow Lane, Keith Curle had signed a new goalkeeper, Bartosz (Bart) Bialkowski, defenders Dean Leacock and Gary Liddle, midfielder Andre Boucaud, forwards Francois Zoko and Yoann Arquin, with winger Jamal Campbell-Ryce soon following. Four victories from the first five league games saw Notts sit top of the table and each of the new signings had made a contribution. Surely, this was the season that Notts would end their time in the 'lower' divisions? Sadly no, eliminated from all cup competitions and a return of only five more wins before the end of December, knocked any prospect of festive cheer for long suffering 'Pies.

I missed the early season away win at Bury to pay my obligatory visit to EFL newcomers, Fleetwood Town. There, I met up with a few other 92 Club members who had the same intention. Mr Baldwin, who had rather short-sightedly booked a holiday before the fixtures had been issued, missed seeing Aldershot lose 4-1.

A couple of weeks later I missed the away game at Oldham (2-2), but won a few brownie points with my son-in-law as I'd got tickets for Liverpool's game at Sunderland. We saw Raheem Sterling for the first time and a future Liverpool goalkeeper, Simon Mignolet, for the opposition in a 1-1 draw. The following day, we both did the Great North Run. He queries this, but I swear I was catching up and would have overtaken him had there been a couple of extra miles!

A weekend in Vienna at the end of October, gave us the chance to see an Austrian Bundesliga game in which Rapid Vienna beat SV Salzburg.

Notts being drawn away to Rotherham United in the 2nd Round of the FA Cup was a bonus as it presented the perfect opportunity to visit the recently opened New York Stadium. After a draw up there, the Millers easily won the replay 3-0.

As the year came to an end, I had permission to join a queue outside Field Mill as tickets for the Stag's 3rd Round FA Cup tie with Liverpool went on general sale. I was there for about two hours, in pouring rain I might add, and there were only six people in front of me when the 'sold out' sign went up. To be fair to the Mansfield staff, they took contact details of those who had just missed out and said they'd be in touch should any more tickets become available. They did, and just before Christmas I was able to pick up a couple. Russ (S-in-L) was unable to come but I had no trouble in disposing of the spare. So, whatever was going on at Meadow Lane, I had this game to look forward to in the New Year.

2013

Stags, who were to be promoted back into the Football League a few months later, were a little unfortunate to lose their big Cup Tie. Daniel Sturridge made his Liverpool debut and scored the opening goal in a 2-1 victory. To this day however, Stags' fans insist that the second goal from Luis Suarez shouldn't have been allowed to stand.

A mixed set of results in January and a defeat at Hartlepool on 2nd February, saw Keith Curle sacked. He'd been in the job for less than twelve months, and once more, there was general surprise at this development, especially as his replacement was immediately announced as being Chris Kiwomya. He had been looking after the youth team, and whilst it was initially a temporary appointment, it was confirmed as permanent by the end of March. This appeared short-sighted as the Club finished the season in 12th place, lower than when Kiwomya had taken over.

I missed the away game at Bournemouth to see York City - they'd been promoted alongside Fleetwood Town - play Accrington Stanley. When combined with the 0-0 draw that Notts had gained on their first ever visit to Crawley Town, this ensured that I was back up to 92.

We had one further long trip before the season ended. I had applied for tickets for the Europa League Final. Liverpool were in the competition, and going well when I applied, and I thought I might be able to do Russ another favour. Not long after I'd heard that I'd been successful, Liverpool were knocked out, on away goals, by Zenit St Petersburg. So much for that plan.

On Wednesday 15th May, Helen and myself set off in my Ford KA for Holland aiming to reach the Amsterdam Arena for the 8.45pm (local time) kick-off. We made it, breaking off to check in to our pre-booked hotel in Utrecht before carrying on. Chelsea were to beat Benfica 2-1 with a Branislav Ivanovic 91st minute goal. Back at the hotel after the game, we shared a drink with a few Chelsea supporters who were fellow guests before, the following morning, beginning the return journey. It was a round trip of 950 miles. Was it worth it? Well, if I'm honest, probably not.

With the security of a now permanent job, Chris Kiwomya brought in Mustapha Dumbaya, Mark Fotheringham, Danny Haynes and Ronan Murray. None will live long in the memory of Notts fans, although the loan signings of Callum McGregor (Celtic) and Jack Grealish (Aston Villa) in the early weeks of the 2013/14 season undoubtedly were.

Following two wins from the first thirteen league games, and with Notts bottom of the table, the Chris Kiwomya 'experiment' was ended early. He'll be remembered, not only for the loan signing of the two youngsters, who following their spell at Meadow Lane have gone on to bigger and better things, but for overseeing a 1st Round League Cup victory (3-1) over Fleetwood Town. The reward was a trip to Anfield. After ninety minutes, the score was 2-2, and had there been any justice, Notts would have earned a replay. As it happened, Liverpool scored a couple of extra-time goals and a plum away draw at Manchester United in the next round.

Shaun Derry was appointed Notts County Manager on 6th November. His first game in charge was a 3-2 defeat up at Hartlepool in the 1st Round of the FA Cup, and it was five league games later before he saw his side win. Another quickly followed, but as 2013 turned into 2014, Notts were in bottom spot and the customary doom and gloom of previous festive seasons had returned.

19th October was a memorable day for one young grandson, although he'll need this reminder to recall why. Ailsa's first child, Finlay had arrived on 4th July 2012, so he was fifteen months old, when he accompanied Grandma and Grumps to his first ever game. It was Belper Town v Mickleover Sports in the FA Trophy. There were 223 there, and for the record, the away team won 3-2 to progress to the next round.

7th December was a memorable day for me. As Notts were out of the FA Cup, they had no game scheduled for that day. As a result, I bought a couple of tickets to see Blackpool play at Pride Park. Then I heard that Notts had brought forward a scheduled midweek fixture with

Gillingham, who had also been knocked out of the Cup, to that same Saturday afternoon. That gave me a dilemma, but the Rams made life a bit easier for me because they then brought forward their kick-off time to 1230 - I don't know why, as I don't think it was televised - and having disposed of the spare ticket, I dropped Helen off in Nottingham in the morning, and headed over to Derby.

Despite having Neil Bishop in their side, Blackpool lost 5-1, although it was only 4-1 as I left this one sided game a little early. I missed the first five minutes at Meadow Lane, but enjoyed what I did see as Notts beat Gillingham 3-1.

Midway through an October weekend break in Amsterdam, Helen and myself caught a train to The Hague and saw, Ado Den Haag win an Eredivisie game. It was a thriller, with the home team coming back from 2-0 down to defeat FC Twente 3-2. That however, was a rare afternoon of joy in what was turning out to be an otherwise miserable football season.

2014

Shaun Derry will have been pleased with the three consecutive league victories to start the New Year, but it was downhill then until mid-March, by which time relegation looked a near certainty.

Heather's first child, Alex, was not yet two when he attended his first game, and he proved to be a lucky mascot as Notts beat Coventry City 3-0 on 8th February. Finlay's first visit to Meadow Lane was a fortnight later. He brought no luck however as Shrewsbury Town took all three points with a 3-2 win. This after them having been 2-0 down after thirteen minutes.

Whilst Notts were bottom of the table, I had the good fortune to have a work visit to a new business in Stourport. This coincided with newly promoted Newport County AFC having a Tuesday night game at home to Fleetwood Town, and with me having been to Field Mill earlier in the season, was the perfect opportunity to top up my 92. There were no goals at Rodney Parade that night!

With nine games of the league season remaining, and Notts in danger of being cut off at the foot of the division, we were treated to a reprise of the *Great Escape* from 2002/03. Six of those games were won, and with only two defeats, Notts required just the one point from their visit to Boundary Park, to ensure survival. It required an Alan Sheehan equalising penalty in that final game to gain the necessary point - as it happens results elsewhere would have meant they were safe anyway – and, once again, the celebration of securing survival was only marginally less joyous than when success had been achieved.

I was not at Oldham that day. I was convinced that Notts would be safe after the previous week's home win over Swindon Town and was more concerned about Arbroath's chances away to Airdrie. They had to win to have any chance of avoiding automatic relegation and I just had to be there to help them. They lost and whilst I was pleasantly pleased, although not surprised, to hear that Notts had avoided dropping into the basement, I was disappointed that my home town team had failed.

After seeing Fleetwood Town join Notts in the third tier after their Wembley play-off 1-0 win over Burton Albion, Helen and myself retired the following week. Far too early I thought, but it was a decision that I've come to accept and don't regret. I make the point because, after a bit of fuss when we packed in, we had a trip to Brazil to look forward to.

Back in the autumn, I'd scoured the dates, times and locations of matches taking place in the 2014 World Cup Finals, and recognising that the likes of Rio de Janeiro and other coastal cities would be popular destinations, I applied for group games scheduled for Belo Horizonte. Again, I came up trumps and was allocated a couple of tickets for the four group games to be staged at Estadio Mineirao.

We booked our flights and accommodation before the draw, and again that proved to be a saving, as well supported nations like Colombia, Argentina and England would be playing games at that venue. We booked a cheap flight from Luton to Lisbon, and after an overnight stay, a direct flight to Belo Horizonte. We were to return by the same route, but as we were flying west to east, had no need of a night in Lisbon.

Our accommodation for the first couple of nights was just south of the city and then, for the rest of the stay, a hotel some sixty miles away in a beautiful little town called Ouro Preto. After some difficulty in finding our first hotel - we were surprised at how little English was spoken away from the city - we settled in and found a good parking spot for the hired car for all four of our trips back into the city for the football.

At our first game, Colombia v Greece, we perhaps shouldn't have been surprised by the number of Colombians there because at least their nation is on the same continent, but it's still a long way. By road, it's 5,000 miles from Bogota to Belo Horizonte. Anyway, they were everywhere, and left the ground happy as they had seen their team win 3-0. They went on to win the other two group games, and like Greece, qualified. Whereas Colombia were comfortable group winners, the Greeks just squeaked through as runners-up.

It was the day after this, a Sunday that we travelled over to Ouro Preto for the first time. Other than our hotel being at the top of an extremely steep and long hill into town, we had chosen well.

Our next game, on the Tuesday, was between Belgium and Algeria. The Algerians were winning at half time and it needed second half goals from substitutes Marouane Fellaini and Dries Mertens to secure a 2-1 win. Belgium also went on to win all three group games and Algeria came through in second place to join them in the knock-out stages. This was the first time that I'd seen Kevin De Bruyne. He was outstanding and it's no surprise to me, that following his move from Wolfsburg to Manchester City, he has done so well. Just why did Chelsea let him go?

We had no problem finding our usual spot for the Argentina v Iran game. Argentina dominated but it needed some individual brilliance from Lionel Messi in the 91st minute to give the South Americans a 1-0 victory. There were many Argentinians at the game and it became clear that there was no love lost between them and the locals. One particular Brazilian behind us, became increasingly loud in his abuse as Argentina struggled to score. As many around us were celebrating Messi's goal, I looked around, and this guy was up and away. I reckon he'd made a wise decision.

On the way back, on a normal two lane carriageway with traffic slowly moving away towards the ring road, a car behind me saw the chance to nip in front, but just as he pulled out, another car travelling in the opposite direction, came over the brow of the hill. I thought he'd got enough time to get past and pull in, until I saw in the mirror that he was pulling a trailer. He did get past, but as he pulled in, the trailer ran right down the side of my car.

He beckoned to stop further up the road, where we could pull out of traffic and examine the damage. It was hard to tell whether or not his trailer had been damaged, but that was not an issue with the hire car. It was a mess. The other driver made a number of Latin apologetic gestures and suggested in pigeon English, that we should follow him, as he knew a man who could sort this for us. We followed him as best we could, but at the first opportunity, he put his foot down and was away.

Helen was a bag of nerves by now, but I was more concerned about how I was going to sort this out, and just as important, how much would it cost as we continued on our way.

Back at the hotel, the receptionist, who was a very friendly and helpful chap - tailor made for that job - came out to have a look at the damage. He said that he knew someone who could probably sort it for us and he'd ask him to come round the following day (Sunday) to have a look. All being well, he'd have it fixed on Monday. This sounded like it might be a bit too good to be true and there might be a catch, but we'd no other option.

We spent that Sunday pottering around the various markets in town and when we got back, our friendly receptionist confirmed that the repairs would be carried out the next day. He had no idea of the likely cost but assured me that his pal was very reasonable. Aha, I thought, that will be the catch. However, as there was little else I could do, and with my credit card hardly having been used on the trip, I thanked him and handed over the key.

On the Monday, we took a train trip up to Mariana, the oldest city in Minas Gerais. It was a lovely day but I couldn't really enjoy it as much as I'd have liked, because I kept thinking that there might be a big bill at the end of the day.

With hindsight, I should have relaxed a bit more as when we got back, the car was neatly parked and looking in better condition than when we'd picked it up from the airport. You could never have guessed what that side of the vehicle had looked like earlier in the day. So far, so good, but how much was it going to cost?

I can't remember exactly how much, but I reckon he said that it was around the equivalent of £200. We'd found Brazil so cheap, that we'd still got plenty of unspent Brazilian Reais. So much so, that I was able to pay in cash, with a bit extra between them for doing such a grand job. I was able to enjoy my drink that night, but it didn't stop Helen from fretting about the trip into Belo Horizonte for the final game, or indeed the drive back to the airport to return the car.

Our last trip up to Estadio Mineirao was to see a game in which the only thing at stake was pride. Costa Rica had already qualified and the England team knew that they would be home before the bulk of the supporters who had made the trip. *Now that's an experience I'm familiar with.*

There was quite a contrast between the two sets of supporters before the game. The Costa Ricans, supplemented I think by many locals, had seen their nation win the first two group games and were loud and brash. English supporters on the other hand, had seen narrow defeats to both Italy and Uruguay, and were simply there to witness the last rites of a campaign that the media back in the UK had forecast would see them do well.

Both sides made changes, and perhaps because nothing hinged on the outcome, it was a drab scoreless draw. The Costa Ricans weren't too bothered about that though as the point from this game ensured that they topped the group. No-one in their right mind would have predicted that beforehand, particularly in a group containing three former World Cup winning nations.

267

After a couple more days in lovely Ouro Preto we began the long journey home. We had enjoyed the Brazilian experience although, a bit like South Africa, the level of poverty we came across surprised us. Favelas are not limited to big cities like Rio de Janeiro or Sao Paulo. They were everywhere. Despite that, the Brazilians seemed happy enough although that might have been a result of the tournament. It's a well-worn cliché that the Brazilian love of football is comparable to a religion, but during our time there, it didn't seem too far-fetched and it would be interesting to note the suicide rate after Brazil's shock 7-1 semi-final defeat.

We'd only been back three weeks when I saw my first pre-season friendly at Nuneaton Town. It was an opportunity to look at some of the new signings brought in by Shaun Derry. These included veteran goalkeeper, Roy Carroll, Hayden Mullins, Gary Thompson, Liam Noble, Alan Smith, Blair Adams, Gary Jones and Nicky Wroe. Other than Noble, and to a lesser extent Adams, these were players who were approaching the end of their careers. To be fair to the manager, he did also promote some of the better of the youngsters at the Club, viz., Haydn Hollis and Curtis Thompson.

Early season results were mixed. A first round exit away to Sheffield Wednesday in the League Cup, was no real surprise. League form however improved and after five consecutive victories, Notts were as high as third and Gary Thompson was becoming a bit of a cult hero after scoring six goals in five games. It wasn't to last. Despite a succession of loan players coming and going - or possibly because of that! - only two points from a possible twenty one saw Notts slip down to 10th position at the end of the year.

Accrington Stanley needed a replay to ensure that any hopes Notts had of FA Cup glory were ended at the 1st Round stage. There was some joy however in the Johnstone's Paint Trophy. Victories over Mansfield Town, Scunthorpe United and Doncaster Rovers saw Notts play Preston North End in the semi-final (Northern Section). A 1-0 home defeat just before Christmas however, closed that particular route to Wembley.

A September trip down the M1 to see Luton Town, promoted back to the EFL the previous season, still left me one short of getting back up to 92. Cambridge United were missing but I couldn't see a convenient free date to enable me to pull that in. It was looking as if I'd have to leave that until 2015/16 - just in case you're wondering, the rules do allow that! - little knowing at the time that I wouldn't have to make a special trip.

A weekend away in Sweden's capital in October - interesting, but expensive - was perfect in many ways, not least because it gave us the chance to see Malmo secure the Allsvenskan (Swedish Championship) with a 3-2 win over home team, AIK Stockholm.

2015

The general feeling around Meadow Lane was that if the Club could just get a bit of consistency, they might still have a chance of at least getting a play-off place. As all football supporters can attest however, 'it's the hope that kills you'. Not literally of course, but there can be no worse feeling in sport than having expectations raised, just to see them dashed.

Notts were to win only four of the twenty four games played in the New Year. There were thirteen defeats and as the gradual slide down the table became more of a plunge, they dropped into the relegation places on 3rd April and stayed there until the last home game of the season. A 2-1 victory over Doncaster Rovers meant that they'd travel to Gillingham the following week with their destiny in their own hands. It was a bit complicated at the bottom but a win, or at least matching the results of any of Colchester United, Leyton Orient or Crawley Town was what was needed.

I didn't go to Gillingham. We'd already planned a full week's holiday in Scotland prior to attending my nephew's wedding on 9th May. When these plans were made, we were unaware of just what the last day of the season would involve. Besides, I'd every confidence that the odds favoured Notts. They just had to do what was required and they'd be safe. That explains why I was sitting in the car outside the Cairn o'Mohr

Winery overlooking the River Tay, watching rain bounce off the windscreen, as I listened to the drama unfold south of the Border.

Things seemed to be going all right. Results in the other games were going the way all we 'Pies wanted, and there had been no goals at Gillingham. Then fantastic news, Graham Burke, on loan from Aston Villa scored and providing Notts held onto the lead they were safe. Within minutes, Gillingham equalised and then took the lead.

Even now though, and despite Gillingham scoring a third, Notts would not be relegated providing Colchester United failed to win. They were playing Preston who, with a win, would be promoted themselves. The odds still favoured Notts. It all went wrong however in the 82nd minute when Colchester took the lead. For those last eight minutes I became a temporary (& long distance) Preston fan hoping that they would at least come back to equalise. They didn't. Notts were relegated. We entered the Cairn o'Mohr winery for a tour. I'd temporarily lost the will to live and could care no more!

Thankfully, the feeling lasted about ten minutes. I'm not a believer in the old Bill Shankly maxim that football means so much that, for many people, it becomes a matter of life and death. Besides, with demotion, I'd no longer have to make special trips to visit the grounds of the teams promoted into the Football League from the Conference because Notts would be visiting them in the new season. What's more, the fixtures would be published in a few weeks' time.

I've not mentioned it, but past history has probably led you to believe that Shaun Derry was no longer in charge. You'd be right. He packed his bags after a 4-1 defeat away to MK Dons in March, and was replaced a few days later by what Ray Trew described as a truly exciting appointment, Ricardo Moniz. The Dutchman had assisted Martin Jol at Tottenham and was highly regarded. OK, he may have been unable to save the Club from relegation, but we were assured of exciting times ahead.

The Notts County revolving door recruitment policy was operating at peak levels of efficiency during the summer and I got the chance to view some of the new signings at a pre-season friendly at Alfreton. There were far too many newcomers for me to record here, but there were some who stood out who I thought would have a good season. These included Mawouna Amevor, Thierry Audel, Elliott Hewitt, Julian Jenner, Genaro Snijders, Civard Sprockel, Adam Campbell, Rob Milsom, Jon Stead and especially Stanley Aborah. He was a gifted midfielder who had the ability to play at a higher level. A look at his history though showed that he may be a flawed genius. Notts were his 11th club, and he'd only just turned 28!

The signings brought a distinct continental feel to the squad and hopes were high as the season got underway. I missed the opening league win, 2-0 at Stevenage, as I (and England) had unfinished business at Trent Bridge. As it happened, the cricketers got the job done quickly and although Hertfordshire was out of the question, I managed to get to Field Mill for Mansfield's 1-1 draw with Carlisle United.

We had to wait until 12th September for the second win when another new signing, Izale McLeod, scored a double as Notts defeated Luton Town 3-2. I missed that home game too as I was at the wedding of Rhona and Phil Henshaw.

Results were inconsistent, and although Notts had a good away win at Huddersfield in the League Cup, and then went on to share eight goals with Villa in the next round (Notts only got three of them!), the feeling was growing amongst fans that perhaps Mr Moniz was not a good fit for the job.

Any goodwill that he may have gained was put to the test in November when Notts went to high profile Salford City - they'd been featured in a BBC documentary - in the 1st Round of the FA Cup. Probably as a direct result of that documentary, the game was live on BBC1, and Notts helped provide what most of the viewers would have wanted viz. a shock result. Without having to play particularly well, the non-league side, operating three divisions below Notts, won 2-0.

That may not have been the final straw, but after less than nine months in the job, the Dutchman was on his way on 29th December, with the

Club 15th in the table. There appeared to be no imminent fear of relegation, but perhaps more importantly, there was no sign of an embryonic push for promotion.

Yes, things may have been gloomy at Meadow Lane, but at least Helen and myself had enjoyed an October weekend in Athens. There we saw AEK Athens, perhaps the least well known of the Greek capital's three big sides, win at the Olympiako Stadio Spyros Louis. They defeated a team from the north called Iraklis who were no match for them, the final score being 5-1.

2016

After Ray Trew's promise of an exciting managerial appointment nine months before, the replacement for Ricardo Moniz almost universally got a response of "Who??" Jamie Fullerton had been working across the river, looking after Nottingham Forest's development squad. He had no previous managerial experience, but Mr Trew assured us that he had never been as impressed by anyone at an interview as he had been by Jamie. He had captivated everyone involved in the recruitment process by his suitability for the job of managing Notts County. 70 days later, Jamie Fullerton was out of a job

To be fair to the lad, some supporters were just not prepared to give him a chance. No matter what he did or said, he would never have been accepted by some of the more opinionated fans. The fact that the team failed to win a home game whilst he was in charge (one point from a possible eighteen) didn't help, but he'd been handed a poisoned chalice, and following a particularly poor home defeat (4-1) to Exeter City, he was made to drink from it on 19th March. The following day, Mark Cooper became the fourth Notts County manager in just less than twelve months.

The new man arrived during a run of no wins in ten games as supporters began once more to work out how many points the Club needed to avoid the unthinkable. A couple of home 1-0 wins extinguished any fears on that score and come the last game, fans were just glad that the season was coming to an end and that we seemed once again to have a 'proper' manager running the show. At, least we thought we had.

On the day of the last game, 7th May, an embarrassing and humiliating 5-0 home defeat to Carlisle United (with Keith Curle in charge) - and which was Daniel, Heather's second son's first ever game - it was revealed that Mark Cooper had accepted a firm offer to take over Conference outfit, Forest Green Rovers.

There were conflicting stories as to how this had come about, but regardless of what or who we believed, yet another appointment would be required. Within days, it was confirmed that John Sheridan was taking over. He would have a busy summer and so would we. We'd got a trip to the 2016 European Championships to look forward to, and with Helen vowing that she was definitely not going to Russia in 2018, and this being the last of the Euro's to be held in this format, we wanted to make the most of it. It was to be our last.

Having only the faintest of hopes that Scotland would qualify and that the *Tartan Army* would be 'on operations' in France the following year, I had applied via the UEFA website for tickets purely based upon location. I tried to get six games, managed four, was happy with that return, and as had become customary every other year, waited for the draw to be made. We didn't get any games featuring the major or fancied nations, but with two games in Bordeaux and another two in Marseilles, we'd put together an itinerary that would allow us to see some parts of the country that we'd not visited before.

With us being based in western and southern France, we booked a Brittany Ferries, Portsmouth to Bilbao crossing. It was less than a three hour drive across the top of Spain and into France. We'd arranged for an overnight stay in Biarritz to break the journey. Too late, we realised that we could have done without this as we were only about ninety minutes away from Arcachon, our first base. We had a meal in our hotel that night, and within twenty four hours, Helen was not feeling too good. She was convinced that something in the buffet meal that she had enjoyed at the time, was responsible.

For our first game in Bordeaux, we took a local train. It was on time and good value. This, despite stories circulating that there would be industrial action during the Championships. We had a good look round the city, one we'd visited eighteen years before of course, before taking the tram out to Matmut Atlantique, a new stadium, purpose built for the tournament and now the base for French League club, Bordeaux FC.

Gareth Bale gave Wales an early lead against Slovakia, but this was cancelled out midway through the second half. With nine minutes to go, Hal Robson-Kanu scored and the Welsh held on to win their first ever game at a European Championship tournament.

Accompanied by many jubilant Welsh men and women, we squeezed onto a tram for the return trip to the station. It was now that Helen's situation became apparent. She'd been gradually deteriorating but had not said anything. However, at the station, when we saw chaotic scenes and heard rumours circulating that there were no trains running at all, and that we'd have to stay in Bordeaux until the morning, Helen was clearly in trouble,

We got a bit of clarity and were told that we'd have to go to a specific platform where a train taking us to Arcachon, would arrive shortly. Ninety minutes later, no such train had arrived and my wife was almost doubled up in pain. I went to find some help and make the case for Helen to either see a doctor or go to hospital. The station staff, I'm sure feigning ignorance at my perfectly phrased French, seemed disinterested. Fortunately, by the time I got back to Helen, there was some activity, and a train backed up alongside this platform. We had to wait a little longer but were then allowed to board.

The match had kicked off at 6.00pm and it was 1.00am before we got to our apartment. This was three hours later than we'd allowed for and didn't help Helen. She had a dreadful night, feeling sick and barely sleeping, and the following day, a Sunday, was pretty much a washout for her. If she felt better, and was up for it, I resolved to drive into Bordeaux for the next game.

We had a leisurely tour of the countryside the following day before climbing the Dune Du Pilat - Helen sensibly stayed down below - where, at the top, I had some interesting football discussions with Austrians, Hungarians, Slovakians and a few cocky Welshmen. I was already well aware of this, but had I not been, it would have been the perfect introduction to man's (or woman's) ability to have a football related conversation anywhere in the world.

After another day of rest Helen felt a lot better and we drove up to Bordeaux for the second game between Austria and Hungary. Waiting outside the stadium, I got a feel for how Hungarian men (& a few women) could knock back the drink. In the huge car park it was like an American sporting event with tailgate parties everywhere. The main difference though was I couldn't see much food, it was just can and bottle, bottle and can as we passed each open boot.

As for the match, the Hungarians were 2-0 winners, but other than meeting a couple of guys from Forfar who, like us, had just got into the habit of attending international tournaments, the game had no special memories. It just never really got going.

We left Arcachon in the morning and headed east towards Carcassonne where we had three nights booked. The medieval walled city is well preserved and with its links to the Crusades and the expulsion of the Cathars, had Helen purring with delight. She loved it, but not enough to brave a boat trip down the Canal Du Midi. I had to go on my own!

After that I met up with Helen, who'd been happy sitting in the sun with her book, and as we strolled back into town, we passed a bar where I could hear football commentary. I popped my head in and saw that it was the England v Wales group match being shown. There were about half a dozen people in there, so it was quiet, and Helen was more than happy to take up the offer and have a cooling drink.

It was early in the second half and England had just equalised through Jamie Vardy and it stayed that way until the 92nd minute when Daniel Sturridge scored England's winner. From what I could see, it was probably deserved, and with England having only drawn their opener, would have been a relief to many back home.

The reason I remember this though is, not for the football, but the comment of the French presenter when they returned to the studio. I'm far from perfect but can get by with French, and after over a week in the country had attuned back into the language. I was surprised then when the main man's opening statement was "Sturridge's goal has just saved the Queen of England." It was not only irrelevant but totally ignored the fact that she's also Queen of Wales.

Something much more important than football had been happening back home that day. When we got back to the hotel, we became aware of the murder of Jo Cox. This was a reminder that whilst we were away, the UK Referendum on continuing membership of the EU, was continuing to bring out the worst in British society. A sad day.

Our next stop was Avignon, a reasonably short train ride away from Marseilles, the location for our final two games. Once more, Helen was purring. This Roman city was not quite as pretty as Carcassonne but was a good base for visiting the likes of Arles, Nimes and the Camargue, not forgetting the Stade Velodrome of course.

We took the train into Marseilles for the Hungary v Iceland game, and after a tour of the cosmopolitan city centre, walked out to the stadium, about four miles away. About a mile short of the ground we stopped at a little pavement café for a drink. We'd been there about ten minutes when a guy on a moped came up, shouting into the various establishments as he passed, "Ils Arrivent. Vous devez fermer!"

We wondered if he was referring to the police and would these little cafes be in trouble for selling alcohol. Very soon, we found out what he was referring to as we heard the increasingly loud noise of a crowd of people approach. It was the Hungarian equivalent of the *Tartan Army*. They had apparently gathered in the port area and were on the communal march. The guy who had been frantically warning shopkeepers must have thought that there would be trouble.

Although this procession, which took about ten minutes to pass us was loud, with many in it clearly having had a bevy or two, they were in good spirits and there was no likelihood of any trouble. Besides, Hungary were playing Iceland that day, and other than the Cod Wars of the past, who had ever heard of Icelanders getting involved in a fight.

Although heavily outnumbered in the stadium, the Viking Thunder Clap from the Icelanders was at its loudest in the 40th minute when their team took a shock lead. They held it until two minutes from time, when the Hungarians equalised and the game ended as a draw. There was general disappointment all round, but in the end, both sides qualified, and as I'm sure many football fans will remember, one of them went on to create the shock of the tournament.

Getting back to the main railway station we found many fans from both nations milling around. It was a repeat of the situation we experienced in Arcachon. Eventually we boarded a train just after midnight. This pulled into every little village and town en route and it was after 2.00am when we arrived back in Avignon. Fortunately, Helen was in fine fettle this time, but I again made the decision to use the car for the final game.

We made good use of our final couple of days, and after seeing Poland defeat Ukraine 1-0 to secure their passage to the knock-out stages in probably our last ever overseas international, the following morning would see us start the long journey home.

We'd pre-booked an overnight stop in Toulouse which was a relatively straightforward journey, but whilst we were in the Avignon area, I wanted to make a detour and head 40 odd miles north east to drive up Mont Ventoux. Keen followers of the Tour de France (which I'm not by the way), will be familiar with this mountain as it is often used as one of the climbing stages.

Those of a certain age, in addition to cycling fanatics, will recall that this was the mountain on which 29 year old Tommy Simpson died in 1967. It rises to over 6,000 feet, and on the day we drove up we overtook countless routine cyclists who wanted to get this big one onto their CV.

I'd love to go back myself one day and give it a go but................I reckon I'm too late.

After our night in Toulouse we headed over the border into Spain, and after a frantic search for the ferry port - we were indebted to a lorry driver who suggested that we 'follow him' - we made it in time. The cabin was comfortable and the crossing smooth but we had a very disturbing experience in the morning. We found out that whilst we had been away, a minority (37%) of the British electorate had condemned the UK to a life outside the EU. It made us wonder what other foolish decisions might be taken in our absence on future overseas holidays!

One thing that we found hadn't changed when we got back, was the fact that John Sheridan remained in charge at Notts County. Well, it had been over six weeks. Anything could have happened!

Like his predecessors, he had been busy during the summer and had brought some experienced players to the Club. These included goalkeeper, Adam Collin, defenders Richard Duffy, Matt Tootle and Carl Dickinson, midfielder Michael O'Connor and former loanee, Jonathan Forte.

The opening day defeat away at Yeovil, when Notts were 2-0 down after 25 minutes, was so abject that Helen and I left at half-time. This disappointment being followed by a home draw and defeat, led to the unwelcome feeling that we were in for another season of struggle. Things did pick up however, and by the end of September and three consecutive victories, Notts had risen to 5th in the table. I was not to see them win another league game however for four months. There was a surprise win at Portsmouth - who would go on to be champions - but I missed out on that rare treat, as I was in Scotland that weekend.

Our latest grandson, Ailsa's second boy Saul, did however prove to be a bit of lucky mascot as he was introduced to Meadow Lane. His first game was on 3rd September and a 2-2 draw with Grimsby Town. Later that month he saw Notts defeat Leyton Orient 3-1 and it was not until November that he saw, what many of his immediate antecedents had seen regularly, viz. his first Notts County loss.

After a 3-2 home defeat to Carlisle United, on 31st December, Notts were just one place away from filling one of the two relegation places. The various cup competitions had brought no joy either, although they did play four FA Cup games after replays with both Boreham Wood and Peterborough. Small crumbs of comfort indeed! Whilst all this was going on, the Club's financial situation was a continuing worry and Mr Trew had been desperately trying to dispose of Notts County for months.

Still, I'd managed to get a ticket to see West Ham play a Europa League play-off game in their new ground, and this, plus Notts County's visits to The Hive to play Barnet and newly promoted Cheltenham Town just left me the away game at Grimsby Town, early in the New Year, to get me back up to 92. Life doesn't have to be complicated to have fun.

2017

After an embarrassing 4-0 away defeat at Cambridge United on 2nd January, Mr Sheridan was on his way. If it was any consolation to him, he had been in the role longer than his two immediate predecessors. A 4-1 away defeat at Morecambe the following Saturday, with Alan Smith in caretaker charge, set a record of ten consecutive league defeats.

Meanwhile, the Club had been sold and Mr Alan Hardy, a local businessman, took over and immediately appointed Kevin Nolan as manager. There was no quick fix with one point from a scoreless home draw with Mansfield Town being the sole reward from his first two games. This left the Club in 23rd place, and once again, facing the prospect of non-league football.

Out of contract Shola Ameobi was signed until the end of the season and Jorge Grant came in on loan from Nottingham Forest. These two helped to improve fortunes, and with nine wins and only six defeats from their remaining games, Notts gradually climbed clear and after four straight wins as March turned into April, Meadow Lane was buzzing.

There were two games in February which convinced me that a big corner had been turned. These were a 3-2 away win at fellow strugglers and eventually relegated Leyton Orient, and a 1-0 midweek win at Plymouth Argyle, a club that would enjoy promotion at the season's end.

The new owner had a number of clever but simple ideas, one of which was arranging with the Home Park club that all Notts supporters who had made the long journey south on the Tuesday night, be provided with a free Cornish Pasty. Not a particularly expensive initiative as there were probably less than 200 'Pies there, but a PR triumph.

I missed the final game of the season, which was a 2-1 loss away to Newport - that result effectively saved the Welsh side and relegated Hartlepool United - as I was up in Scotland, seeing Arbroath clinch promotion with a 1-1 draw away at Stirling Albion. Great joy, and as it was on my birthday, the perfect excuse for a double celebration.

Kevin Nolan, who in the owner's eyes (and at this stage the view of most supporters) could do no wrong, brought in the likes of Lewis Alessandra, Shaun Brisley, Terry Hawkridge, Nicky Hunt, Dan Jones (no not my three year old grandson!) and the returning Liam Noble and Robert Milsom during the close season. He also brought back Jorge Grant from Nottingham Forest with the added bonus of Ryan Yates joining him.

Given the way the previous season had ended and the encouraging transfer activity during the summer, the opening day 3-0 defeat away at Coventry City was not expected. The following Tuesday night, on a very wet Glanford Park (Scunthorpe United) pitch, Notts went out of the League Cup on penalties after a 3-3 draw and extra time. It was however, the first time we'd seen Yates and I could see that he would be useful. The on loan midfielder would go on to play the next twenty five league games, and by the time Forest recalled him - only to then immediately send him out to Scunthorpe - Notts were sitting 2nd in the table.

Attendances were considerably higher than in recent seasons and with more crowd pleasing incentives from the owner, by the end of the year, it looked as if Alan Hardy's claim that Notts County would be flourishing at no lower a level than the Championship (2nd Tier) within a few years, was not just a fanciful dream.

Besides, although the Checkatrade Trophy campaign had proved short lived, Notts had overcome both Bristol Rovers and Oxford City, and as a result, had a trip to Brentford in the 3rd Round of the FA Cup to look forward to. What could possibly go wrong?

2018

The last game with Ryan Yates in the side was the trip to Brentford where a Jon Stead goal was enough to see Notts progress to a home fourth round tie with Premiership side Swansea City. Stead scored again when Swansea came to Nottingham. This time though it was the equaliser and the replay, ten days later, was the worst ever - to date at least - defeat that I've seen the Club suffer. Swansea City 8 Notts County 1. I'm pleased to say though that I was there when Noor Husin scored for the second game running and reckon I'm one of a very small number of people to have seen all three of the Afghan international's goals in English senior football.

Notts had lost only two league games when Yates was in the side. They were to lose a further seven without him, and whilst at the beginning of the year they were strongly fancied to win promotion, come May, they had slipped to 5th place, seven points adrift of the third automatic position and had to face Coventry City in the play-offs.

Notts took the lead at the Ricoh Arena in the first leg and would have returned to Meadow Lane with a one goal advantage but for a poor refereeing decision resulting in an equalising penalty. Decisions didn't favour Notts in the second leg either although there was no denying Coventry's deserved victory. 5-2 on aggregate though gives a totally false impression.

Under normal circumstances we'd have been preparing for a trip overseas for more football. Helen had been adamant all along that she was not going to Russia and even when I dangled the prospect of two weeks in St Petersburg, she remained unmoved. She did say (and I think she meant it), that I could go on my own. It just wouldn't have been the same though, so, like most of the world's population, I had to make do with watching a few games on television.

Although England progressed to the semi-final stage, they never quite gave the impression that they could go on to win it. Fans at home were obviously hopeful, enjoying the run while it lasted and were understandably disappointed when they lost to Croatia. I think though that the general view was that the best team in the competition, viz. France, even though the needed luck in the Final, were worthy winners.

Incidentally, had I succeeded in getting tickets for the group games being staged in St Petersburg, I'd have seen, amongst others, Morocco v Iran. That was a close run thing then and just goes to show that, ach well, sometimes things do work out best for a reason!

Meanwhile, despite the poor second half of the 17/18 season culminating in the play-off defeat, there was still an air of optimism around Meadow Lane during the summer. Most fans thought better times lay ahead, but I was not one of them. I'd become a little tired of the manager making excuses and of giving the impression in post-match interviews that he and I had been at different games. He could clearly talk a good game and had enjoyed success in the early days, but I think he'd been found out.

Still, the signings of David Vaughan, Enzio Boldewijn, Kane Hemmings, Andy Kellett and Kristian Dennis looked encouraging, and although there was no indication in pre-season friendlies that the Club would bounce back from the play-off defeat of a few weeks previously, most fans still remained positive. I equally stubbornly remained unconvinced. Vaughan in particular failed to impress me.

On 26th August, with only an opening day 0-0 draw to savour, and with Notts County already out of the League Cup and sitting bottom of the entire Football League, Kevin Nolan was on his bike. Some people, especially Mr Nolan himself, expressed surprise, but not me. It's interesting to note that he has not held another managerial position since, although eighteen months after leaving Notts, he was appointed as first team coach at West Ham United. Whatever, five days later,

Harry Kewell left what looked like a secure position at Crawley Town to take over at Meadow Lane.

It was the tenth game of the season before Notts gained three points, the first of three consecutive wins to lift Notts to the giddy heights of 17th. The third of these wins, 1-0 away to Macclesfield on 6th October, was Finlay's first ever away game. Once more, it was a false dawn and Harry Kewell was not to see another league victory whilst manager of the Club. Ten weeks after his arrival, he was gone. A humiliating 4-0 FA Cup defeat at Barnsley was his last game. Ten days later, Neil Ardley became the 16th Notts County Manager since the Munto Finance fiasco, ten years earlier. At least, unlike Harry Kewell, he hadn't given up a secure job to come to Meadow Lane, having left AFC Wimbledon a few weeks earlier.

Once more, a change of manager failed to bring about an improvement, and Neil Ardley must have been wondering what he had let himself in for as he saw in the New Year. He had enjoyed just the one win in his first seven games and Notts were sitting rock bottom of the entire Football League.

2019

It would be 9th February before Notts were to win again. The surprise 2-1 victory at Forest Green Rovers had been followed by an even more surprising 1-0 win over Mansfield Town at Meadow Lane. It had been such a long time since a League victory over their Nottinghamshire rivals that I swear I saw grown men cry that afternoon. They then had Newport County at home on the Tuesday night and a win over the South Wales team would take Notts out of the relegation zone. They lost 4-1, and other than for sixteen minutes on the last day of the season, they were to remain in the bottom two.

The manager had brought in some experienced players, e.g. Mitch Rose, Jim O'Brien, Michael Doyle and Craig Mackail-Smith on either loan or short term contracts, and there was definitely a bit more fight about the team. They were getting no breaks however, and I can well remember how at Tranmere, a defensive header from around the half way line from Jim O'Brien, fortuitously set up Connor Jennings. He had a clear run at goal and put away the only goal of the game. I came away from Birkenhead, convinced that our proud claim to be the *Oldest Football League Club in the World* was soon to be passed on to another.

Notts were never quite cut adrift although the 8,519 turning up at Meadow Lane on 27th April knew that if the Club were to lose at home to Grimsby Town and Macclesfield were to beat Port Vale that day, our fate would be sealed. Grimsby were overcome 2-1, but the sad news from Moss Rose, was that the Silkmen had also won. The only way out now was for Notts to beat Swindon Town away on the final day and hope that whilst we were doing that, Cambridge United do us a favour and beat Macclesfield.

Down at Swindon on 4th May, Notts went in at half-time level, buoyed by the news that Cambridge had taken the lead and provided they didn't concede in the second half, all Notts would have to do is score. In the 52nd minute, Kane Hemmings converted a penalty and the thousands of 'Pies who had travelled thought they just might be witnessing a miracle in the making. It wasn't to last. In the 68th minute we heard that Macclesfield had equalised, and almost immediately, Swindon did the same. They went on to win 3-1 and it no longer mattered what happened up in the Fens. Notts County would be playing non-league football in 2019/20.

All this was assuming of course that the Club continued to exist. Alan Hardy was in deep financial trouble and had put Notts County on the market in January. He kept putting out optimistic statements about various interested parties but couldn't reveal any more information because of the sensitive nature of negotiations. I took all these claims with a pinch of salt, because of immediate concern were the threats that the Club would be wound up. Money was owed to a number of creditors, not least of whom were HMRC. Various dates for a winding up order to be heard were adjourned, but the more we became aware of, the less likely it seemed that the Club would survive the summer. Alan Hardy had to find a buyer who would not only clear all debts but satisfy the FA and National League that Notts County remained a viable concern.

On top of all this, we'd became aware that Alan Hardy had brought personal embarrassment upon himself. Helen and I were out In Australia for four weeks earlier in the year when Ailsa sent us a link to a story that had appeared in *The Guardian*. The content was never denied, and on the assumption that it was true and that Mr Hardy's financial position had deteriorated to such a level that NCFC staff were being paid late, I thought that with him being a lifelong fan of the Club and the man at the helm as they lost League status, he'd have surely considered topping himself.

It was not until nine days before the first game of the National League season, that we knew that the Club had been saved. Alexander and Christoffer Reedtz, who are brothers originally from Denmark, and who had set up a successful football analysis company, claimed to have always wanted to run their own professional club. As the clock was ticking, both metaphorically and practically in terms of persuading all those who needed to be persuaded that their intentions were genuine, they had arrived at the fifty ninth minute of the eleventh hour.

There was a collective sigh of relief from the few thousand fans who had stuck with the Club through the occasional thick, but mainly thin times of recent years. We were all aware that fans of other clubs, and by that I mean those who chase the glory primarily from their armchair, regarded us as a bit of a joke organisation that had once had its day but now belonged in the past. Well, those of us who have remained loyal know that you cannot truly appreciate the good times until you've been made to suffer, and that doesn't mean the 'agony' of missing out on a Champions League place!

All true football supporters will tell you that when Nick Hornby had *Fever Pitch* published back in 1992, he spoke for us all, when he said that 'you can change your wife as many times as you like, but you can never change your football club. You may fall out occasionally but the bond will never be irredeemably broken. *NB – these days, in an effort to ensure political correctness, he would probably have include husband or partner in his profound statement.*

The 2019/20 season began with Neil Ardley still in charge - top marks to that bloke for sticking with the Club - and a squad of players that had been hastily put together. This was reflected in the early season results, with only two wins in the first ten league games and the Club disappointingly in the lower half of the table. However, although consistency remained a problem, there were generally more good performances and better results as the season progressed and the year ended with three straight victories and Notts in a play-off place.

Now, from the way I've planned this book, you'd expect me now to break off here and have you wait until the chapter entitled **The Twenty-Twenties** begins before recording how the season evolved. However, as I'm writing in August 2020 and haven't seen any live football for twenty weeks - and if the truth be known, according to some prophets of doom, may never attend another game in my lifetime - we are living in unprecedented (one of the most overused words of the past four months!) times. As a result, regardless of how the coronavirus crisis develops, I'm going to bring things to a close.

Up to the final game on 14th March, Notts continued to progress and with three players (Kristian Dennis, Kyle Wootton and Wes Thomas) each having scored over ten goals, had climbed to 3rd position in the National League and reached the semi-final of the FA Trophy. As I write, promotion via the play-offs remains a possibility. Unfortunately, as things stand, I won't be able to personally see how this evolves.

It's a shame, but as has been often said in recent weeks - in fact, almost as frequently as the word unprecedented - there are more important things in life than sport.

On that note, although I will come back to football, in the summarising chapter, I'll move on.

Chapter 15

Twenty-tens – more experiences (both old & new)

I made reference in an earlier chapter of how Helen had discovered the joy of attending a 'day at the races' and of how we had begun visiting various courses around the country. Well, when we set out to achieve something, generally speaking we manage it and on 31st October 2016, after a visit to Hereford Racecourse, we could proudly claim to have spent at least one day at all 60 courses in Great Britain.

There were 60 in the country when we started out on this mission. It then briefly became 61 as Chelmsford's 'all weather' track was opened in Essex, but then fell back to 59 as both Folkestone and Hereford were closed. We'd completed the 59 when visiting Taunton in 2015, but just because 'it's there' as mountaineers claim to justify their obsession, we had to visit Hereford when it re-opened. OK, we've very rarely managed to match the return on the 'investment' that we achieved at that very first visit to Doncaster in 2000, but it's been fun, and providing you don't try to 'chase your losses' it doesn't have to be expensive.

Ever since Helen had seen the film Goldfinger, she had told me that one of her ambitions was to have a mint julep. If you're not aware, this is a cocktail synonymous with America's southern states and is associated with horse racing and the Kentucky Derby in particular.

We did a tour of the Deep South in 2011, and when I discovered that we could easily arrange to be in Louisville on a Sunday when a race meeting was taking place at Churchill Downs, I got to work.

For a remarkably low price, I pre-booked a box - it was shared with another family - which not only allowed us a fantastic view of the track but the package included unlimited food and drink. Helen could have as many mint juleps as she liked!

A lady had been assigned to our box, and those of our immediate neighbours to make sure that our every comfort was catered for. She took particular interest in us - the British accents always work well - and asked if we'd like to have a tour of the course. She added that she'd see if she could get us into the parade ring before one of the races. We took up the offer. I can't say if the owners we subsequently rubbed shoulders with in the ring were curious about the 'high profile' British visitors or not, but we certainly enjoyed the experience.

It wasn't a particularly profitable afternoon for us - we had a couple of short priced winners - but it's difficult to put a value on an afternoon like that. For us, it was priceless. *NB – she'll deny this, but I almost had to 'pour' Helen back into the car after the last race.*

We introduced Finlay to horse racing at Nottingham on 3rd August 2017. We only had time for five of the seven races scheduled, but with him making his selections before we set off, he picked three winners, and like his Grandma on her first 'day at the races', made a tidy profit. For the record, he picked Crotchet in the 2.10pm and with a SP of 5/1 after I'd managed to get 6/1 on the rails.

As I write, the very last race meeting that we attended was in February 2019 whilst in Australia. We had an afternoon at Warwick Farm, Sydney, and Helen had one of those days, opening with an 18/1 winner. The Aussie bookies, well one in particular, were glad to see us fly out the following day!

Having seen just the one Rugby League game prior to this decade, I've now been to quite a few. In part, this is as a result of Heather now living in a village between Warrington and Wigan. As regular visitors to that part of the country I went to the Halliwell Jones Stadium (Warrington RLFC) a few times and began to get a better feel for the game. This then led to what has become an annual visit to at least one Super League game with a couple of former workmates.

I guess I got the bug in the unlikeliest of places. We had three weeks in Canada in 2017 and on our plane as we flew over the Atlantic, were the players and officials of Coventry Bears RLFC. I got into conversation with some of them and found out that they were due to play recently formed Toronto Wolfpack in a League 1 game a couple of days later.

Helen and I went to see that game, and although it was a total mismatch, (54-12) in favour of the home side who were to go on to win promotion to the Championship, I found the game really entertaining. Since then, and please don't blab to Helen, I've resolved to visit all Super League grounds.

As for Rugby Union, admittedly after only the two games seen live, I just can't seem to get into it. When Nottingham RC were using Meadow Lane, all season ticket holders were given a one off opportunity to watch a Championship game with a scheduled kick-off an hour after whatever football match had taken place that day. London Welsh were the opponents and won quite convincingly. It was OK, but I didn't really feel as if I'd been entertained.

Our next, and to date last experience of the sport, was at Twickenham in 2013. It wasn't cheap, but the chance to see a Calcutta Cup encounter couldn't be ignored. Although Scotland took the lead, England went on to win by 38 points to 18. Again however, despite investing in audio equipment to enable me to listen in to the referee, I just couldn't get into it. Unlike Rugby League, where the spectator can see exactly what's happening, it's not the same in Union as there are too many times when the ball is hidden from view. I know the game is popular in a few countries and have a theory that to fully appreciate the sport, it is probably better to have played it at some time.

The other thing that I found difficult to accept, was the amount of alcohol being consumed. Spectators were up and down throughout the game to bring back up to four pints. Not only was this a distraction, but there was a lot of boorish behaviour, probably brought on by drink, that I found annoying. There was never any hint of trouble, and I did like the non-segregated crowd and generally good-humoured banter from most, but there were too many who had more drink inside them than was good for them. I'd probably go again to give the game another chance, but I won't be sorry if it never happens.

My understanding and appreciation of baseball has grown with each visit to the USA. After that first game in St Louis, whenever we've been in the States during the MLB season, we've managed to see at least one game. I've no real favourite club, although I suppose that if we were permanently based over there, that might change. I will concede though that my favourite ballpark is what is now known as Oracle Park in San Francisco. The location, McCovey Cove overlooking scenic San Francisco Bay towards Oakland, is worth the visit on its own.

I may have given the impression in an earlier chapter that I was a good runner. If I did, I must apologise and qualify that by saying that, for my age I was competitive, but never ever good enough to challenge those natural athletes who, even in their 60's/70's were ahead of runners half their age. Having said that, when I wasn't selected for the London Olympics in 2012, I was disappointed/not surprised in the least (take your pick) and suggested to Helen that for us to be involved, we'd need to apply for tickets. After all, there was very little chance of this festival of sport ever again being held in the UK during the rest of our lifetime.

We didn't get all the events we had asked for, but on 5th August 2012 we had prime seats at the start/finishing line of the Ladies Marathon. There was steady rain at the start - and a five minute cloudburst that left us soaked - but we were oblivious to this as the race developed on a figure of eight course. This meant that, as well as hearing commentary from when the runners were out of sight, they were regularly running past us in the finishing straight.

The winner was Tiki Gelana, an Ethiopian, who set an Olympic Record of 2:23:07 as she finished five seconds ahead of the runner-up. We weren't aware of it at the time but the Ukrainian, Namibian, Peruvian, Colombian, Montenegrin, Tunisian and Burundian athletes all set national records that day. Now, before you think what a fantastic memory I have, I've just googled the official race result. I've not done this because I'm pedantic, but to give you the opportunity, should you find yourself in any of these countries in the future, to begin a conversation with, "I knew a bloke who was present when........" You just never know when that might get you out of a sticky situation.

We had intended seeing a boxing session in the afternoon, but as we had to wait for some of the slower ladies to finish the Marathon before we, in the prime seats, were allowed to leave, we hadn't enough time.

That was a shame but it did give us the opportunity to buy some much needed dry clothing before heading over to east London to see the evening boxing session.

Neither of us had seen boxing in the flesh before, and I guess, based on this particular experience, we probably won't again. Professional boxing might be a bit different but this wasn't particularly exciting. Having said that, we did see Luke Campbell win one of his early bouts en route to becoming the 2012 Olympic Bantamweight Champion.

The whole Olympic experience was a pleasure and the organisers, after a few scares in the early days of the Games, fully deserved the credit that came their way. In addition, the volunteers were knowledgeable, helpful, and many of them seemed natural born entertainers. In fact, we enjoyed the day so much, that we decided we'd get up to Glasgow for the 2014 Commonwealth Games.

We didn't get all that we'd asked for, but still managed to get four of the seven events listed on our application. We booked three nights in Troon and set off early on Friday 25th July 2014, heading straight for the newly built Hockey Centre on Glasgow Green. We made it in time and saw two games, India overcoming Wales and South Africa beating Scotland in the men's tournament.

In the afternoon we headed over to Kelvingrove to see some action in the Lawn Bowls competition. There were a number of matches taking place concurrently and it was interesting although not wildly exciting. The fact that it was a warm sunny day was appreciated.

On the Saturday, we travelled up from Troon to the SSE Hydro to see the morning session of ladies Gymnastics. You can't help but admire the grace and physical effort put into the various routines and it was quite a spectacle, but not a sport I'll be rushing to see again.

On the Sunday, we were at Hampden Park for the opening day of the Athletics. There were a number of preliminary and qualifying events on that afternoon, but the highlight was the 5,000 Metres Final won by the Kenyan, Caleb Ndiku. The crowd gave their loudest applause however, for Roseefelo Siosi, representing the Solomon Islands, who was triple lapped by the leaders and came in nearly four minutes after the winner and almost two minutes after the next to last. He deserved a medal for his guts alone.

Again, like London, the Games were a credit to the nation, and for us mere punters, a joy to attend.

I'm tempted, to record in detail, the cricketing highlights of the Twenty-Ten decade. There are however, far too many, so I'll resist and just summarise.

In 2011, India played the second of a four Test series at Trent Bridge. England were 124/8 and needed 64 from Stuart Broad to reach a mediocre 221. In reply India were going well at 267/4 when Broad took the wicket of Yuvraj Singh. He took four more, including a hat-trick as India added only 21 more runs, nonetheless gaining a useful lead of 67.

England had a much better second innings and with Bell (159), Pietersen (63), Eion Morgan (73), Tim Bresnan (90) and Broad scoring another 44, India needed 477 to win the Test. They fell well short, and with Tim Bresnan taking five wickets, lost by a mammoth 319 runs.

Amongst other things, this particular Test will be remembered for the running out of Ian Bell from the last ball before the tea interval. Bell had played a shot which the chasing fielder appeared to indicate had crossed the boundary. Although the umpire had not yet signalled four, the English batsmen began to walk off in anticipation of the end of the afternoon session, when the ball came flying in from the boundary and Bell was run out. The umpire had no option but to raise his finger.

During the interval some sensitive discussions had apparently taken place, and as the players returned to the field of play after their twenty minute break, Ian Bell came out carrying his bat. A tannoy announcement confirmed that MS Dhoni, the Indian captain, had withdrawn the appeal, and as a result, Bell had been re-instated. Common sense, and the all-important spirit of cricket, had prevailed.

The 2nd Test of the three match 2012 series against South Africa took place at Headingley. Russ joined me on the Saturday where we saw

Pietersen make 149* (he was out without addition on the Sunday). Overnight he showed his true self however when it was revealed that he had humiliated James Taylor, questioning his right to play at this level. Even worse, and for this offence he was suspended, he was found to have been making derogatory remarks about some of his England teammates in phone messages to the South African captain. Which just goes to prove that you may be able to take the Afrikaner out of South Africa but ....! In other words, once a self-centred prat always a self-centred prat!

Oh, and by the way, the Test was drawn.

The 2013 Ashes Test at Trent Bridge was, for me, another missed opportunity. I couldn't make the second day as I attended the funeral of a former work colleague. A shame really because with England having batted first and made 215, and Australia on 73/4 at the close of play on the opening day, I'd anticipated an exciting day in what was shaping up to be a tight Test. I was right.

As I was to find out, midway through that second morning, Australia had lost five more wickets and were still 98 runs behind. At this point, Ashton Agar began his first ever Test innings. He and Phil Hughes more than doubled the score in what turned out to be, at the time, a record breaking last wicket stand of 163. Agar was last man out, having made 98.

On the third morning, as we took our seats, England had already lost two of their second innings wickets, but at least they were now fifteen runs ahead. Kevin Pietersen and Alistair Cook made half centuries but then departed fairly quickly. By the time Matt Prior was dismissed, England had crept to a lead of 153, but with only four remaining wickets, Australia were favourites.

Stuart Broad came out to join Ian Bell who had himself just passed 50. Their partnership, of 138 swung the game England's way, and although the last four wickets fell for 20 runs, Australia needed 311 to win. An opening stand of 84 suggested that they might well reach their target. Wickets began to fall at regular intervals however, and at close of play of the fourth day, England just needed four more wickets to win the first Test of the series with Australia requiring a further 137 runs.

The fifth day, a Sunday, was as dramatic a conclusion to a Test as I've been witness to. Australia were still 80 runs short when the ninth wicket fell and we expected it to be all over by lunch. However, despite England taking the extra half-hour, Brad Haddin and James Pattinson were still batting and required only twenty more runs at the interval.

The tension had got to me and I just had to break from usual custom and go for a long walk around Trent Bridge to settle my nerves. It didn't really help, nor did the addition of five more runs upon resumption of play. However, Jimmy Anderson then took the most important of his ten wickets in a man of the match performance. The catch by Matt Prior, off Brad Haddin, was not given initially, but eventually overturned after review. England had won by fourteen runs. Phew!!

The first of the 2014 five Test Series with India was played at Trent Bridge. As a high scoring draw it lacked the drama of the previous year. It did however, give us the opportunity to witness the Test record for a last wicket partnership being broken only twelve months after it had been set at the same ground. As I've explained, we missed that one, but saw every run of the new record.

India had scored 457 in their first innings (Murali Vijay 146) and England looked like conceding a big lead when the 9th wicket went down. Jimmy Anderson came out to join Joe Root and they jointly added 198 runs (the new record) before he was dismissed for his highest ever Test score of 81. As a result of their efforts, England had somehow gained a lead of 39. With no real prospect of victory on a pitch which came in for criticism, India opted for batting practice.

2015 was the year when I first introduced a grandson to the delights of cricket. Along with Heather, I took Alex to Old Trafford on Wednesday 15th July for a floodlit T20 game. Coincidentally (believe that if you like!), Nottinghamshire were the visitors.

In truth, Alex (three years old at the time) was more interested in the flame throwers and the enormous ice cream that he managed to eat in its entirety, than he was in the cricket. Well, for the record, it gives me no great delight (well, just a little), to remind/inform him that, needing six runs from the last two balls, James Taylor scored successive fours and Notts won by three wickets. If it's any consolation, Lancashire went on to win the competition.

England had the opportunity to regain the Ashes in this year. They did by winning 3-2, taking an unbeatable 3-1 lead after winning the 4th Test at Trent Bridge. Prior to that I was happy to be in attendance at both Sophia Gardens and Edgbaston on the last day as the 1st and 3rd Tests were won. They had been on top for much of those two Tests but had lost heavily at Lord's in between. As a result, an England victory in Nottingham would ensure the return of the famous little urn.

I had tickets for all five days but as the opening day, Thursday, coincided with Littlewoods Pools collection night, and I'd have had to leave Trent Bridge no later than the tea interval, I decided to give my tickets away. What a day to miss! In just under 100 minutes, Australia, who had been asked to bat, were all out for 60, blown away by Stuart Broad who took a career best 8/15. By close of play, England were 214 ahead with six first innings wickets in hand. The Ashes were effectively already 'in the bag' and I had opted to miss it!

Joe Root scored 130 in England's total of 391, and when Mark Wood bowled Nathan Lyon before noon on the third morning, victory was confirmed. England had won by an innings and 78 runs. In the post-match presentations, Michael Clarke, the Australian captain, who had been vilified by the visiting press corps, made a dignified but highly emotional announcement that he was to step down after the final Test. He went out on a high, as the Aussies won that Test by an innings.

Pakistan were the visitors in 2016. We had tickets for the first two days of the 1st Test at Lord's and saw Jake Ball (Nottinghamshire) play the first of his four Tests. It was an unhappy debut as Pakistan, with Misbah-ul-Haq scoring a 1st Innings century at the age of 42, were always on top and eventually won by 75 runs.

I went up to Old Trafford for the Saturday (the second day) of the 2nd Test with a couple of old - OK, to be fair, they were a lot younger than me, so make that former! - colleagues. England began the day on 314/4 with Joe Root unbeaten on 141. England went on to declare on 589/8 with Root progressing to 254 which, as I write, remains his highest Test score. At close of play, Pakistan were 57/4 and not only had we seen a good day, but it looked almost certain that England would win and level the series. They did, by 330 runs, but despite winning the next Test at Edgbaston, they lost at The Oval and had to settle for 2-2.

England were 3-1 winners in the four match 2017 Test series with South Africa. Unfortunately, we saw every ball of the sole defeat. That's not quite true, as we didn't get down to Trent Bridge until just before lunch on the second day. It was raining at home and, we were led to believe, also in Nottingham. On that basis, confident that there would be a delayed start, we pottered about at home with a view to setting off when the weather cleared. Shame really because we probably missed England's one good session.

Play had in fact started on time, and Jimmy Anderson had taken four wickets and South Africa were all out for 335 having only added 26 runs to their overnight score. By the time we arrived however, England had already lost two wickets and never regained the initiative. They went on to lose by a whopping 340 runs. Still, they did win the series!

2017 was a memorable season for Nottinghamshire and I managed to achieve one of my ambitions viz. see them win a one day final at Lord's. I ought to qualify that by saying that I saw most of that game as I had to leave with 20 overs remaining. At the time, Notts were recovering from 150/5 but still looked unlikely to exceed Surrey's total of 297. Thanks to Chris Read's 58, and his role in a match winning stand of 137 with Alex Hales, they were to win by four wickets with thirteen balls remaining. Hales was unbeaten on 187, the highest ever individual score in a Lord's final. Sadly, I was not there to see the climax and resulting celebrations. I was already on the M1 as I had to get back to babysit Finlay & Saul.

That Lord's match was on Saturday 1st July and nine weeks later, Notts were to win the T20 trophy for the first time. Sadly, I wasn't at Edgbaston that day but was just up the road in beautiful Burslem, watching the 'Pies beat Port Vale 1-0. Cause for double celebration then when I got home that night!

Maintaining a record of being there on the day that England clinched victory, I was at Headingley on the third day of the 2nd Test v Pakistan in 2018. The Pakistanis had won at Lord's in the first of a two match series but were to lose this Test by an innings. Sam Curran made his debut at Leeds, making 20 with the bat as England gained a lead of 189 on first innings. They had added 61 runs for the loss of their final three wickets on the Sunday morning. Pakistan were unable to make England bat again and we were on our way home by 5.00pm.

Later that summer, India lost 4-1 in a five match series. Once again, Helen and I saw the first three days of the Trent Bridge Test, by which time there was only ever likely to be one outcome as India had set England a victory target of 521. At close of play on the third day, they had reduced that by 23 runs but I took the decision not to bother travelling down to see the inevitable and gave away my tickets for the fourth day. With hindsight, perhaps we should have gone as England did manage to bat all day and Jos Buttler scored his maiden Test century. They had only the one wicket remaining however, and the end came quickly on the fifth morning.

Nottinghamshire had initially announced at close of play that it would be only £10 to enter Trent Bridge on the fifth day. There was such a furore about it that common sense prevailed, and on that final morning they reversed the decision. Apparently around a couple of hundred spectators turned up and were allowed free entry into the ground.

2018 was the year that six year old Finlay first visited Trent Bridge. He'd been enjoying the coaching sessions of *All Stars* cricket arranged by the local village club in Selston and it just felt right that we take him.

Friday, 20th July saw Leicestershire defeat Notts by 17 runs. The result was probably of no real consequence to Finlay, but as he seemed to enjoy the experience, we took him again a few weeks later. This time, he saw Yorkshire thrashed by 63 runs and joined in with the crowd's joyous celebrations as this victory appeared to confirm that Notts would make it to the Quarter Finals.

England had the chance in 2019 to regain the Ashes. They didn't, although they came from behind to draw the series 2-2. As Trent Bridge had not been allocated a Test I didn't see any play in the series, although I was at the ground on the afternoon that Ben Stokes, for the second time that summer, became a cricketing hero.

We were watching Notts beat Yorkshire in a T20 match, aware before the first ball had been bowled, that England faced likely defeat at Headingley. Like many others, I'd given up all hope as England had lost wickets immediately after the lunch interval. However, around 3.30pm, a distinct murmur went round the ground. This intrigued me, but I dismissed it. Around fifteen minutes later, a number of cheers were heard and the ground gradually erupted. England had won by one wicket and I now assume that the earlier murmur had followed Australia's unsuccessful DRS appeal against Jack Leach. With Notts winning as well, it was quite a day.

Stokes of course was 'man of the match' in the World Cup Final that had taken place a few weeks before. I wasn't at Lord's on that never to be forgotten day, but recorded the entire Channel Four coverage of the game and have watched it through a couple of times. I've retained the highlights package shown later that night and occasionally invite the grandsons to watch the best bits of what is generally regarded as the best ODI ever.

Helen and I did manage to see six - there should have been seven, but one was abandoned without a ball being bowled - of the group matches at various venues earlier in the tournament. As I'm sure all who attended any of the games will attest, it was a fantastic experience. The summer of 2019 was a glorious time to be a cricket fan in England.

One of my hopes when we went to Australia in the early part of 2019 was to see some Test cricket. Ideally, I have liked to have gone to both

SCG and MCG, but the cricketing schedule and our itinerary wouldn't allow for that. I had to make do with seeing part of the last day of the 1st Test v Sri Lanka at The Gabba (Brisbane) and the first two days of play in the 2nd Test when the Manuka Oval, in Canberra, was used for the very first time. Australia won both Tests comfortably but that was irrelevant. It was an experience to savour that, as Helen will testify, had me once again purring with delight.

One other feature of that trip was a visit to Bowral. As really keen cricketing fans will know, this was the NSW town in which Don Bradman grew up. There is a museum there attached to the ground, now named Bradman Oval in his honour, that not only covered Bradman's life and career but cricket in general, and was well worth more than the couple of hours I could spare.

Sadly, as I write, there is no immediate prospect of first class cricket being played in front of spectators in the near future. Now, you may not agree with me, but that is surely just cause to be gloomy!

The Epilogue

Right now (August 2020) is a very sad time for sports fans. As a result of Covid 19, the general public is barred from attending almost all sport played anywhere in the world. Some major events are however, being televised, which whilst far from satisfactory, is better than nothing.

I'm as disappointed as anyone about this state of affairs but recognise that it is what it is for a reason and I'm resigned to a long wait. Although sport has been an important part of my life - and if you've got this far, you'll have come to appreciate that - I accept that there are many more important things in life.

I've just recently reached my biblical 'three score years and ten', so realistically (& statistically!) I'm likely to have enjoyed more sporting experiences in the past than I can look forward to in the future. There's not much I can do about that other than look after my health as best I can.

I do however, have a few remaining sporting ambitions. Some, I hope, are achievable. Others, like being (or even seeing) the first Scot to lift the World Cup are probably no longer possible and yes, I accept that the first of those options never was.

It may not be possible, but I would like one more trip to the USA to see a few more games of baseball. I'd also like to see more Rugby League action and hopefully add to the number of Super League grounds that I've visited.

Finally, from a purely personal viewpoint, I'd like to complete the full set of Scottish football grounds. Back in 2009, after a visit to Firhill (Partick Thistle), I suggested to Helen that we slowly 'pick off' the grounds that she's not visited. As I write, she has been to 25, plus Berwick Rangers (where she has fond memories!) and Hampden Park. I've been to a few more of course - well I had the advantage of a head start - and I'd like to think we could complete the set (42) together.

I hope to be around long enough to see all four grandsons develop a keen interest in sport. If they can have fun playing the sport(s) they particularly like, all good and well. If they've got real talent in any given sport, I hope that they make the most of whatever skills they've been blessed with. The key thing though, is to get maximum enjoyment from the physical effort and camaraderie that participation provides.

Failing that, I hope they enjoy a lifetime of watching a wide range of sports, providing they never lose perspective and always remember that there are other aspects of life which are more important. On rare occasions, I've perhaps not been the best of role models, but I'd like to think I've not done too badly. You, dear reader, and in the fullness of time, Alex, Finlay, Daniel and Saul, will be the best judge.

A Commissioned Publication Printed by

MOORLEYS
Print, Design & Publishing
info@moorleys.co.uk · www.moorleys.co.uk